Praise for TRUST YOUR VIBES

"In an increasingly complex world, intuition is our necessary super-skill. And no one teaches it better than Sonia Choquette."

— **Vishen Lakhiani**, entrepreneur, author, and CEO of Mindvalley

"There's no one better! In my years of producing world-famous experts, there is no one more skilled at helping real people develop their sixth sense than master intuitive and teacher Sonia Choquette! As Sonia guides you through her signature teachings with boundless joy, expect massive life shifts and a new understanding about what is possible for you. Yes, you have a hidden superpower. And yes, Sonia can help you learn to use it to up-level your life beyond your wildest dreams."

— **Sheri Salata**, former executive producer, *The Oprah Winfrey Show*

"Sonia's ability to help us navigate out of our heads and into our hearts where we find life-changing inner guidance is masterful. Trust Your Vibes *is a must-read for anyone wanting to tap into where their real power and magic lie."*

— **Craig David**, British singer, songwriter, music producer, and DJ

"The unprecedented disruptions going on in the world require we access new creative ways of thinking and acting. This can be found in our innate intuitive intelligence more than anywhere else. Trust Your Vibes *shows us how to activate and act on this inner guidance to lead us forward."*

— **Andrew Horn**, co-founder and CEO, Tribute.co

"Trust your vibes and read this book! The straightforward, practical advice (backed up with solid examples of how well it works) will show you how to access your most valuable asset—your sixth sense."

— **Cheryl Richardson**, the *New York Times* best-selling author of *The Art of Extreme Self-Care*

"In this timely guide of world change, Trust Your Vibes *not only helps us tune in to our intuition but shows us how to immediately put it to use in a grounded, practical way. It is life changing."*

— **Fearne Cotton**, author and English television radio and podcast presenter

T0188603

TRUST YOUR VIBES

ALSO BY SONIA CHOQUETTE

TRUST YOUR VIBES

Live an Extraordinary Life by Using
Your Intuitive Intelligence

SONIA CHOQUETTE

HAY HOUSE, INC.
Carlsbad, California • New York City
London • Sydney • New Delhi

Published in the United States by: Hay House, Inc.: www.hayhouse.com®
Published in Australia by: Hay House Australia Pty. Ltd.: www.hayhouse.com.au
Published in the United Kingdom by: Hay House UK, Ltd.: www.hayhouse.co.uk
Published in India by: Hay House Publishers India: www.hayhouse.co.in

Editorial Supervision: Linda Kahn
Cover design: Sandy Cull
Interior design: Karim J. Garcia

Originally published as *Trust Your Vibes* 978-1-4019-0233-9.

Cataloging-in-Publication Data is on file at the Library of Congress.

Tradepaper ISBN: 978-1-4019-6959-2
E-book ISBN: 978-1-4019-6960-8
Audiobook ISBN: 978-1-4019-6961-5

11 10 9 8 7 6 5

1st printing, March 2004
2nd edition, June 2022

Printed in the United States of America

*This book is dedicated to my daughters,
Sonia and Sabrina. Thank you for the gift of your
delightful spirits, your wise insights, your glorious
intuition, your endless sense of strength and humor, your
honesty, and your profoundly generous, forgiving, and
loving hearts. It is my greatest honor and joy to be your
mother and friend as you carry the light forward
into the world. You are my dearest soul mates.*

*And to my mother, who taught me to trust my vibes,
no matter what. I shall be forever grateful for
the gifts you have given me.*

*And to my beautiful granddaughter Sufiya Rose.
You are pure joy and the light of the future.*

CONTENTS

WELCOME

I have an extraordinary life. What I mean by *extraordinary* is not defined by money, fame, or material success. My life is filled with magic and miracles. I am constantly connected to support, am quickly led to solutions whenever problems and challenges arise, meet opportunities at my front door, and feel creative and fulfilled in my work. I regularly attract exceptionally good luck, meet the most magnificent people, receive countless bountiful gifts and blessings in the most unexpected ways, and feel connected, confident, valued, and loved. I trust myself, others, and the Universe to bring all that will enhance my soul, improve my life, and help me become a better, more loving, secure, contributing person. I'm never disappointed. If anything, I am humbled by the endless flow of blessings that come my way. I have had many heartaches, sorrows, and disappointments and much grief, as these inevitable experiences come with life. But through it all, I have never felt alone and have always felt guided through the storm to a better place on the other side. This is what an extraordinary life is.

Over the past 50 years, I've taught millions of others to have an extraordinary life, as well. An extraordinary life is available to everyone because it is our natural birthright. It isn't something we hack into with our clever intellect. It's something we *surrender* into. An extraordinary life comes from connecting with your authentic Self, your Divine spirit, your inner guidance, and letting this part of you become the navigator of your life.

The *only* way to live an extraordinary life is to *trust your vibes*, the turn-by-turn directions coming from your spirit. This means letting go of the safety of the known, the place of certainty and control that keeps you small, stuck, and limited. It means taking a leap of faith and doing something different. An extraordinary life asks you to step into the unknown, where you will meet an entire constellation of hidden support that lies far beyond our limited logic and perception. This leap is not into the void. It is a leap back into your true Self. Trusting your vibes is trusting your spirit and letting go of the fear that keeps you from living authentically. It's your spirit, after all, that moved you to pick up this book. Stop for a moment and recognize how true this is. These same vibes will continue to guide you to live your best life as long as you trust them to do so. After all, you followed your vibes this far.

If you are ready to experience the biggest, most positive shift of your life and leave the ordinary behind, continue following your spirit to your own extraordinary life. I'll show you how.

INTRODUCTION

Ever since I was 12 years old, I have been an intuitive guide. I've dedicated my life as a spiritual teacher and writer, working with people worldwide and offering intuitive guidance and spiritual direction. I know that's difficult to believe, but it's true. I entered this lifetime with a clear sense of mission and purpose to teach—or perhaps, more accurately, remind—others that we humans are spiritual beings with six, not five, senses available to guide our lives. And that we need access to this sixth sense—our intuition, our inner guide, our *vibes*—to be the best versions of who we are and live the best lives possible.

I was born into the perfect circumstances to support my spiritual purpose because, in my family, the sixth sense was considered the most important sense we have. We relied upon our sixth sense for guidance and direction for everything. My mother, a Romanian-child war refugee separated from her family during an evacuation in World War II, relied on her intuition to survive. When she was only 12, she ended up in a German work camp, became deathly ill with rheumatic fever, lost her hearing, and was in constant grave danger of losing her life. She survived only because her inner guidance protected her and navigated her to safety throughout this entire ordeal. Her vibes further guided her to a chance encounter with a young American soldier who was part of the liberation army named Paul Choquette. Shortly after, in 1946, when she was 15 years old, she married him and moved with him to the United States. Eleven years later, my life began. My parents had seven children. I was number five and named after my mom, Sonia. As a child, I was completely enamored with her because she was exotic, beautiful, creative, unstoppable, and most of all magical. She taught my siblings and me about the spirit world, explaining that we always had help from the subtle realms and were never alone. Her vibes brought with them constant miracles and magic of every sort.

According to my mom, it didn't matter what our other senses told us. The most important one, the one that would guide us, protect us, open doors that appeared closed, connect us to people when we felt alone, even lead us to love when it seemed nowhere in sight, was our sixth sense. It revealed what was hidden and what we needed to know most. And because our sixth sense was in our heartbeat, we could never lose it like we could our other senses. In fact, she regularly claimed that the best thing that ever happened to her was becoming deaf because it spared her from having to listen to all the misery, fear, and ego nonsense that comes with not tuning in to your vibes.

"Trust your vibes, your spirit. It's all you need to be safe in life," she said. "It will show you the solution to every challenge you meet. All you have to do is tune in to your heart and ask for help." That was our way and what we did.

I believed my mom because I saw the benefit of her trusting her vibes all the time. She knew who was calling on the phone way before a caller ID was ever even imagined, let alone invented. She knew where the parking spaces were, even in the most crowded downtown streets. She always found the lost keys, or lost anything, in seconds. She was first in line at surprise sales. She arrived at opportunity's doorstep before it had even opened. Nothing was impossible. Her vibes made things possible.

Because my mom was deaf, not formally educated past the age of 12, a foreigner, and a stay-at-home mom with a house full of kids, she lived in her own world. She didn't have many authority figures interfering with her. What other people said or thought didn't matter to her. She couldn't hear and didn't listen to those who blocked her way, and she told her kids not to either.

We were instructed, by her example, to first and foremost check in with our vibes for answers, not with others. We were empowered to listen to what our spirit said because it told the truth, even if doing so meant standing up to authorities. When I asked her a question as a child, before she'd answer, she'd often reply, "What does your spirit say?" I was expected to tune inward to find my own answers, and I did. I didn't know it at the time, but that was the most empowering gift she gave me.

By six years old, I was in regular conversation with my spirit and the spirit world in general. These conversations did not take place in my head. They occurred in my body. They didn't come in words either. Instead, they came in energetic waves that originated in my heart and spread throughout my body, sometimes settling in my gut, sometimes in my throat, sometimes even causing the hairs on the back of my neck to stand up, always guiding the way.

My task was to interpret these energetic transmissions to understand what they were trying to convey. Believe it or not, that was easier than it sounds because it was all so natural to me. Just as my eyes received vibrations of light and my ears felt vibrations that tapped on my eardrums and I understood the meaning of those sights and sounds, what my heart and gut told me was also perfectly clear. All I had to do was get quiet, tune in to my body, and listen.

When I started school, I noticed that trusting vibes was not something everyone did. It was peculiar to our family, and we were considered "weird" at best by others. I thought everybody else was weirder. Why on earth would you ignore your sixth sense? You might as well walk on the highway blindfolded, at night, against traffic. Going through life without access to your vibes seemed to be tantamount to a death wish. I preferred to withstand other people's negative judgment over being in danger. Besides, I had enough support in my own large family that I didn't need to seek it from outsiders.

By the time I was 12 years old, I was so good at reading vibes that my mom's friends and neighbors came to see what I had to say. I also studied with two master teachers who transformed my understanding of intuitive energy and of life. The first was a theosophist and psychic from England named Charlie Goodman, and the second was a teacher of spiritual law, Dr. Trenton Tully.

Charlie taught me the psychic arts, which are psychometry (the art of tuning in to vibes through touch), clairaudience (tuning in to your inner voice), clairvoyance (seeing things with your inner eye), clairsentience (tuning in to energy through your feeling body), and prophetic knowing (intuitively knowing something without a shadow of a doubt), and how to tune in to this subtle energy with accuracy.

Dr. Tully taught me that vibes are not random. Vibes are thoughts sent and received by people, near and far. He showed me how thoughts create our experiences. Tuning in to vibes was simply dialing in to creative thought energy. If the vibes you tune in to feel good, carry on. If the vibes don't feel good, change course. Through his lessons, I came to understand that we create our own realities and how. Our thoughts and intentions determine our outcomes. We are not powerless victims of our life circumstances. We are Divine co-creators.

By the time I was 15, I had realized that not using our vibes presented a significant handicap in life. It pained me to stand by and watch people flounder and suffer when their problems could so easily be corrected. It wasn't as if other people didn't have vibes. We are all naturally endowed with six senses. But most people had turned off—or had someone turn off—this subtle sixth sense. It was if they had turned off the light and were going about their affairs in the dark. I needed to show them how to turn this inner light back on and why.

Thus began my unwavering purpose in life. I've been committed to this purpose for more than 50 years. My commitment has led me to write 28 books over the years and the first version of this book nearly 20 years ago. Over that time, the world has been catching up and many people now recognize that we indeed have an intuitive sixth sense just as surely as we have sight, hearing, taste, touch, and smell. The interest in trusting our vibes is exploding around the globe.

I wonder if this mass intuitive awakening is finally coming about in response to the challenges that have befallen us. First, of course, is the global pandemic of 2020, which none of us could have imagined. This virus reminded us that we are all vulnerable. It also encouraged us to look inward for guidance and answers, as there was little clarity in the outer world. Second, our world economic systems turned upside down, again reminding us how much we depend on and affect one another, something the ego, which ignores vibes, denies. Necessity is the mother of invention here, too, so we are now turning to intuition to lead us forward. Third, global warming can no longer be ignored. Because a problem cannot be solved with the same thinking that created it, we've been forced to look for answers in new directions. Those directions now include looking inward. I'm confident our intuition will help bring solutions to all these crises and more. Ultimately, they remind us that we are all spiritual beings who have a temporary shared human experience on a shared living planet.

The more we listen to our inner guidance, the more we will overcome ego limitations that have pitted us against ourselves, one another, and the planet and find solutions to the disasters bearing down on us now. Trusting our vibes will also help restore our integrity, enhance our self-respect, re-instill respect for others, increase love for ourselves and others, activate our creativity, and help us heal the beautiful but suffering earth that we occupy and have so deeply hurt.

In the spirit of forward movement, I've been guided to update this book with all the practices, tools, and tips I've developed since the first version of *Trust Your Vibes* was released. I know in my heart that when every one of us trusts our vibes, we will find the solutions to our collective problems that humanity so desperately needs right now. Just as whales need their sonar and bats need their echolocation to survive, we need our vibes to survive as well. Beyond survival, trusting our vibes will restore our peace and bring back our joy. This is our natural design and birthright. It's time to reclaim it.

How to Use This Book

This book will teach you specific practices for activating and sharpening your intuition and trusting your vibes as quickly as possible. In it, I share the best intuitive practices I have developed over the course of my life so far for turning on your sixth sense and letting this innate superpower lead your life. Each practice is designed to remove your ego resistance, pique your curiosity, capture your imagination, and—best of all—bring about quick, positive results.

Over the years, I've discovered that a lighthearted, nonthreatening approach works best when easing people into an intuitively guided way of life. These practices are easily integrated into your life and work well; they quickly convince your ego that it is safe and beneficial to let go of control over your life and allow your Divine spirit and brilliant intuition to take over. As you work with these practices, you will soon naturally see that trusting your vibes isn't a reckless or dangerous risk to take but rather the best way to live. Your inner guidance does a far better job of making your life work than your limited and fearful ego ever can.

In these pages, I will show you how to think, feel, and act intuitively, as if it were the most natural thing in the world to do—because it is. Some of the practices will make immediate sense, while others might seem a bit strange or risky. Just try them out, then judge for yourself if they are worth incorporating into your life. Nothing I suggest is dangerous. A lot of my suggestions, however, may feel different. The ego often doesn't know the difference between different and dangerous, so please remember this and know you will always be safe, even if you briefly feel a little uncomfortable at times. We always feel awkward when learning new things, so relax. If you feel this way, know you are making significant progress.

The more you use your intuitive radar, the stronger and more precise it becomes. In time, with practice and positive feedback, trusting your vibes becomes automatic. By engaging with these practices one at a time, you'll quickly activate your inner guidance system. You'll soon be able to distinguish accurate inner guidance from doubt, fear, and wishful thinking.

In a short time, you will naturally and spontaneously follow your vibes rather than get stuck in your head, trying like mad to figure out the way forward to no avail. Nor will you hesitate, question, second guess, ignore, resist, or deny your vibes as you might presently be doing. I call this quitting the "woulda, coulda, shoulda" club of missed opportunities that all ego-controlled five-sensory people unhappily belong to.

As you introduce each new practice into your life, you will quickly experience an undeniable grace, what nonintuitive people call "good luck." This is the natural consequence of listening to your spirit instead of your ego. Just as we can thank Google Maps for navigating us from one unfamiliar destination to another and saving us from having to frantically figure our way out in the dark, so, too, can we rely on our vibes to relieve us from fumbling with our fear as we move through life.

Trusting your vibes takes the angst out of life and puts more clarity, confidence, and joy in. Gorgeous surprises unfold. You will find yourself being less influenced by other people's opinions and interference, feeling less stressed and exhausted by fear, and being less indecisive.

Each intuition-strengthening practice is a blueprint for a new way to live. Your energy will increase because you are removing the hidden burden of fear that comes with fumbling around in the dark. Before you know it, trusting your vibes will make life work in ways you never thought possible—the way life is meant to be.

ONE STEP AT A TIME

I introduce these practices one at a time, beginning with the most basic and graduating to more and more advanced ones as we go. I want to ease you into intuitive living, much like easing into the shallow end of a warm pool as you learn to swim. It's important to feel safe in these new energetic "waters." Only when you are at ease will I suggest you dive in deeper. No practice will throw you into the deep end by asking you to take uncomfortable risks before you are ready. Approach this journey with curiosity and a sense of adventure. I've taught enough people over the years to know which tools work best, bring quick results, and are the most effective, and fun.

LET THE ADVENTURE BEGIN

The goal of each tool or practice is to quiet your ego, wake up your spirit, and help you tune in to the unseen world of energy. The tools in this book can also help you shift your identity from ego-centered fear and control to spirit-centered lighthearted ease. I want you to be able to expand your sensory bandwidth from a limited AM radio bandwidth (ego) to an elevated and expanded FM bandwidth (first-level protective vibes) and ultimately to an unlimited satellite bandwidth (energy from your Divine Self and the Universe).

There are 34 intuitive practices in all, divided into 9 parts. Each part builds on the one preceding it, gently moving you further into fluid partnership with your spirit.

At the end of each chapter is an exercise, what I call a "Woo-Woo Workout," to help anchor what you've just learned. I call these exercises "woo-woo" because the five-sensory people among us, who do not *yet* feel vibes, generally dismiss the subtle unseen world of energy as nothing but woo-woo. This is the biggest mistake anyone can make. Woo-woo energy opens the way to the extraordinary benefits and bountiful outcomes we deserve and can have. Embracing the woo-woo factor frees you from the limitations and stress of facing problems from the ego alone, which often leaves you feeling trapped and powerless. This leads you instead to recognize all the bounty-bringing possibilities inherently hidden in all challenges in life. Plus, it's fun to unapologetically embrace a little woo-woo in your life. It lets the world know you are choosing to follow your inner guidance and spirit over automatically submitting to the rules of the highly limiting five-sensory ego-perspective approach to life.

After each exercise, I've included a message that helps summarize and simplify the chapter's lesson. This Woo-Woo Wisdom will make it easier to remember the practice and incorporate it easily into your life.

Be sure to read this book at your own pace, giving each suggested practice a try for a few days. Then see what happens. This gentle process provides a solid system on which to strengthen your personal intuitive muscles. Some tools you may already use, while others may be entirely new for you. Be curious and give each one a genuine try. Experiment with each practice until it feels natural to you. It's helpful to write down your results. That way, after a week or so you will have concrete evidence that your vibes are trustworthy.

I've literally taught thousands of people to trust their vibes and create extraordinary lives, so I know what works and what doesn't, as well as where the traps are. Going through these practices little by little works—trying to become an "expert" overnight doesn't. When you start trusting your vibes, you change the way you run your life. You get in touch once again with your authentic Self and let the real you, your spirit, take over. It's the antidote to the famous frustration in the U2 song "I Still Haven't Found What

I'm Looking For." When you start to trust your vibes and begin to live your spirit, you finally do find what you are looking for—the authentic, empowered *you*.

A FINAL SUGGESTION

Even though we all have the potential to be full-blown intuitive beings guided by our spirit, wanting is not enough. In the same way that watching an exercise video won't give you abs of steel, neither will reading this book make you an intuitive aficionado. Unless you train your intuitive muscles and use them daily, they won't improve.

At first, you may feel awkward or even worry that you're just "faking it" when practicing the suggestions in this book, but if you stick with them, that will soon change. Leaving the ego-driven space of your head and moving into the spirit-driven space of your heart is a significant shift and initially takes some getting used to. However, it won't be long before you have evidence that this is the best way to go. Once you decide to turn the light back on in your heart, it's simply a matter of finding the switch. The wiring is all in place. The light still works and always has.

I believe we all know on some level that "something is wrong with this picture" when we don't trust our vibes or when we ignore our spirit. If you want to move away from fear and retrieve the missing link in your awareness and are ready to make the commitment to do so, you can. If you want to follow your spirit and see beyond appearances and into a deeper understanding of yourself and others, and live an extraordinary life, you can. If you want to be able to make confident, clear decisions, knowing with certainty that you are on the right path for you, this is the way.

In my first book, *The Psychic Pathway*, I introduced you to your sixth sense. In this book, I'll show you how to develop this sense into the powerful inner guidance system it's intended to be. If your desire to trust your vibes and live a magical, extraordinary life matches my desire to teach you how, I've no doubt we will succeed.

Quiz: How Intuitive Are You Now?

Before we dive in to the tools and practices, it can be helpful to recognize how presently attuned and responsive we already are to our vibes. Therefore, complete the following questionnaire, checking one choice after each statement.

		Rarely	Sometimes	Often
1.	When I'm with someone, I easily understand how they feel.	_____	_____	_____
2.	I love to physically move and exercise.	_____	_____	_____
3.	I listen to my gut feelings, even if they don't make sense.	_____	_____	_____
4.	I'm aware of when someone is lying to me or manipulating me.	_____	_____	_____
5.	I can tell if I'm on the wrong track, and I change it.	_____	_____	_____
6.	I know when someone is misleading me.	_____	_____	_____

	Rarely	Sometimes	Often
7. I tend to get overly involved with other people's problems.	_____	_____	_____
8. I get immediate answers even when I don't fully understand the problem.	_____	_____	_____
9. I change my plans quickly if I get a bad feeling.	_____	_____	_____
10. I share what I have and don't worry about having enough.	_____	_____	_____
11. I feel protected in some way, as though someone were watching over me.	_____	_____	_____
12. I can say no even when it's difficult.	_____	_____	_____
13. I express my true feelings, even when they're unpopular.	_____	_____	_____
14. I trust myself to make the final decision.	_____	_____	_____
15. I'm careful whom I ask for advice.	_____	_____	_____
16. I like to take risks and try new things.	_____	_____	_____
17. I take care of my body.	_____	_____	_____
18. I pay attention to people and listen closely when they speak.	_____	_____	_____
19. I know things before they happen.	_____	_____	_____
20. I often think of people and then they call me the same day.	_____	_____	_____
21. I sense whether people and situations are good for me.	_____	_____	_____

	Rarely	Sometimes	Often
22. I'm a creative thinker and love to doodle or play when I have a free moment.	_____	_____	_____
23. I have a great sense of humor.	_____	_____	_____
24. There are a lot of coincidences in my life.	_____	_____	_____
25. I believe I have helpers on the Other Side, such as guardian angels.	_____	_____	_____
26. I'm spontaneous and love to dance.	_____	_____	_____

When you've completed the questionnaire, go back and look at your answers. Give yourself one point for each "Rarely," two points for each "Sometimes," and three points for each "Often."

- **If your score was 26–39:**

  You're not presently in the habit of noticing your intuition—but this will change rapidly when you use the practices and tools in this book. As you open to your intuitive Self, your sense of adventure and vitality will increase significantly.

- **If your score was 40–59:**

  You're already quite tuned in to your sixth sense, although you may not call it that. You may just consider yourself "hypersensitive" or "lucky." As you work with these practices, you'll experience an increasing sense of safety, guidance, and creativity, and your life will become much more exciting and satisfying.

- **If your score was 60–78:**

  You probably realize that your sixth sense is exceptionally developed, but you may not trust it completely. As you practice the tools in this book, you'll develop the confidence you need to begin living the joyful life of a fully awakened six-sensory being. You'll learn how to navigate life with grace and ease and soar above problems rather than struggle through them. You'll awaken your spirit and learn to fly.

So now that you know you're ready to become the empowered, intuitive, six-sensory being you are naturally designed to be and start trusting your vibes, let's begin.

PART I

BEGIN WITH THE BASICS

EMBRACE YOUR INNER WOO-WOO

The first step in living an intuitively guided life is to recognize that you are a spiritual being, that you are naturally designed to be intuitive, that you feel your intuition through "vibes," and that trusting your vibes is *necessary* if you want to experience your best life.

Some people dismiss vibes as "woo-woo." This is the worst decision you could ever make because "woo-woo" is the way to go. What people call woo-woo is transcending logic and tuning in to the voice of your spirit, your true Self, your Divine personal power. We all need a little woo-woo to rise above the fray of an ordinary life of struggle and survival, to free ourselves from the tyranny that comes with endlessly trying to figure things out, and to happily get on our way to living a life of wonder, grace, and flow.

WHAT ARE VIBES?

As I said, your vibes are the voice of your authentic Self, your spirit (as opposed to your inauthentic ego Self) guiding you through life. Your spirit does not communicate to you through thoughts or words. Instead, it transmits information energetically, through your body, just like your other senses do. You don't think vibes. You *feel* them. And I don't mean "feel" as in feeling an emotion. I mean sensing subtle energetic vibrations or signals that convey a more accurate understanding of what is happening in your life than meets the eye or is evident at the moment. Your vibes work like energetic traffic signals, such as red, yellow, and green, or like merge, caution, and stop signs, depending on the message. Your spirit communicates like a satellite GPS radar, helping you navigate the road ahead by sending advance warnings and helpful directions as you go. Once you become aware of vibes, you will begin to seek out these signals from your spirit to guide you.

Like road signs, vibes are easy to miss if you aren't paying attention or are distracted. And you don't want to miss them, because if you do, you may get turned around, led off course, and even completely lost. Through vibes, your spirit quickly tells you how to get to where you want to go in life in the most direct way possible. Your spirit also points out marvels along the way that you might otherwise not see because you didn't even know they were there. And vibes, of course, also keep you from crashing. That's why it's important to be on the alert for vibes and follow your inner signals.

Many great people who have changed the world for the better have attributed their phenomenal success to somehow embracing the woo-woo transmissions coming their way. Thomas Edison once said, "The first step is an intuition—and comes with a burst." Oprah Winfrey said, "Learning to trust your instincts, using your intuitive sense of what's best for you, is paramount for any lasting success. I've trusted the still, small voice of intuition my entire life. And the only time I've made mistakes is when I didn't listen."

But the person who summed up trusting your vibes better than any other is Albert Einstein when he said, "The intuitive mind is a sacred gift and the rational mind is a faithful servant. We have created a society that honors the servant and has forgotten the gift."

Your ego, or rational mind, is like your pet dog: a faithful companion to the spirit, your authentic Self. Your ego is not a problem in and of itself. Indeed, it provides you with support and service. But it isn't the true leader of your life. Your spirit, your sacred Self, is the leader and it's capable of guiding your life in the highest possible way. That's not to say you need to abandon your pet dog or your ego. Instead, you need to *train* your ego, so it doesn't wreak havoc and mess up your life much like an untrained dog. You want your ego to follow and support your spirit, as a cooperative, faithful companion, head and heart working together, to create your best life.

Once you recognize the difference between your ego and spirit, trusting your vibes becomes easy. Simply listen to your spirit and train your barking dog ego to be quiet and of service to your spirit. Ignore your barking dog when it gets out of line and tries to take over. Speak to the spirits in others and don't listen to or fight with their barking dogs either.

THE DIFFERENCE BETWEEN FIVE-SENSORY AND SIX-SENSORY PEOPLE

The difference between a person who listens to their vibes and someone who doesn't is simple. A five-sensory person only pays attention to their five external senses, ignores their spirit, tunes out or denies the unseen world of energy, and prefers to be guided in life by their barking-dog ego. The basic problem with this is that the ego is limited, insecure, and highly fearful, and can lead you astray if not directly in trouble. The ego perceives life through the lens of "me against you." Therefore, it puts up a barrier and keeps the world at bay, fearing everything and every-one. The ego is subjective so does not convey accurate informa-tion. Drawing from its biased, limited, and more often than not incorrect conclusions, it can distort reality and can even lie about what is actually happening. Ultimately, the ego never feels good enough, smart enough, strong enough, sexy enough, or enough of anything to truly relax and let the world in. The ego jockeys for position, constantly offering up your power in its quest for approval and reassurance from others. And because the ego is so insecure, it can get confused, become defensive, feel suspicious, over-give, or withhold, or a combination of all the above. In other words, it's way over its head and cannot manage your life with any grace because it is a limited Self and not connected to Source. It is not the leader it tries to be, and deep down it knows this.

Trying to protect us from perceived danger, our barking dog becomes manipulative, competitive, dishonest, and calculating. It has limited perception, so it misreads the world most, if not all, of the time. That is why five-sensory people rarely feel deeply secure or at ease with themselves and in life. Instead, they settle for survival. It's an endless, exhausting dogfight in which a person can never relax.

Six-sensory people use all six senses and put the sixth sense first. They know they are spiritual beings, co-creators with the Universe, here to connect with their heart's desires and contribute to the world's betterment. So they let their spirit lead in confidence and follow its guidance without hesitation, knowing that if they do, everything will turn out better than they could have possibly imagined.

These people recognize the spirit in themselves and others, and seek to connect with that spirit in every way. A six-sensory person is deeply attuned to the body, listens for the signals from spirit, and expects positive guidance and outcomes every day.

Six-sensories feel secure because they are connected to their sacred gift, their Universal Light, and while they may have flickering moments of fear, they know they will always receive Divine support to help them overcome it.

The fundamental difference between being a five-sensory and a six-sensory is simply the channel you are listening to: your barking dog or your sacred spirit. Five-sensories have become disconnected from their spirit much the way a lamp can become disconnected from an outlet, its source of power. The source for our sixth sense is our heart, where our spirit resides. The five-sensory is temporarily plugged in to the head and needs to reconnect to its source. Once this happens, the inner light of spirit turns on right away.

BEGIN ALL IN

There is a Chinese saying that I've learned to be true throughout my life: "The way it begins is the way it ends." If you begin this adventure wholeheartedly, committed to letting your spirit lead, your intuition will take off and so will your life. If you begin half-heartedly, sometimes listening to your spirit, sometimes to your ego, you won't make much progress.

So please begin this adventure with a total commitment to reconnect with your spirit. Try the tools and practices in this book and see what unfolds. Explore and experiment with a sense of adventure and curiosity. Tell your barking dog to hush, and tell your spirit to speak louder. Believe it or not, your ego actually prefers this arrangement. It can watch and learn, happy to relinquish control and step out of the way, allowing the master—spirit—to take care of everything.

Woo-Woo Workout

Begin this adventure by identifying your barking dog. What kind of dog is your ego? Picture its breed and temperament. Is it a nervous Chihuahua, or a German shepherd? Is it an energetic puppy, or an old dog, set in his ways?

My ego is a fancy-pants poodle named Fifi. When Fifi tries to be in charge, she's very snooty and vocal about it. She expects special treatment and has very little patience. She is definitely *not* my Higher Self.

Have fun identifying your barking dog, and don't get too serious. If you laugh, the ego cannot control you. Some among you will inevitably say, "I don't have a dog for an ego. I have a cat." No problem. Go with the cat. That just says your ego wants to be special. Just be aware of this.

Now turn your attention to your spirit. What name best describes your beautiful, sacred inner Self? I named my spirit *Bright Light* because that is exactly what my spirit brings to my life—a big bright light illuminating the path ahead so I can move forward with confidence and make the best decisions. Maybe your spirit is named Jewel or Sparkle or Treasure. Again, don't overthink this—it's just a way to find the light in the dark room.

Then, after you've named your barking-dog ego and spirit, begin to notice which one is in charge. What brings out the barking dog? What brings forward your spirit? There is big difference in the way each of these channels feels. If you are tuned in to the ego, you will feel tense, threatened, and territorial. Your barking dog usually makes a lot of mental noise. If you are tuned in to your spirit, the noise in your head will be much quieter and you will feel more present and at ease. When in your spirit, you feel physically more open and at ease, your mental chatter is quiet, you breathe deeply, you feel present, and your heart feels light and content. The difference between the two, barking dog and spirit, is significant. Check in with your body to determine which is in charge. You'll know it by how you feel.

Woo-Woo Wisdom

Listen to your spirit, not your barking dog.

GET BACK IN
YOUR BODY

Vibes are energetic waves of subtle energy that arise from several places, some from inside your body and some from the world around you. All this makes up your vibes. Intuitive messages come from your heart and gut. Others come through the back of your head, on your arms, the back of your neck, even in your throat. These waves of energy reverberate throughout your entire physical being, sending you messages. We sense them more than we realize. The vibes traveling to and through our gut, for example, earn the expression "gut feeling." Vibes that travel up our spine can give us a chill. Vibes can affect the hairs on the back of our neck and make them stand up. Often when we hear something that feels energetically incongruent or untruthful, we'll say that it doesn't "sound right." Vibes can also affect our vision, hence the expression "I just can't see that," or "I see what you mean." We even say, "That leaves a bad taste in my mouth" or "I smell a rat" when something does not feel quite right. We may not realize it, but when we say these things, we are describing our vibes.

To sense your vibes and come to trust them, your body must be in good working order. If you tend to live in your head and tune out your body, your vibe radar will dial way down and possibly turn off altogether. If you want to tune in to a higher frequency than that of the dense physical plane, it is necessary to give your body what it needs.

BE PRESENT

Putting your body into an optimal vibe-receiving state starts with being present. Try this right now: set this book aside for 10 seconds and look around the room. Notice three separate things, with three different textures, right in front of you. Name them out loud.

For example, you might notice a window with a smooth, cool surface. Next, you might notice the floor, perhaps carpeted, or made of wood, with a warm, heavy feeling. The third thing you notice might be a plant with a soft, delicate, velvety texture.

Next, turn your attention to your body and take a nice, slow breath and notice how you feel inside right now. Tense? Relaxed? Holding your breath? Notice the feelings inside your body. Don't concern yourself with why you feel what you do. Instead, just name out loud what you feel and where in your body you feel it.

You might now feel more relaxed in the shoulders, or sense more space in your chest. Acknowledge that. Then, exhale slowly, releasing the sound "Ahhh." Repeat this a few more times.

Breathe between each feeling you notice in your body. Then turn inward once more and do it again. For example, you may notice that you feel slight anxiety in your chest on one inhale. Say that aloud, exhale, inhale, and check again. The next time you may notice you feel antsy in your lower back, as though you need to stretch or move. Keep breathing and see how much more aware of your body you become with this exercise.

Before doing this exercise, many of my students said they were numb to their body, and until they checked, they didn't feel a thing. Being aware of your body is essential to intuitive living. This is where you look for your vibes, because your body is the receiver. If you ignore your body, you miss your vibes.

This simple practice being present, done several times throughout the day, brings you back to your body. Once you are back in your body, take notice of how you feel.

If your body is stressed out, thirsty, tired, sitting too long, hungry, had too much coffee, or is deprived of a basic need, your intuitive radar weakens. Like a car that runs out of gas, the radio stops working if your body's battery is drained. When this happens, you miss the most obvious things around you and are unable to tune in to the more subtle frequencies traveling through the airwaves around you.

GET ENOUGH SLEEP

Not getting enough sleep is death to our vibes. When you look up the word *intuition* in the dictionary, one definition is "to notice," and another is "to pay attention." When you're sleep-deprived, it's challenging to focus on what's right in front of your nose, so chances are you won't notice much on the more subtle psychic plane of energy either. When you get overtired, your body tunes out—it stops feeling and only thinks.

One of the most practical suggestions for tapping into your vibes is to "sleep on it." My teacher Charlie Goodman once explained that sleep allows the emotions to rest and the spirit to get through. I know for a fact that this is true. Years ago, I struggled over whether I should keep my office manager or let her go. Even though she did a fantastic administrative job, my vibes told me something was terribly off with her—yet I couldn't quite put my finger on what it was. Firing her for no reason would have been disruptive and caused me more trouble. I wrestled with my uneasiness, trying to tune in for answers until I wore myself out. Finally, I decided to sleep on the matter and revisit it in the morning.

In my dream state, I saw my office manager opening the drawers to a dresser in my bedroom and then rifling through my closets like a thief in the night. She opened a bottom drawer and pulled out my personal diary and put it in her briefcase. Then she ran past me and into a large department store. I woke up. That was enough for me—I no longer struggled over my decision. For reasons I didn't understand, my vibes told me that she was somehow stealing my work and taking it for herself.

I confronted her the next day. I told her point-blank that I knew she was taking my writing, and because of that, she was fired. I didn't tell her I saw it in a dream. I stated it as a fact. She was surprised by what I said but didn't deny it or argue. Instead, she looked me in the eye and said, "I'm sorry." Then she gathered her things and walked out the door.

My sleep vibe was impressive. The takeaway from this is: get enough sleep so your vibes can get through.

EAT REAL FOOD

If you want to tune in to your vibes, it's important to eat properly. You can't eat junk and expect to always be on top of your game—you've got to pay attention to the foods you eat and how they affect you. Many people are sabotaging themselves with foods that aren't good for them. Not surprisingly, they often feel fatigued, headachy, or restless, and they can't focus or take in much of anything, let alone notice their subtle vibes.

It's not necessary to follow a strict diet to live in a more energetically attuned way; just make sure that what you eat is good for *you*. Sugary pastries, large cups of coffee, salty fast-food items, and frozen dinners just don't work for me. I can't do proper intuitive readings if I have too much sugar and not enough protein. I need a lot of energy to focus, so when I work, I eat oatmeal or eggs and avocados to help me concentrate. This simple choice makes all the difference in the world in the quality of my intuition.

You don't have to take my word for it—simply pay attention to how you feel when you eat. Make the connection between good food and good feelings, and bad food and bad feelings. You'll see that it's obvious. It isn't necessary to become a vegetarian or exclusively eat sprouts and tofu; just make sure your diet is as healthy for you as possible. In other words, use common sense and pay attention to the connection between the food you eat, the way you feel, and the vibes you sense.

Here's an example of what I mean. My friend Valery, a seasoned flight attendant, came to see me after seeing her doctor for extreme fatigue. She said her doctor had just informed her that her tests showed she might have thyroid cancer and suggested she have surgery to remove it as soon as possible to be on the safe side. Needless to say, the news was extremely upsetting, and she wanted a second opinion, so she came to see me. While I never offer medical advice, I did see in her reading that her diet played a significant part in her poor physical condition. I told her to look for answers there. Valery said that she had the same vibe and decided to postpone the surgery for a few weeks and consult a nutritionist. Through a series of tests with this doctor, Valery discovered she was highly gluten and dairy sensitive. This was taking a significant toll on her body. She then decided to further postpone her surgery and stop eating gluten and dairy for a month. Valery wanted to feel better before she underwent surgery and knew this change would help.

Four weeks later, Valery had a second thyroid scan. In those few short weeks since the first scan, the results showed no need for surgery at all. She also felt better than she had in a long time.

Valery *had* changed her diet dramatically. Being an "all-in" kind of person and not wanting cancer, not only did she give up gluten and dairy, but she also gave up the fast food she often grabbed at the airports. Her vibes would simply not allow her to eat it anymore. So she started making vegetable soup and salads and took those with her on trips instead. "My vibes just told me that nonstop airport food was making me sick. I couldn't ignore this, so I stopped."

Her vibes also said she didn't need surgery. Her doctor was surprised to see how much her thyroid had changed since the first scan and her diet changes, and he ultimately supported her decision not to have the surgery. Five years passed, and Valery never did have surgery on her thyroid. She has trusted her vibes ever since.

The ego misses the hidden connections between diet and awareness, while intuition sees it all the time. To this day, Valerie rightly attributes her healing to a gluten-free, dairy-free, home-made, healthy-food diet and listening to her vibes. Now, I'm not suggesting that food or intuition should replace a medical diagnosis and treatment. I'm simply suggesting we all pay attention to what we eat and notice how it affects our health. Intuition, nutrition, and health all work together. No matter how you look at it, we need to eat correctly to have our bodies and senses working at their best.

TAKE A BREAK

Tuning into vibes requires a little more downtime. Besides refreshing your body, doing nothing creates inner space to open up your intuitive channels. If you are too busy, you have a high chance of missing the subtle signals of spirit. Fear and stress create so much inner noise that you cannot hear your vibes. While your ego might urge you to keep going no matter what, your soul needs to rest and let the Universe take over for a while. When doing nothing, your intuitive channels turn up, letting intuitive downloads drop in.

My friend Bill learned this lesson firsthand a few years ago. Bill and his girlfriend were on vacation in Paris. One day, they decided to go their separate ways early in the morning and then meet back at a café next door to their hotel at five. They were staying in a small, quaint inn with a unique room key, and Bill said that he'd keep the key with him. His girlfriend insisted that she'd be more responsible with the key, but he wouldn't relent. So their rendez-vous was set.

After sightseeing and shopping, Bill headed for the café, exhausted and ready for a nap. It had begun snowing and was getting colder by the minute, and although it was only four o'clock, Bill realized he'd had enough for one day. As he sat down to enjoy a cup of café au lait, he reached into his pocket for the key. It wasn't there. He searched his pockets, but to no avail. Stressed not only about the key (which the hotel clerk had warned him not to lose because it couldn't be replaced) but also about losing face with his girlfriend, Bill was nearly frantic. Yet instead of panicking, he focused on his steaming, inviting cup of coffee, and decided that the best thing to do now was to drink very slowly and relax.

Bill sat there sipping and contemplating the passing scene, refusing to give in to panic. Finally, after 45 minutes had passed, he felt the urge to get up and walk to the first metro station he'd entered that day. He remained relaxed as he trudged through the snow, which was piling up fast by now. Ten paces before the metro entrance, he looked down, and there, lying in the snow, was his key. It must have been there all day, and amazingly, no one had taken it. Not believing his luck, Bill picked up the key and strolled back to the café, arriving at precisely five o'clock.

His waiting girlfriend was thrilled to see him, as she was loaded with packages and looking very tired. "How are you?" she asked.

"Great! Do you want some coffee?"

"No, I just want to get back to the hotel. Do you have the key?"

"I do," said Bill, holding it up and smiling.

Bill still insists that the secret was in deciding to sit, drink, and do nothing for a moment. He gave himself some room to breathe instead of going into panic mode. He made the right choice. It worked.

My teacher Dr. Tully said the most powerful thing you can do is nothing. When you relax and step back, you make room for your spirit to step up, step in, and work its magic on your behalf. He taught me that when guidance isn't forthcoming, if you sit still and do nothing but relax for a while, it will show up. I've applied that rule religiously for more than 50 years, and it really works. This was how I was directed to meet with the dean at my university in Denver to apply to the Sorbonne and ended up with admission and a full scholarship. It is how I received the guidance to walk the Camino de Santiago after my father and brother suddenly died, even though I had zero hiking experience. That was one of the most remarkable healing experiences of my life, and it set me off in an entirely new direction, including getting a much-needed divorce and moving to Paris, where I now live my extraordinary life. It's also how I receive the inspiration for all of my books. These are just a few examples of life-altering guidance I've gotten from my spirit by giving myself a little space.

Good things happen when you also give yourself some room to breathe. Your nerves relax, your ego quiets down, and your spirit begins to shine a light on your path. This is what happens when we say that a person radiates, and it's why we draw a light bulb over a person's head to demonstrate inspiration. There's a perfect French saying that describes this centered broadcast from spirit: *Je me sens bien dans ma peau*, or "I feel good in my skin." We create the perfect conditions for our intuitive channels to open up when giving our body and soul some rest, nourishment, and space.

RESPECT YOUR BODY

One of the most valuable things I learned in my apprenticeship with Charlie Goodman was the importance of respecting your body if you want to wake up your intuition. If your body is chronically neglected, exhausted, or abused, your spirit leaves via what's known as the "silver cord." This is a shimmering cord of light extending from your solar plexus to your auric field.

And when your spirit leaves, it shows. Your eyes appear dull, your face is flat and ashen, and it looks like nobody's home. On a soul level, nobody *is* home, so you won't feel much inspiration.

Even if you think that you're getting away with something, you aren't. When you abuse your body by using drugs, drinking too much, or even smoking cigarettes, you're just kidding yourself. Your body can't live in endless toxicity. Eventually, it will tell you this truth by becoming weak and thinning your aura. A thin aura allows negative energies and entities to move in, and believe me, when this happens, there's nothing "high" about that vibration. I see this all the time when I read for clients. They may think that they're sitting all alone in the chair during a reading, but often they really aren't. As I look psychically at these individuals, I often sense a crowd of little psychic critters camping out in their auras. These stowaways are lower-vibration energies composed of the generic psychic pollution of mass thinking, including general malaise, cynicism, judgment, and paranoia, and they can drive us into a funk.

The way to get rid of these unhappy campers is to become responsible for your body by giving it rest, proper food, and downtime. In addition, a good Epsom-salt bath works wonders for clearing your energy field and cleanses you of what's not yours. Put two cups of Epsom salt in a hot bath and sit and soak the psychic pollution out of you.

Woo-Woo Workout

Take good care of your body. If you've been careless about what you eat, make some changes. Give up junk food and anything that depletes your energy. It kills the vibes. Figure out which foods support you and shop for them. Stock up on fresh foods, such as fruits, veggies, and grains, and prepare them so that they're ready to grab and go. Notice how much better you feel and aware you are when you eat healthy food. Preparing food and cooking for yourself doesn't have to be difficult. You can simmer soup in a big pot and eat it all week. Plan at least one balanced, fresh meal a day, and make it or have someone make it for you. Skip that fourth cup of coffee and drink water instead. You will be surprised at how much more intuitive you become when your battery isn't dead. Intuition improves with water.

If you have chocolate (and I personally believe we all *must* have it now and then), let it be good-quality dark chocolate for your brain and mood.

To fully recharge, turn off the news, hide your phone, get a good pillow, and take a warm, relaxing bath. Listen to some healing music while in the tub. This clears the aura and relaxes the brain. Read a book that takes your mind off the present. As you lie in bed with your eyes closed, focus on your breathing. Breathe in light and breathe out everything else. Using your imagination, breathe into your heart and out through your belly. Imagine melting into the bed as you breathe. If you struggle to fall asleep, instead of trying to sleep, focus on rest and relaxation. Your body can restore itself if you let go.

Create an inner space to take "psychic breathers." Don't schedule every moment; instead, leave some free time here and there to just hang loose. Make sure you *keep* those appointments.

Be sensitive to your body's signals and respond instead of ignoring them—for example, go to the bathroom when you need to instead of postponing it until you finish a project. Stretch when your back hurts instead of staying hunched over. And try to drink at least six glasses of water a day.

Don't ignore your basic needs, but don't be too dramatic about meeting them, either—a few simple, intelligent choices go a long way toward living well. Follow the "put on your oxygen mask first" philosophy of life. Love others, but don't leave yourself behind. It's all in the attitude. A five-sensory perspective pushes you to hurry up and do more. A six-sensory one says that responsible self-care is necessary to maintain your holy temple.

P.S.: If you have addictions, not only do they ruin your sixth sense, but they ruin everything else as well. Keep in mind that as you reach for higher ground, it's necessary to leave the swamp. Before you can go one step further, be honest and admit if you need help. Then get it. It's time.

Woo-Woo Wisdom

Take care of your body.

GET GROUNDED

You must be grounded to tune in to your vibes. This means that you need to be in your body and connected to the earth. When you are ungrounded, you are unplugged. You are too energetically unsupported to accurately tune in to higher awareness. As a result, you lapse into overreaction, anxiety, worry, restlessness, and impatience, and you lose perspective on reality.

You know you are ungrounded when you experience any or all of the following: You exaggerate your problems, fret over imagined things, or act like a drama queen. You feel insecure, get angry over little things, cry easily, and react too quickly. You generally feel "off" or out of sorts, are restless, or are indecisive. You overgive, overcommit, then melt down: drop the ball, trip over your feet, go in circles, or repeat yourself for no reason. You can't focus or concentrate, or you spend a lot of energy accomplishing very little. When ungrounded, you don't have the support of the earth *or* the higher awareness of your spirit, leaving you in a mental and emotional void.

Being grounded is fundamental to tuning in to your vibes. Our bodies, like all things in nature, need to be connected to Mother Earth to function best. Grounding makes that connection. Your ego has no connection to any support other than its own fear—it's not connected to either the Divine Father or the Divine Mother, so it will try to convince you that you don't need either of them to exist. This is simply untrue. Like a cut flower in a vase, we'd perish if we were disconnected from our source.

I must admit that this has been one of the hardest lessons for me to learn. I can get caught up in in my head as much as anyone else can, even though I know it's a mistake to do so. When I'm ungrounded, I can't hear my vibes, so I become impatient, defensive, reactive, and crabby. And, to my frustration, becoming ungrounded always sneaks up on me, just as it will with you. The only difference is that I can recognize when it is happening, and I know how to fix it.

STAGES OF BECOMING UNGROUNDED

It's important to recognize the signs that you are becoming ungrounded. They are as follows:

Stage one: You get a little anxious. *Stage two:* You start getting crabby. *Stage three:* You begin to cause a little drama, letting everyone know you don't feel okay. *Stage four:* You lose your cool altogether and become unglued, unfocused, angry, weepy, or miserable. The key is to pay attention to these minor shifts and get grounded before you unravel.

Fortunately, the way to re-ground and plug back into Universal support is simple: Just reconnect with the earth by doing something physical. Every time you feel out of touch with yourself or overwhelmed, step away from others for a few minutes, stand up, stretch, and move your body. If possible, go outside and take a brisk walk for 10 to 15 minutes. As you walk, notice the world around you. Name the things you see, hear, and smell as you breathe deeply and slowly. For example, "I see a red car." Breathe. "I hear kids playing on the porch." Breathe. "I smell the lilac bush I am passing." Breathe.

Refocusing your attention on physical activity and the physical world puts you back into your body, reconnects you with the earth, and releases the adrenaline and cortisol coursing through your veins. This practice calms your nervous system and plugs you back into the earth. Moving quickly while breathing as deeply as possible gets your heart pumping, providing your body with the life force it needs to raise your vibration and elevate your awareness.

If your body were a computer, being ungrounded would be like freezing up. Doing something physical is the energetic equivalent of rebooting the system. Going outside, taking some deep breaths, and walking resets your energy system and gets everything moving in the right direction once again. It will quickly calm you down and ground you, I promise.

Physical activity also expels any accumulated negative or overloaded energy in what scientists now call your biofield and I call your aura. This is the energetic field that emanates from you and between you and others. When you are ungrounded your biofield looks a bit like Pig Pen, the *Peanuts* character who walks around in a cloud of dirt. In the same way that a rainstorm clears the atmosphere, physical movement clears psychic pollution, refreshes your biofield or aura, and resets your nervous system view.

My teacher Charlie habitually went for a brisk 30-minute walk before he met his clients to do an intuitive reading. This cleared his energy field of any lingering psychic debris he may have accumulated during the day, and it sharpened his awareness for the task ahead. It freed his mind from all distractions, so he was a clear channel when he focused on his clients.

Grounding your energy keeps you from emotionally melting down when you feel overwhelmed. It calms your nervous system and quiets your mind so that you can actually hear your vibes.

Shifting your energy from an overactive mental activity to a grounding physical activity often jump-starts your creativity as well. I have a client, Anna, who had wanted to write a memoir for years, yet she couldn't write a single sentence worth reading when she went to her desk. Her mind either went blank or she got flooded with so many ideas she couldn't make sense of them or know where to begin. Frustrated, she came to see me for guidance on how to get out of this mental sand trap.

I suggested she start her day with yoga, Pilates, or some gentle stretching, and then go for a short walk before writing. None of these interested her, so she signed up for hula lessons. Within a week of swishing her hips and heels around for 45 minutes then walking home, her inner voice started dictating her memoir to her loud and clear. Not only did she begin writing, but what she wrote was so beautiful and surprisingly organized that she felt as if she were being guided from a higher plane. Her spirit, and not her ego, was doing the writing. That's why it flowed so well. Now that she was grounded, her ego quieted down, letting her vibes do the writing for the first time. She continued her morning hula-walk ritual for four months during the summer, and by the time the hula class ended, she had a complete first draft of her book.

She refined it over the next few months, and the following spring, she self-published her completed memoir. "It was a dream come true," she said. "I don't even care if it sells. I wrote it for myself because I wanted to make sense out of my life. It was the best therapy I've ever had." Shortly after, she got the intuitive guidance to become a family systems therapist, an idea that sprouted from her writing and had never occurred to her before. She also volunteered to teach the hula class in the park the following spring. Moving her body in a hula class every morning eventually led her to her true purpose in life. That's how vibes work.

I have another client, Walter, a waiter in Chicago, who lost his job in the early months of 2020, during the pandemic. Sitting at home with no prospects for work, Walter came to me for a reading because he was deeply depressed. I suggested he take up running to get his imagination working and kick his inner guidance back into gear. "You've become ungrounded by this pandemic and need to reset." He wasn't surprised by this suggestion, even though he was far from a physical guy. He intuitively felt he could no longer sit around waiting for something to happen, so he went for it.

He started out running slowly, more like shuffling, he later told me, as he was completely out of physical shape. But he soon picked up the pace, and by the end of the first month, was running two miles a day. Each day he became more and more clear-headed as he ran. During his run, his vibes urged him to move from Chicago back to Indiana. His parents had invited him to move home months earlier, but he ignored them. Suddenly, he knew it was exactly what he must do. His vibes also told him to enroll in an online animation school, a dream he had had in high school but had abandoned. If he lived with his parents, he could do this now. If nothing else, it would be something to keep him occupied while in lockdown, and he needed that.

Following his vibes, Walter called his parents and asked them if he could come home. His parents welcomed him with open arms and even supported his plan. He was excited to have a tangible goal and no rent. Eight months after enrolling in his course, he got a sudden intuitive download for an animated kids' show, complete with an entire cast of characters. "The entire thing marched into my imagination over coffee one morning, just like that," he shared with me later. "I felt like Walt Disney dreaming up Mickey Mouse for the first time. In fact," he said, still laughing, "this is so weird, but I even wondered if the spirit of Walt Disney sent me this idea since my name is also Walter!" I didn't laugh this off. I was sure it was.

Last we spoke, Walter was in the process of creating his show and getting it into the world. He was on fire with enthusiasm and on his way to fulfilling his purpose. "It all started with running," he said, "instead of sitting around, trying to figure my life out, which only made me miserable." He fell into the flow because he got grounded, as I told him he would.

GROUNDING WHEN THINGS FALL APART

My greatest need for grounding came after the sudden death of my older brother, Anthony, followed six weeks later by my father's death and the implosion of my 30-year marriage with my then-husband Patrick, who suddenly moved out to Colorado. Blindsided with grief and traumatized by all these unexpected endings, I received guidance one morning to walk the Camino de Santiago, an 800-kilometer pilgrimage in Spain. It was unquestionably Divine Guidance because I had just had knee surgery a few weeks earlier and wasn't walking anywhere at the time. Moreover, up until then, all I had ever hiked were a few blocks to the grocery store, so hiking was hardly my idea of a healing experience. I had vaguely heard of the Camino, but it had never crossed my mind to go on it myself until that download dropped into my awareness like a telegram sent straight to me from God. Strange as it was, I knew I had to say yes.

A month later, I was on my way. The next 36 days were some of the most challenging, healing, mystical, life-transforming days of my life. While walking, I accepted and let the past go and found the inspiration and courage to leave Chicago, where I had lived for most of my adult life, and move to Paris, a dream and calling I had felt for years, and the beginning of yet another phase of my extraordinary life. (I share both adventures in my books *Walking Home* and *Waking Up in Paris*.)

You can often recognize reliable guidance and distinguish it from wishful thinking because what you receive surprises you. Believe me, being guided to walk the Camino was a *complete* surprise. I'm so glad I trusted those vibes and went. I walked out of a life where I was unhappy into one that freed my spirit. I've continued to walk every day for at least 30 minutes. These walks are my daily grounding practice in which I check in with my spirit and receive my daily download. On these walks, I listen for and receive clear direction on all matters, great and small. They leave me grounded, guided, inspired, and with a clear sense of where I am going.

Woo-Woo Workout

This week, exercise or do something physical every day for at least 15 minutes. Start with a short walk around the block and then build up to more extended efforts. During this time, simply enjoy yourself and allow your mind to relax. Notice how negative energy starts to drain out of your body, leaving you more relaxed the more you move. You can amplify this effect by exhaling all anxiety and worry and inhaling health and vitality with every deep breath you take.

Observe how physical activity increases your intuition and awareness. For example, thoughts become sharper after you go for a walk than while you're sitting in your office all day. Doing something physical opens intuitive pathways, leaving your mind clear, your aura cleansed, and your attention sharp and attuned to guidance.

Woo-Woo Wisdom

Your body is your intuitive receiver.

LISTEN
TO YOUR
BODY

Perhaps the most immediate way to tune in to your vibes is by listening to the energetic feedback of your physical body. Your head listens to your ego, which filters out and distorts information, believes what is not true, or convinces you that it's okay to do what's harmful. Your body, however, listens to your spirit, which tells the truth. It honestly and accurately reflects how energy impacts you on a vibrational level through physical signals, such as aches, pains, flutters, ripples, tightness, fatigue, or even sickness to keep you safe and aligned with your spirit. Of course, the signals change depending on what they are trying to tell you.

The good news is, not only is the body an honest, intuitive channel, it's also straightforward. In other words, if you're on the right track doing what supports your soul and spirit, then you're going to feel more at ease, full of life, relaxed, and peaceful. Your heart will open and beat steadily. Your energy will increase, and you'll be relatively free from stress. If, on the other hand, you're making choices that compromise or betray your spirit, or if you find yourself in circumstances that threaten or disrupt your energetic well-being, your heart will pound, your stress will rise, your sleep may be harder to come by, and your body may even hurt.

If you ignore these signals for a long time, your physical body will turn up the volume and try even harder to get your attention. These louder signals result in greater tension, irritability, insomnia, reactivity, anxiety, or any number of little to bigger physical disturbances. And if you ignore your body's signals completely, a "red alert" siren turns on in the way of more significant physical disturbance, and there's a good chance that you could become ill or depressed.

YOUR BODY TALKS

Fortunately, your body's signals are easy enough to read. It's mostly a matter of deduction. For example, problems with your legs or feet usually reflect where you're going in life, if you are grounded, or whether you are standing on your own two feet. Problems with your sexual organs and lower abdomen often reflect blocked creativity, or an absence of pleasure or sexual safety. They also reflect danger or distress about the person you are sexually engaging with.

My client Elaine had recurring bladder infections and extreme PMS the entire time she dated and lived with her boyfriend, Jim. She was at a doctor's office every other month. However, instead of being compassionate, Jim acted annoyed with Elaine's chronic physical distress, which didn't help Elaine feel any better. Finally, six months following their breakup, after she learned he was a chronic cheater, she realized she had not had a single bladder infection in a while, and her PMS was substantially better as well. She didn't connect the two at first, but one day it occurred to her that her relief had everything to do with Jim no longer being in her life.

Gastrointestinal difficulties, irritable bowel, reflux, and other digestive troubles can signal a feeling of being overwhelmed, not feeling nourished, or that you're unable to digest life or "stomach" certain conditions. My client Maria had suffered from severe reflux and diarrhea for three years. Eliminating every dietary and medical reason possible, one day, just before going to sleep, she asked her body why this was happening. She was tired of suffering. Ten minutes later, she was flooded with a desire to quit her job at a not-for-profit food-distribution organization. While she believed in the ideals of the job, Maria often said she couldn't stomach her boss, an incompetent, arrogant director, as far as she was concerned. There was such an obvious connection between her sick gut and her sickening boss that she couldn't believe how she could have missed this.

Maria was married to an extremely wealthy man and felt guilty that she enjoyed such abundance while so many other people starved in the world. She recognized that perhaps she was punishing herself for having such good fortune by sticking with this poorly paid yet "noble cause" job that was making her sick. After she quit her job, Maria joined a volunteer group that grew a local community garden. Through that, she learned of a volunteer position at a local inner-city middle school in Chicago that had just started their own experimental community garden. These kids were learning to grow food that they could take home to their families and eat. Her time spent between these two new commitments was fulfilling and fun. It took almost a year, but eventually, her reflux subsided, and her bowel troubles started to ease. Maria was able to reduce her medication by half. "I resented my body for giving me so much trouble. Then I realized it was just trying to save my soul and I was too stubborn and willful to listen," she admitted.

Heart concerns are often associated with feeling disconnected from your emotions or may reflect difficulty giving and receiving love, while neck and throat issues may relate to speaking up or out, being heard, or listening to the world with an open mind and heart. Difficulties with your eyes often indicate problems with perception, outlook, and point of view, not wanting to see what's in front of you, or even fear of seeing what's ahead. Brain problems may reflect deeply held, even karmic emotional pain.

This, of course, is a highly simplified version of how the spirit communicates with the body—and it's certainly not intended to say these are the *only* reasons our bodies experience illness. The spirit signals the body for all reasons, and some of those reasons are warnings. If such warning signs are ignored for some time, they can increase in intensity to the point of causing a physical disturbance. Therefore, taking care of the body should include listening to your emotional and intuitive signals along with other factors. More and more doctors are now recognizing this mind-body-spirit connection to health and asking their patients about their intuition as a way to treat them.

Our bodies are highly sophisticated and complex. We need to love our bodies, listen to them, and give them all the support they need if we want to be healthy.

NOTICE THE SUBTLE SIGNALS

Start noticing what is going on in your body instead of ignoring it. If something is off, don't deny it. Instead, be interested and wonder why. Observe with interest and ask your body what's up—your body will directly tell you what's wrong and why if you want to know.

Even though there are some general similarities in everyone's psychic-feedback system, each has its own unique set of signals. For example, when I'm exposed to something or someone potentially dangerous or harmful to my spirit, my body warns me by giving me a rapid heartbeat and a sense of "ants in my pants," as if I need to run away as fast as possible. The minute I get this signal, I know that I'm into something I should avoid, so I do.

My friend Dave gets his strongest intuitive warning signals in his back. Whenever his back aches, he knows he has been taking on too much responsibility for his family and friends and needs to cut back. A generous man by nature, he easily gets taken advantage of and becomes buried in others' problems. However, he is developing better boundaries, as he doesn't want the pain anymore.

When I was young and my mother felt that something wasn't right for her (or was "off," as she called it), she got a buzz in her ears. I remember dozens of times being in the middle of a sentence, and she'd shush me because her ears started ringing with a warning that she needed to pay attention to.

One time after school, when I was 13 years old, I was sitting with my best friend and my mom, recounting the day, when suddenly she shushed us, cocked her head to the side, and said, "Quiet! Something just happened." She was silent for about 10 seconds and then said, "Anthony has been in an accident." Five minutes later, my brother called from the hospital located just three blocks from our house. He had been in an accident, just as my mom had felt. He was pretty banged up but, thankfully, nothing more than that. The thing that struck me was how my mom sensed the minute the accident happened. This occurred all the time with my mom and was always impressive.

In teaching clients, I've observed that sometimes they are overcome with fatigue and cannot stay awake in class. Usually, this happens when I suggest a change that they are not quite ready for, such as leaving a bad relationship, quitting a job that's not good for them, or admitting a self-defeating behavior, such as an addiction. They go unconscious because they are not yet ready to be conscious about this subject. I point this out when it happens, and those guilty of falling asleep on themselves usually laugh and admit it's true. This is an example of how our ego shuts down our inner guidance.

On the other hand, shutting down may also signal that something is just so wrong for you that your body won't cooperate at all. When I was in high school, I took a job at a men's clothing company, working in the back office, posting monthly statements and mailing them to the clients. I can honestly say it was the worst job I've ever had. I could barely keep awake after arriving each day. It was pure torture. I knew it was all wrong for me, mainly because, apart from being dreadfully boring, my boss was a terrible alcoholic and so toxic she frightened me. One day I nearly passed out at my desk from resistance to being there. All of a sudden, the machine I was posting the monthly bills on started smoking. My boss screamed, "What is happening?" I didn't know because I was asleep. Waking up with a jolt, I said, "I quit" at the exact moment she said, "You're fired."

I ran out with the machine smoking behind me, thrilled to have escaped this terrible situation. After that, I vowed never again to work in an office. It wasn't suitable for me or safe for any office, given how the machine had just blown up.

Physical signals are "psychic telegrams." Read them. What is your body telegram telling you? Any gut feelings, tightness in the chest, flutter in the throat, or chills on your arms? These intuitive signals are usually subtle in the beginning and may never become strong, but they are always there and will get your attention if you make them important.

I have a client, a successful restaurant owner, who has strong gut warnings every time he gets involved with unscrupulous people, which often occurs in the restaurant business. He finally learned his lesson to never ignore his gut after getting into a partnership with a person he had had a terrible gut feeling about. Sure enough, a year later he was caught stealing money. My client had to take him to court and go through an awful ordeal after that. So now, if he gets even the *slightest* warning in his gut about something, he refuses to be involved.

Another client, Stephanie, who used to work in sales, explained that she felt a lump in her chest whenever she made a deal with someone who wasn't going to pay her. This became so clear that in time she decided to leave sales altogether. "Why should I work so hard on commission when clients take products they don't pay for, and I don't get paid? I finally listened to that lump in my throat and said, 'I quit.'" Stephanie now teaches at a school for the blind and loves her job.

Once you start paying attention to your body's vibes, you'll appreciate how faithfully they keep you informed, not only about what's really going on around you, but what's going on with your body itself.

YOUR BODY IS YOUR ALLY

Listening to your body's signals can keep you balanced and safe. After all, your health-care practitioners and advisors are only human, so they need your help to keep you healthy. I've spoken with several doctors over the years who admit that in some of their patients' cases, they're merely guessing at a diagnosis and can use all the help they can get in figuring out the problem. Knowing this, you can see how limiting it is to completely surrender your well-being to others, regardless of how talented they are. A far more enlightened approach to health care is a partnership with your medical experts.

My client Tracy is another example of how strong the body's signals can be. After numerous attempts over five years to become pregnant with in vitro fertilization and fertility drugs, Tracy had no luck conceiving a second child. Frustrated and demoralized, she came in for a reading to learn what the problem was. The doctors could only guess at the trouble, but my reading showed that neither Tracy nor her husband had any specific physical trouble, but emotionally, she was resistant to conception. I picked up on a soul level that she'd long been concerned about world overpopulation and had once made a commitment to help the problem by mothering an abandoned child. On a conscious level, she'd forgotten about this; her body, however, had not. Tracy's body had remained faithful to the commitment by not conceiving any more children of her own.

After sharing what I'd picked up, I asked her, "Does any of this make sense to you?"

Tracy wasn't surprised, and replied, "Yes, actually, it does. I've always secretly felt that I should adopt a child, even before I was married. But after the birth of my son, I forgot about it. I never even discussed it with my husband. He's so set on having another baby that I haven't brought it up. But I feel guilty about continuing our efforts when children are waiting to be parented in our own city and I can help. It bothers me, but I've been ignoring it."

I didn't hear from Tracy for two years, at which point she sent me a note saying that she and her husband had adopted a four-year-old girl. Nine months later, she notified me that they'd adopted a little boy, too. Her body was faithful to what her soul really wanted, even if she didn't consciously realize it at the time.

No matter how confusing your body's signals may appear, they always make sense if you just listen and learn the language. Listening to your body's vibes for guidance and feedback may seem odd at first, but keep in mind that your body is a direct conduit to your Higher Self, and it won't mislead you. Every signal it sends has direct meaning and essential information for your physical well-being, spiritual balance, and safety. It doesn't take a mystic to read and understand your body's messages—after all, it's *your* body. The more you pay attention to it and want to understand what it's trying to convey, the easier it becomes.

Consider your body signals carefully. If you have a bellyache every time you go to work, perhaps it's telling you not to go. If you can't sleep at night, maybe your body can't get your attention during the day. If you get tired every time you go out on a date with someone, perhaps that person is draining you. It doesn't take a detective to figure it out—just a little attention.

Woo-Woo Workout

Try something I call a vibe check. By this I mean run a mental scanner over yourself from head to toe and see if you're receiving any signals. Do you sense any psychic telegrams in the form of aches, pains, tingles, illness, or tension? If so, ask the feeling directly what it is telling you. Then answer out loud. Don't overthink it and try to figure it out, because you'll get stuck back in your head. Instead, sound it out by speaking directly from the heart and do it quickly. The faster you acknowledge what you're feeling in a vibe check, the more precise the answer coming through will be. Be curious about the message and let your body do the listening.

While taking your shower, vibe check again. Water washes away mental debris and interference and leaves your mind quiet so your heart can be heard. Something in you opens while under running water that frees the intuitive voice inside. Mentally scan your body from the feet up, slowly. Check to see if you notice anything at all, however slight, that is trying to tell you something. Remember, vibes are subtle. If you pause or hesitate at any part of your body, your body is trying to tell you something. Instead, ask it directly what's going on. Ask what it wants you to know, what is essential that you haven't noticed before, and what it needs. Then let it know that you're now paying attention.

If you curse, reject, or criticize your body regularly, please stop, because you're really hurting yourself by attacking your primary intuitive receiver. Your body is your ally, so quit diminishing, poisoning, harming, or ignoring it. Don't shoot the messenger—after all, your body can only work with what you give it, and it's just trying to protect you either from yourself or from something in your world.

If you have a particular physical challenge, ask your body what you can do to ease the problem. Resist the temptation to dismiss this as a waste of time. Dr. David Edelberg, one of Chicago's most respected holistic physicians, my good friend of 25 years, and the author of *Healing Fibromyalgia*, once told me that after 55 years of medical practice, he's observed that the best way to stay healthy is to talk to your body first: "It's the best diagnostician I know."

Don't dismiss what you feel as if it's only your imagination when your body talks to you either—even if it is, what you're imagining will have meaning. Instead, pay close attention and voice these body messages out loud so that you can hear what your body is saying. The more you acknowledge your body's signals out loud, the clearer and more precise your body's messages will be.

Vibe check often throughout the day. Be alert for any tension, tightness, rumbles, tickles, flickers, uneasiness, pain, loss, or surge of energy, or fits of restlessness—and see if they correlate to the situation you're in. For example, does the tightness in your chest correspond to entering your workplace? Does the burst of energy you feel have anything to do with the great new friend you just met or the class you enrolled in? Notice how your body communicates the red and green lights of intuitive feedback, and don't censor or dismiss a thing.

Opening a dialogue with your body is the beginning of creating better physical and psychic health.

Woo-Woo Wisdom

Your body tells the truth.

PART II
<hr />

MIND OVER
MATTER

TAKE IT EASY

It helps to maintain a peaceful and relatively calm attitude and inner state when learning to tune in to your intuition. When you're tense, nervous, or anxious, your mind gets worked up and blocked, and it is difficult to shift into your heart center, where your spirit and vibes communicate.

Remaining calm despite what's going on around you is incredibly challenging. However, calming down even a little will help you tune in to your vibes for guidance and will probably add a few years to your life as well—after all, getting worked up about things only makes them worse. Life will always be full of drama and challenges; we all know that. But you don't have to freak out or overreact to any of it if you train yourself not to. You have the option of being less emotionally reactive and, instead, trusting there is always a solution that your vibes will reveal if you remain calm and tune inward.

Martial arts students are taught that their best defense is to maintain a calm state of mind so they can sense trouble before it occurs and step out of harm's way instead of running into it head-on. When you practice being calm, it becomes far easier to tune in to your vibes on demand so you can sense trouble before it happens. One of the primary benefits of having vibes is being warned instead of being caught off guard in life. Sensing this danger is far more possible if you're open, relaxed, and at ease.

PSYCHIC ALERTS

Animals are good examples of this phenomenon. In her book *The Highly Sensitive Person*, Elaine Aron writes that when antelopes feel a stampede, they move away 30 minutes before it arrives because they're so calm. We humans have an intuitive self-defense system that's even more sophisticated, and if we don't get hysterical every time something challenging happens, we can access it. When we become agitated and overwhelmed, it doesn't take an intuitive to see that we're creating so much commotion within ourselves that we'll misread the energy around us.

My client Adam, a software salesman, was on his way to an early-morning meeting, quietly listening to classical music on his car radio, as he usually did, so he would arrive calm and collected when he arrived. As he drove this morning, however, a few minutes after leaving the house, he had a sudden overwhelming urge to go back home. He ignored the feeling for a block or two, but it was so strong the car almost turned on its own. Not sure why, Adam wondered as he drove into the driveway if perhaps he had forgotten something. This wasn't the first time Adam felt the vibe to do something he didn't understand, so he was curious as he walked through the door, wondering what the reason would be. Immediately after entering, he found out, when he smelled acrid smoke coming from behind the dishwasher, which he had started just before leaving. Rushing to turn off the circuit breakers to the kitchen, he immediately called 911. Within minutes two fire trucks arrived and six firefighters stormed into the place. They pulled the dishwasher out and used their axes to break into the wall behind it, where they discovered smoldering wires and the beginning of an electrical fire, which they quickly put out.

Once the bedlam was over, one of the firemen turned to Adam and said, "Wow, you are so lucky you caught this when you did. Good thing you were home."

"The thing is, I wasn't home," Adam answered, shaking his head in disbelief at how glad he was that he followed his vibe to come back. "I was on my way to a meeting when suddenly I felt the need to turn around, so I did." When he heard this, the fireman raised his eyebrows then said, "Well, sir, you must have some kind of angel upstairs!" "I do," Adam agreed, relieved his house hadn't just burned to the ground. After they left, Adam sat down and took a breath before calling the insurance company to report what had happened. Amazed at how lucky he had been, he was grateful he was calm and not in a rush that day, or he might have ignored his vibe and lost his house.

BREATHE

Being calm is a skill that starts with proper breathing. Dr. Tully taught me that breathing deeply and regularly is the key to remaining calm and instantly connects us to a higher vibration. When we're stressed or fearful, we tend to hold our breath, which traps us in the head and cuts us off from our hearts, our spirit, and our intuitive vibes. Breathing shallowly puts our bodies into fight or flight, and we don't even know it. In this state, we shut out any chance of receiving guidance. Dr. Tully said that it's almost physically impossible to be uptight and breathe deeply simultaneously. It is also nearly impossible to get caught in someone's dramatic reaction if you both breathe together. This is called sharing a breath. It's a way to steer clear of a conflict and tune in when someone is agitated and truly tuned out.

The way to do this is to start breathing in sync with that person, then slow your breathing to a deeper, calmer pace. The upset person will automatically follow your breathing and calm down too. This is actually easier to do than you think, because humans naturally fall into sync with one another. It may take up to 10 breaths to achieve synced breathing with an agitated person. When you are both breathing calmly, you reduce the drama and even eliminate it. What's more, this is when your vibes can get through and offer a solution to the problem causing all the drama in the first place. Try it, and you'll see for yourself.

Jane, a commercial interior designer, didn't believe this could work but gave it a try. She was working with a co-worker whose constant drama made her desperate for some relief. I suggested she try this breathing technique. The very next day, Jane's co-worker dashed into her office all worked up over the news that the carpet scheduled for delivery that day wasn't coming. As she ranted and raved at what a disaster this was, Jane just started breathing with her and said nothing. The woman eventually stopped talking and noticed Jane was quietly breathing. "What are you doing?" she asked, both annoyed and confused. Jane took another long, slow, deep breath, and simply said, "I'm listening," then took another long, slow, deep breath. As if compelled to follow, the co-worker took a deeper breath herself.

"The funny thing is," Jane shared with me later, "once I started breathing, I stopped listening to my co-worker and started listening to my vibes. The delay in the carpet did present a huge problem, as we had scheduled many other installations around this, so we needed help. I asked my vibes for guidance and suddenly felt the need to call the owner of the carpet company and ask him to help."

Not letting her intellect argue, she asked her co-worker, "Do you have the owner's number?"

"No, but I can get it," she responded.

"Please do," Jane said, still breathing slowly. Once the co-worker handed it over, Jane dialed, and the owner picked up. Still remaining calm, Jane explained that they were just informed of the delay and shared that this would be catastrophic for their project. "Can you do anything?" she asked. The owner was surprisingly receptive. "I'm sure it was because I was so calm," Jane said.

Rather than say it was out of his hands and in the hands of the delivery company, which he certainly could have, he said, "Give me a minute," and put her on hold. She was on hold for 10 minutes but remained calm and continued to breathe as slowly as she could. Her co-worker stood in her office, saying nothing. Her hysteria had drained out of her body by now, and she was as quiet as Jane was.

It seemed like an eternity, but eventually, the owner came back on the line and said, "You're in luck. You called just in time for me to get the delivery company to reschedule you back in for today. You are on their docket, and the carpet will be there by three this afternoon. Good timing. A few minutes later, and there would have been nothing I could do."

Jane thanked him profusely and hung up. Then she turned to her co-worker and said, "Problem solved." Her co-worker was silent for a full 10 seconds, then said, "That was amazing. Thank you."

"No problem," Jane answered. "If you remain calm and breathe, a lot gets solved."

"No kidding," her co-worker responded. "I have to remember this."

Please do, Jane thought, but only smiled.

THE POWER OF "AHHHH . . ."

My favorite breathing technique is to inhale and then slowly open your jaw wide, and exhale while saying, out loud, "Ahhhh . . ." This practice immediately centers and calms me.

Try it right now—you'll see that it works. Dr. Tully had me breathe like this for a few minutes every day, starting with two breaths and gradually extending it until it became second nature. It took a while, but breathing in this way is now a habit, especially when under stress.

Another great breathing exercise is to place one hand on the belly and the other on the chest and breathe in through the nose and out through the mouth slowly, as if blowing out candles, until you feel calm. Using this stress reliever when you feel scared or unsure will signal your vibes to kick into gear and help you attain higher ground and gain direction in minutes.

When training your mind to trust your vibes, be aware of what sends you into orbit, and if possible, eliminate the trigger at its source. It took me years to realize that loud noises caused me to melt down. It feels as if I'm being electrocuted. Unreasonable deadlines almost always cause my friend Julia to hyperventilate and block any intuitive inspiration, while too many commitments tie my neighbor Celine into a knot and shut her vibes down.

Knowing these things, we try to avoid these stress-inducing situations: I regulate the noise level around me, Julia negotiates her deadlines well in advance, and Celine says no.

What can you change in your life so that you're calm and peaceful?

OUT YOUR INNER CONTROL FREAK

Another way to remain calm is to stop your barking dog from trying to control everyone around you. The more controlling it is, the more you'll fight with life and everyone in it. Sometimes you aren't even aware when your ego is controlling you. It cleverly tries to fake you out and make you believe you are spiritually motivated when, in fact, it's only more of the same old ego stuff in disguise. Here's a clue: If you are spirit-led, things run peacefully. If you are ego-driven, there's usually a struggle or fight. That's how you tell who is running the show.

For example, my client Marion saw herself as very spiritual. The truth was that she rarely actually listened to her spirit—instead, she was always figuring things out in her head. For example, she insisted that she loved her teenage children, and to show it, she got up every morning to prepare breakfast for them before school. Now, this sounds very loving of her, I agree, but her kids weren't hungry in the morning and repeatedly told her so. Marion insisted that they eat anyway because of all the trouble she went through to prepare breakfast for them. The kids just fought back. Consequently, her good intentions deteriorated into daily power struggles, and everyone in the family started their morning miserably.

Finally, Marion stopped micromanaging and listened to her vibes for guidance. They told her to make her own breakfast and then go for a walk before the kids got up. Just thinking about doing this made her feel better, even though her brain said it was selfish. As a result, Marion's mornings became her favorite time of the day, and her kids were happier too.

TBS

People often ask me, "How can you tell the difference between your spirit and your ego?" This is a good question. The answer is that the energy you feel in your body is significantly different when listening to your spirit as compared with listening to your ego.

First of all, when your spirit is guiding the way, your body feels relaxed and open, even expansive, like you have a little more internal room to breathe. You also tend to feel somewhat playful and spontaneous. Your mind is generally quiet, and you feel at ease and fully present. You are not focused on the future or the past. You can easily see the humor in things and laughing comes easily. Because your heart is open, you also tend to be more forgiving, tolerant, and compassionate toward others, and don't easily take offense. You quickly tune in to solutions to problems or at least have confidence that solutions will show up. Even when your spirit warns you of a need to change course or alerts you to danger, you tend to be calm and centered instead of feeling agitated, confused, or ambivalent.

In contrast, when your ego is running the show, your body tenses up and becomes more rigid, as if unconsciously bracing for the worst. Your muscles contract, your jaw sets, you stop listening, your breathing becomes shallower, and you disconnect from others. I playfully call being controlled by the ego TBS, or Tight Butt Syndrome, because when your ego is running the show your buttocks tighten, your hips tend to lock, and you have a wooden Howdy Doody smile as opposed to a real one plastered across your face.

When your spirit is in control, if someone asks, "How are you?" your eyes will light up, you'll smile brightly, and you'll likely answer, "Great!" When your ego is in control, your response is usually a dry, "I'm fine," which you and everyone else knows is not the truth but is the most your ego will reveal. The ego typically throws up a subtle energetic barrier between you and other people for fear of being hurt or found out, so no one can get too close.

The truth is, our barking-dog egos are just trying to take care of us like the faithful servants they are. They just fail miserably because they are not capable of leading well. Your spirit, by contrast, is a natural leader. If your barking dog is trying to control things, recognize it as a failed attempt to make your life better, then take a deep breath or two, squeeze your buttocks really hard for five seconds, and relax your entire body with a loud, audible, "Ahhhh."

This muscle contraction followed by release drains the tension out of your body, frees your jaw, opens your heart, and tunes you back in to your spirit.

Woo-Woo Workout

Let's train your ego to relax and let go. Begin each day with a few minutes of deep breathing—inhale and then exhale to the sound of "Ahhhh," and repeat this for a minute or two. When you're in stressful situations, remember to place your hands over your belly and chest and breathe in through your nose and out through your mouth. If possible, get a relaxing massage. If you can't, take a bubble bath every night and stay in the tub long enough to unwind.

Imagine that your spirit is in charge, even if you don't feel it. Fake it 'til you make it! Training your ego is like training a puppy—it takes consistency and patience. Give your ego a good idea of what a trained ego looks like. Watch funny and entertaining movies with characters who stay cool under pressure, such as The Pink Panther or Cool Hand Luke. This is the quickest reset from ego to spirit. Pretend you are relaxed like the characters on the screen, and you soon will be back in spirit.

If you get into any reactive arguments, try to remember to pause and breathe. And if you're brave, say, "You win," and drop it. (I know this one is challenging, but try it.) If you can't quite surrender straight away, don't worry about it. We're striving for progress, not mastery. It takes time and repetition to train the ego. It learns to quiet down a step at a time. It will eventually settle down if you keep at it.

Talk to your barking dog. Ask what the problem is, what triggers it and causes it to freak out. Anxiety? Insecurity? Restlessness? Boredom? Impatience? Fear?

Remember to breathe as you do this. This calms and soothes your ego and reconnects you with your spirit. And go to bed early, secure in knowing that your spirit and the Universe are in control, not your barking dog.

Tension-Buster Bonus

Practice tightly tensing and relaxing your muscles: squeeze your muscles for 10 seconds, then release. Start with your neck and shoulders and the muscles in your face: tense, hold, release. Next, move to the muscles in your stomach, chest, and back: tense, hold, release. Next, go to the muscles in your buttocks: tense, hold, release. Finally, tense the muscles in your legs and feet: tense, hold, release.

When you finish tensing all the muscles in your body, shake them out, as if you were a bowl of Jell-O, and let out a few belly sounds, such as "Aaaah" or "Oooh." Repeat until you feel all the tension in your body drain away. Notice how much more aware you are when you're not tense.

Woo-Woo Wisdom

Squeeze, then breathe.

MAKE TIME
TO BE QUIET

You must first tune in to your vibes before you can trust them. And to do this, you have to quiet your noisy mind. Your vibes are subtle and unobtrusive, and even though they're always present, they can easily get drowned out by your clamoring mental chatter. It's not that your spirit is reticent or shy; it's just low-key and doesn't often interrupt. So, until you are mentally quiet enough, you can easily miss your vibes. Just as it's nearly impossible to listen to two people talk at the same time, you can't hear your vibes if your ego is blathering nonstop over your spirit, competing for attention.

CHILL OUT

However, as we all know, quieting the mind is easier said than done, at least in the beginning. Your ego, the source of all this inner chatter, is willful, highly opinionated, and does not like to give up the floor. The key is to look for ways to silence it without a fight. Start by noticing the times in which your ego naturally quiets down. When working in the garden, for instance. Or cooking dinner. Or on a drive. These are great times to tune in and receive guidance.

For example, Kim, a client of mine, a sales representative for a pharmaceutical company, had to drive 40 miles to appointments twice a week. She liked to commute with the radio turned off so that she could receive intuitive downloads from her spirit as she drove along. One day, on her way to a regular appointment in the next town, Kim felt a sudden strong vibe that today was the perfect time to request her long-wanted transfer to San Francisco, where her family lived.

Kim was surprised because she was recently told the company had no openings there. Even though her vibes flew in the face of the unlikelihood of success, given her recent rejection, she listened anyway. "Okay, I will ask again," Kim said aloud to her inner voice as she cruised along the highway. Kim put in another transfer request that afternoon, and just before she sat down to dinner, the San Francisco office unexpectedly called her, saying a long-term employee had a sudden health issue and they needed someone to take his place fast. She could have the transfer if she was ready to move right away. She jumped at the chance. As Kim later told me, "Had it not been for my quiet drive, I'm positive that I would have missed my opportunity. It was the quiet that allowed me to hear my spirit loud enough to follow through and ask that day."

DAYDREAMS CAN BE INTUITIVE VISIONS

My friend Lara is a vegan baker who started a gluten-free bakery in her small town years ago that has since grown into a regional success. Her bakery started long before most people realized eating gluten was not good for their bodies and she was frequently laughed at for her niche bakery concept. I asked her how she had known to start her business when she did, even though most of her friends and family were unsupportive.

Lara said she was daydreaming in her hammock in her backyard one afternoon when the idea came to her. "In my daydream, I saw people lined up as clearly as if they were physically standing in front of me, all wanting my gluten-free cookies and bread. I knew it was a vision that would come to pass if I opened a bakery."

I knew a sculptor who created beautiful steel and granite pieces. When I asked him how he got his inspiration, he said that in the night, when everyone was asleep and the house was so quiet you could hear a pin drop, he got visions. "All of a sudden, I see these sculptures in my mind's eye in three dimensions," he explained. "I walk around them and study them very carefully. I can almost touch them; they feel so clear. Then I can re-create what I see. But the visions only appear when it's completely silent."

Over the years, I've received many unexpected intuitive messages in quiet moments like these, especially when taking a short afternoon nap, which I often do. A favorite memory is when Eric, a close friend from France, called to tell me that his father, Serge, had suddenly died. Serge was someone I had loved dearly; in fact, it was his family that had taken me in when I was a student at the Sorbonne the first time I moved there. Eric was shocked and devastated by his father's death, and since he was on his way to Chicago for business later that week, I invited him to dinner.

Before Eric arrived, I took a quick 20-minute nap in my favorite chair. Not quite awake but not quite asleep, I clearly heard twice in my mind, *Cherry clafouti*. I knew that cherry clafouti was a French dessert, but I didn't know anything else about it. I wondered why I had received this message, since I'd never had the dessert or even thought about it. Nevertheless, it sounded interesting. When I roused myself, I knew I should serve that to Eric for dessert, even though I didn't have a clue how to make it.

Inspired by the challenge, I found a recipe and made the dessert. During dinner, Eric was quite emotional, mainly because he hadn't been able to say good-bye to his dad and tell him how much he loved him. After dinner, I wanted to comfort my friend, so I said, "Well, Eric, I know this won't necessarily cheer you up, but I have a special dessert for you this evening—cherry clafouti. How does that sound?"

Eric nearly jumped out of his chair. "Mon Dieu!" he cried, stunned. "Cherry clafouti was my father's favorite dessert. He adored it!"

"He must have asked for it himself this afternoon as I was resting," I told my heartbroken friend. It was as though Serge was telling his son that he was still near him. And somehow, that cherry clafouti offered Eric some comfort and some closure.

We naturally quiet our egos and give our spirits room to speak when doing certain "mindless" activities—tidying up, folding laundry, taking a catnap—but for most people, unless we pay attention, these moments slip by unnoticed. But your quiet moments don't have to be random or lost. You can intentionally tune in to your vibes by recognizing what makes your barking dog naturally settle down and doing that activity when you need to check in with your vibes.

PUT THE PHONE AWAY

Long before technology started holding our attention hostage for so many hours of the day, people had more time to let their minds wander, rest, daydream, imagine, and tune inward. But unfortunately, electronic gadgets—especially cell phones—steal away this precious inner time and keep us from connecting to our spirit and inner Self more than any other obstacle. This is a big problem because when we don't have time to make this essential inner connection with our spirit, our egos take over and lead us offtrack while our spirits get pushed to the back of our awareness.

It's essential to preserve our quiet time by putting away the phone, letting go of the outside world for a bit, and turning inward to our heart and spirit every day. It helps if you deliberately carve out this time in your day, knowing now is the time to be quiet and free of outside stimulation, so you can mentally relax and tune inward.

Larry, a high school biology teacher, suddenly found himself working at home due to the pandemic. For months, he was glued to a computer screen for long, frustrating hours at a time. By the end of the school year, he was so burned out that he impulsively quit his job. "I knew I had to do it but hadn't thought it through," he said, suddenly facing the practical ramifications of not having a paycheck. With a lot more time on his hands, he got his bike out of storage and started riding every morning along the lakefront of Chicago to unwind from the stress. Leaving his phone home, Larry listened to the sunrise instead, finding the quiet hour music to his soul.

After three weeks of early-morning rides, Larry spontaneously got the vibe to look for work in landscape gardening, something he loved but had had no time for. "The minute that idea came to me, my entire being lit up," he shared. "I knew it was right for me." That same day he rode his bike over to the local garden center and asked for a job. "I was immediately hired at fifteen dollars an hour and thrilled about it," he said. Within four months, Larry was transferred to the landscape department, helping people design their gardens. Within six months, he became their main designer. "I got a significant raise, and the garden center created a position for me that didn't exist before, sending me directly to people's homes so I could design their gardens on site."

Larry started his own business the following spring and had so many requests he could barely keep up. "I've never been happier or busier in my life," he continued. The surprise bonus was that during all of this, he met a woman, and within a few months, they fell in love and decided to get married. They are setting out on this new path together. "This all came about because of my phone-free sunrise bike rides," Larry said at dinner while visiting me this summer. "I would have never made this turn in life if it had not been for that."

MEDITATE

My spiritual teachers taught me that the best way to ensure quiet moments is to meditate every day. I agree, at least in theory. While I encourage meditation in all my books, in working with so many people over the years, I've observed that most people still don't do it, despite all the information out there confirming how valuable this practice is. In addition to helping us tap into our intuition, meditation reduces stress, helps us feel peaceful and grounded, sharpens our senses, and increases our patience and creativity. And yet, so many people resist. They are confused about how to do it, or don't do it in the traditional way, which is to get comfortable, relax your mind, center your attention, and breathe peacefully and calmly for 5 to 20 minutes while emptying your brain of thought and worry.

It doesn't take talent to meditate, only patience, consistency, and reasonable expectations. If you have these in place your mind will get used to the idea and begin to cooperate. If you meditate daily at the same time, for example, each time you sit down to meditate, it will become easier and faster to reach the state of inner calm you seek. The key to success is not to expect anything other than giving yourself a little peace and quiet. If you think you must drift into nirvana to be "really" meditating (which is your ego talking), you'll just get frustrated and quit.

CREATE CALM OUTSIDE TO FIND CALM INSIDE

To meditate, it helps to get quiet inside by creating calm around you. This means turning off your cell phone, the music, the TV, the computer, and anything else that might distract you. Also, you don't necessarily have to meditate in the sanctuary of your home. Several of my clients have found more success meditating in the most unlikely places. For example, Lee found herself meditating far more easily in the Episcopal church next to her shop in Chicago during her lunch hour than she did at home with three teenagers in the next room. Even though she wasn't Episcopalian, this was the perfect place for her to meditate. "The atmosphere was so calm and conducive to being mentally quiet, I found I could quickly silence my thoughts there."

Martin found his meditation spot on a bench in Regent's Park near his home office in London, where he simply sat and fed the geese for 30 minutes at noon every day. "My apartment is small, and the neighbors are noisy, and it frustrated me to try to meditate there, so I gave up. While I'm not sitting with my eyes closed, I'm not thinking either, which counts as meditation for me," he said. I agree—it's called mindfulness.

Michelle paradoxically found tranquility when sitting in a busy Denver shopping center, watching infants and toddlers play in the little playground in the middle of the mall. "As I watched these little kids having so much fun, I relaxed, forgot my own worries, and enjoyed the innocence before me. I stopped fretting about my problems—they just faded away," she marveled.

Getting quiet by sitting still doesn't work for everyone. Some people are just too fired up to relax easily, and meditating in a traditional way is too difficult for them. If you happen to fall into this category, get creative about what does work for you. Traditional meditation, though powerful, has no monopoly on providing access to your sixth sense—there are some days when even I can't sit still. The solution is to understand your nature and try nontraditional, alternative ways to achieve the same result. Try getting quiet by engaging your hands, for example, and doing some sort of silent task for a while.

David was as restless and anxious as a person could be. He was constantly tapping his fingers, shaking his foot, or moving in his chair, and although meditation would clearly have been good for him, he had no luck doing it. When I did his intuitive reading, his guides suggested that he take up a hobby that would capture his imagination, consume his attention, and silence his thoughts—like building model airplanes. He loved the idea and gave it a go. He started small but soon found the activity so relaxing that it became his after-work passion. He spent about 45 minutes a day unwinding his mind as he focused only on his project. After a while, he began to occasionally receive intuitive guidance and solutions to the problems he faced at work or in life as he worked away on building his newest model airplane or car. One afternoon while assembling the wings on a model airplane, David distinctly felt his brother's spirit enter the room, although they hadn't spoken in years. He was so connected to this feeling that he realized how much he missed his brother and decided to set his ego aside and call him that night. As he was about to pick up the phone, it rang—and it was his brother. He was calling to tell David that he'd just been diagnosed with prostate cancer, and even though it looked as if he was going to beat it, it made him realize what was important to him, so he wanted to reestablish contact. David's quiet daily hobby allowed his ego to step aside and his spirit to step in, which is what being intuitive is all about. He was receptive and open to his brother's outreach, and the quarrel that had caused their estrangement in the first place became insignificant.

The more you practice being quiet, the quicker and more clearly you'll sense your vibes. It doesn't matter what approach to meditating you use as long as in the end you are mentally quiet for a short time each day. Do whatever works. My mind becomes quiet when I fold laundry, organize my drawers, or go for long walks. My daughter, Sonia, gets quiet by playing her guitar.

My dad's quiet time was when he washed the car every Sunday morning, and we knew to leave him alone during this time. My mother's daily meditation was sewing. She spent hours and hours in her sewing room, listening to her spirit and her guides. She received inspiration and endless creative ideas during this time. Her spirit showed her how to make beautiful dresses, find exquisite fabric on sale, design and make jewelry, and more. Even though it was just a large closet, her sewing room was her temple, her sanctuary, and we were not allowed to enter, as something sacred was occurring there.

The key to having quiet time is to value it. If it's important to you, you're going to find the time. Be consistent. Schedule quiet time at the same hour each day. Plan in advance instead of hoping to steal a few moments here and there. You train your mind by being consistent. When your mind realizes that it is quiet time, it cooperates and helps your thoughts settle down. The more internally quiet you are, the more you'll be able to hear your vibes. And the more you listen to them, the more you'll trust them and let them guide you to your best life.

EASY MORNING MEDITATION

If you'd like to try traditional meditation but are new to the practice, begin the day with this easy five-minute meditation: Sit quietly and look around the room. Notice one or two things in front of you, then gently close your eyes. Once your eyes are closed, turn your attention inward to your breathing and notice how good it feels to deeply inhale, then exhale. Continue this for 10 more breaths, counting each one in and out as slowly as possible. Inhale . . . one. Exhale . . . one. Inhale . . . two. Exhale . . . two . . . and so forth. On the next 10 breaths, say "I am" on the inhale and "at peace" on the exhale. You can also repeat "I am" on the inhale and "calm" on the exhale. Enjoy the quiet that settles in when you do this. Then smile and stretch and begin your day.

If your brain jumps into hyperdrive at any time, don't fight it. Just keep breathing in and out, and finish with a smile. Even when it doesn't feel as though something positive is happening, it is. By repeating this mantra, you train your mind to relax and be less reactive and noisy as you breathe. It's subtle and barely noticeable at first, but within weeks you will recognize a difference.

MORE HELP MEDITATING

There are excellent apps now available for meditation training if you want to go that route. Two of my favorites are Headspace and Calm. Both are easy to use and can gently train your brain to be quiet with much success. There are hundreds of others, including many of my own guided meditations, which can be found both on my website and the Hay House app. The important thing is not to jump out of bed in the morning like the house is on fire, and instead, ease into your day, grounded and calm, tuned in to your heart and spirit and not your noisy, overreactive ego. Learn to meet the rest of the day in the same way.

Woo-Woo Workout

This week, take at least 10 minutes for quiet time each day. If you like to meditate and it isn't a struggle, then do it, for it really is the best way to tune in to your spirit and hear the voice of Divine Guidance. If traditional meditation doesn't work for you, listen to relaxing music, or just sit silently for a few moments each day. Sift through your life to discover if there are any built-in opportunities to be quiet already in place. Do you drive a lot, for instance? If so, can you turn off the radio during the drive and spend this time quietly? Do you like to iron? This can be a perfect quiet time for you. It is for me. Do you enjoy cooking or cleaning? Don't laugh. Many people do, and this, too, is a perfect time for quietly calming down. The more quiet time you give yourself, the easier it is to hear your intuition.

Meditation Bonus

Guided meditation is another favorite form of tuning out the noise of both the world and your ego brain and going inward to hear the voice of your spirit. I love channeling guided meditations and have done so for years. The following link will take you directly to a guided meditation I created for my students to help them achieve this calm, relaxed inner state I'm talking about. Using headphones, listen to this meditation morning or night or anytime you want to quiet your ego and connect with your spirit.

Visit https://www.hayhouse.com/downloads and enter the Product ID **9592** and Download Code **audio**.

Woo-Woo Wisdom

Meditate at least once a day, if only for a few minutes.

OBSERVE, DON'T ABSORB

It's not enough that your vibes work; you want them to work *well*. Why? Because unless you're discerning, you may unwittingly tune in to what you don't want. Psychic airwaves are like radio frequencies, broadcasting many levels of information at the same time. Think of the signals from your spirit as the psychic equivalent of a classical music satellite station—that is, a beautiful channel for high, spiritual guidance and healing. In contrast, what I call "psychic riffraff"—or the generic relay of other people's feelings, moods, fears, thoughts, anxieties, and even nightmares—is the psychic equivalent of low-vibration AM talk radio. In other words, useless noise.

If your intuitive channel is plugged in, but your tuner isn't dialed to your spirit, you may accidentally pick up that low vibration negative energy without even knowing it. For example, you may unconsciously tune in to another person's anxiety, depression, or fear and absorb it, even believe it is your own when it is not, which will cause you to become depressed, exhausted, insecure, fatigued, and perhaps paranoid. Or you may absorb someone else's anxiety, anger, and even illness and suddenly feel irritated and drained for no reason. As one client wondered in despair, "Sonia, I think I'm channeling everyone on the subway! By the time I arrive at work, I feel as if I'm carrying all their aches and pains and worries in my body." She was—believe it or not.

Have you ever been around a very anxious, agitated person? How long does it take before you find yourself infected with the same energy? Even if you were feeling perfectly at ease before contact, you might suddenly become overwhelmed by their funk. To avoid this "psychic contamination," stay focused and committed to your own priorities and goals. The more defined your aims are, the more likely you will avoid the riffraff and not wander into energy that doesn't belong to you, serve you, or possibly derail you. The stronger your intentions and priorities, the better your intuitive GPS, as well as your energetic boundaries, will become, and the more insulated you'll be from any unwanted influences.

Those among us who have wide-open intuitive channels but no filters to decide what gets in and what gets out can become highly saturated with energy we don't want to experience. I'm susceptible to this myself, so I must keep reminding myself, again and again, to keep my focus clear and my energetic boundaries in place so I avoid sponging up others' funky low-vibe frequency.

AVOID PSYCHIC VIRUSES

Just as you keep your distance from someone who has the flu, so too should you keep your psychic distance from someone who doesn't feel energetically healthy. Even though this is basic common sense, I must remind myself to do this. For example, when I'm around a stressed, miserable person, if I'm not grounded in my own body and clear about my priorities, I can easily absorb their anxiety in about three minutes. It's like catching a psychic virus.

Years ago, I lived next door to a moody, highly anxious, reactive neighbor named Phil, an older man who had just lost his life partner of 40 years and was beside himself with grief. Phil's partner Gary had been the calm one in the couple, while Phil was the "emotional" one who got worked up over every little thing. Gary paid the bills and managed the difficult things in their lives, while Phil was the cook, designer, and gardener, making their home and lives beautiful. After Gary's passing, Phil frequently came running over, distressed over some little thing. I recall one time when Phil came over, nearly in tears, terribly upset after seeing a young kid carelessly drop a candy wrapper on his highly manicured lawn. This sent Phil into a raging fit. When he knocked on my door, ready to download this egregious offense on me, I found myself bracing myself for an emotional storm. Sure enough, within minutes of Phil's purge, I found myself becoming just as worked up and enraged as he was. My body was so saturated with all this negative energy, I felt ill. My heart was pounding, I was holding my breath, and I could feel the tension rising in my spine.

Then I remembered a technique my teacher Charlie had taught me years earlier to stop this body hijack. While continuing to nod, I casually turned my torso ever so slightly to the right side instead of being face-to-face with Phil. Then I gently crossed my arms over my belly and started breathing slowly, inhaling to the count of four and exhaling to the count of four as Phil kept talking. During this time, I mentally surrounded myself in white light, an energetic shield of love, and deflected everything he said away from my body. This maneuver kept me from absorbing Phil's negative torpedoes as they headed straight my way. A few minutes after having dumped all his upset in my direction, Phil calmed down. Thankfully, with my turned body, crossed arms, and slow breathing, I was intact. Phil felt better, and I survived unscathed.

PSYCHIC PROTECTION AGAINST BAD VIBES

Breathe in slowly and exhale fully. Next, turn your body slightly to either the right or left of the negative energy being directed at you, and casually cross your arms slightly above your belly button. This is your solar plexus, the place in your body where you most absorb energy from the atmosphere around you. Continue to breathe slowly, inhaling to the count of four, then exhaling to the count of four, slowly. Remain in this position and keep breathing for as long as you need to. This may be challenging when in the eye of someone's intense emotional storm, so it helps to practice beforehand when things are calm. That way, your body has already done this and will do so automatically again when the need arises.

PSYCHIC GASLIGHTING

A more insidious negative energy we also need to be on the lookout for is psychic gaslighting. It's one thing to get caught up in the whirlwind of someone's obvious and outward psychic download, but quite another to be victim of a psychic sneak attack. These are more damaging to the spirit because we aren't prepared, don't know what hit us, and the other person usually denies it. People trigger one another all the time into overly reactive emotional states, and when this occurs, it is toxic. No less painful than getting physically hit in the head, getting psychically hit by another person's negative vibes harms our spirits and causes deep confusion and emotional pain.

These covert psychic bombs occur when a person is filled with their own dark energy, whether from insecurity, anger, jealousy, frustration, or a sense of failure, but instead of dealing with it, the offender spreads this toxic energy around, blatantly denying that they're doing so. Such people leave a trail of heavy, angry, resentful bad vibes wherever they go, like a dark, miserable, polluted cloud, stinking up the place and sucking the joy out of the room. Then, if confronted about their lousy energy, these people turn the tables on the accuser and become defensive, saying they're crazy and they don't know what they're talking about. It's infuriating, to say the least.

This kind of psychic gaslighting is far more common than overt outbursts and sometimes causes people to feel like they are losing their minds, yet it happens all the time. For example, my client Margaret shared that she got into terrible fights with her then-husband, William, because he was always in a bad mood, criticizing her for no reason and acting passive-aggressive, withholding, mean-spirited, and unfriendly. And he denied everything when he was confronted about it. Rather than "own his crap," as Margaret called it, he told Margaret that she was crazy and that she was projecting her own anger onto him. He never took responsibility for being such an angry sad-sack.

For years Margaret put up with it, but she eventually put her foot down and said enough was enough when he started gaslighting their sweet five-year-old son. "I wasn't going to stand by and watch him play these games with our son." I understood what Margaret was describing. In my house, we called those energetic stink bombs "poopy diapers" lying in the middle of the floor.

When Margaret first described her situation to me, she questioned if she was, in fact, the one with the bad energy. After all, around William, she was as angry and agitated as he was. But, as I pointed out, she wasn't like that with anyone else.

Margaret decided to end the marriage because she knew in her heart that living with him sickened her and hurt their son. The important thing for her was to know she was making a clear decision. Her husband had nearly convinced her he was perfectly fine, and that *she* was the miserable one. The last I heard from Margaret, she had found a new partner with wonderful energy who loved her and her son and treated them both with tremendous kindness. "I feel like I went from living in a chronic electrical storm to a peaceful, sunshiny day. What a difference!"

We've all known people like William. Margaret's solution was to divorce and move on. It worked for her but may not work for everyone. No matter what long-term solution you choose, if you are regularly exposed to this kind of toxic energy, the short-term solution is to simply walk away from it. If you need an excuse, just say, "I don't feel good. I have to go." And then stay as far away from the poopy diaper as possible.

People rarely lay claim to their energetic poopy diapers, so don't think you will get anyone to admit it is theirs. Don't even try. Instead, just take care of your spirit and give yourself space.

TOXIC PLACES

Just as people can be toxic or have bad vibes, so can places. For example, when I used to go to my local post office in Chicago, it felt as if there were some sort of psychic infection in there. The minute I walked in, my entire body seized up in self-protection. The building itself was old, dark, dreary, and depressing, and the people who worked there were clearly affected by its terrible vibrations, for they were indifferent, rude, and disinterested. And this infection spread throughout the crowd waiting in line. People often walked in smiling, but within minutes began to shut down, close their hearts, and become more and more agitated while they endured the line. Unless I completely shielded myself from this energy, by the time I left, I would be in such a bad mood, I could chew nails.

I continued going to this post office, however, because it was close and convenient. I decided it gave me a chance to practice what I preach, something I learned when I was training with my teacher Charlie. The next time I went in, I decided to just *observe* and not *absorb* the vibes when I went in. I would have compassion for those infected with the "funk vibe." Some days I succeeded better than others. It depended on how well I felt before going in. I learned not to go if I was tired because it was a recipe for disaster. When I was well rested and in good spirits, I was able to remain detached and keep my shield intact.

You, too, can practice detaching and staying psychically centered and grounded when exposed to chaotic, intense, stressful energy in various places and situations. Waiting in the security line at the airport, eating in a busy restaurant, sitting in a movie theater, visiting a hospital, attending a sporting event, utilizing public transportation, and—the hardest one of all—sharing holidays with your family are all occasions when you might be inclined to absorb negative vibes that aren't yours and lose your cool if you aren't paying attention. Since the pandemic of 2020 began, the amount of this kind of chaotic, stressful energy bouncing around has heightened to an even greater, nearly ridiculous degree, hence more reason to learn to observe and not absorb other people's energy and fast.

As you practice, it helps to keep this intuitive secret in mind like a mantra—"observe, don't absorb"—until it becomes a habit.

LEARN TO DETACH

When I was a student training with my teacher Charlie, he asked me look at photographs and drawings of intensely emotional scenes, from newborn babies to people running from burning buildings and everything in between, while remaining detached. My assignment was to study these images without becoming emotionally reactive. Until I could do this, there was the risk that their energy would override my vibes and confuse me.

Because some of the pictures were so intense, it took months for me to study the scenes and remain neutral instead of throwing my emotions into the mix. Day after day, Charlie would toss me a photo of something horrible or bizarre, and I'd recoil, squealing, "Oh my God! How awful!" He'd agree and laugh but say that it wasn't necessary to get my emotions involved.

I worried that being unemotional would mean that I didn't care. Strangely enough, the opposite happened: the less emotionally reactive I was, the more accurately I could tune in to my intuition for guidance and at the same time feel compassion and love for my fellow human beings. When I was more reactionary, my vibes didn't work, so I felt neither.

When I think of the challenges in my life and my struggle to remain detached, I often think of rescue workers and how selfless they need to be to dive into life's horrors and help the victims without getting emotionally overwhelmed. I'm humbled by those incredible and masterful souls—what would we do without them? This was what Charlie was teaching me; the rescue workers of the world are my role models. God bless them.

Learning to detach proved to be tremendously helpful in my intuitive practice. Now, no matter how emotional a client is or how intense a situation becomes, remaining detached allows me to sense guidance instead of getting caught up in the drama of the moment.

I recently met with a client named Macy who was very angry at her abusive family, especially her in-laws. Through buckets of tears, Macy gave me her side of the story, which included them threatening her, taking her money, snooping into her personal effects, constantly accusing her of awful things, telling her she was jealous, and not inviting her to family gatherings anymore. They certainly sounded like terribly hurtful people whom she should avoid.

On an emotional level, I felt her pain and could understand why she felt her family was cruel. Yet, remaining detached, I used my intuition to look deeper into the situation. When I did I discovered another scenario altogether, one that didn't correspond at all with Macy's version. I intuitively saw that even though her family and in-laws were no prize, she had a severe addiction to pain medication, alcohol, and spending which she failed to mention or even acknowledge. Unless she sobered up, they wanted nothing to do with her. Her addictions were out of control and causing chaos, and her family was trying to keep her from ruining their lives, too.

I suggested that she get sober and get some counseling—and, not ready to look at herself, she proceeded to get as angry with me as she was with everyone else. She was in severe psychic distress, but not for the reasons she'd stated. Had I sympathized with her emotional state, I may have missed the real problem and the opportunity to help her.

Learning to detach is a difficult skill for those of us who are naturally empathic. In picking up vibes, we tend to pick up *everything*, and it takes serious focus to avoid doing so. Because some people, like Macy, have accused me of being insensitive when I advise them, it's essential to understand that staying detached in the face of intense emotional energy doesn't mean that I don't care. It just lets me open my heart more so I can accurately see how best to respond.

It's a myth that caring requires commiserating. Caring means giving someone space to sort things out without throwing your own emotions into the mix. It's also important to listen to your vibes and not overtax your system. If you're bothered by the clerk at the dry cleaner, the rude guy at the grocery store, or the other passengers on the train, then don't frequent those places.

Whenever you can, remove yourself from problems and practice detachment when you can't. (And in either case, try to maintain your sense of humor!)

My favorite technique for detaching is to imagine that the world around me is a wonderful movie to learn from and enjoy, but I'm not the star of it. Just as I'd never get so lost in a film that I'd jump out of my seat and run toward the screen, I restrain myself from feeling the urge to absorb the energies around me and call them my own. Using this technique, I can observe the events around me with creative detachment. The same thing may happen to you. If you get embroiled in the negativity around you, just remind yourself that it's only your movie—it's not you.

WHOSE VIBES ARE WHOSE?

If you are in the habit of absorbing someone else's energy, pay closer attention to your vibes and then ask yourself if they are, in fact, your vibes. The depression or anxiety you're feeling may not really be your own; it may be the result of absorbing too much of what's around you. For example, I once had a client who worked in the office at a prison and, because of the general vibes of the place, often felt depressed. When she quit and began working in a not-for-profit instead, her depression immediately lifted. The bleak energy at the prison was simply too much for her to endure—in her quest to serve society, she was much better off doing so in the not-for-profit, where the energy was less intense.

Another way to keep other people's energy from invading you is to stop whatever you're doing and name everything you see around you, out loud if possible, for a few minutes. For example, right now, you might look around you and say, "I see a black desk lamp, a beige telephone, three magazines, a white vase with a red carnation in it, three yellow pencils, a brown wastebasket, my boss smiling at a client," and so on. Continue doing this for three or four minutes, or until you're completely relaxed, calm, and neutral. This exercise trains you to get out of your head and be present instead of being emotionally hijacked into your own or someone else's drama.

The benefits of detachment in the face of intense emotional activity can't be overstated. It doesn't cut you off from your heart center; it opens you more. When you refrain from absorbing the energy around you, you'll remain clear and grounded, you'll be able to easily access your creative and intuitive channel, and you'll be able to act on the messages you receive from your Higher Self.

Woo-Woo Workout

Set aside time to watch several TV shows or movies to practice observing without getting caught up in the drama. Choose various themes, from love story to action to suspense and even comedy.

Be patient and keep your mind focused on remaining detached and neutral while at the same time appreciating what's going on. Notice how much you resonate with the actors' energy. Study your reaction to what you are watching and think about why you may stay neutral in some areas while losing yourself in others. Ask yourself if you react the same way to real-life dramas as you do to the movies.

Practice being objective and observe how much more intuitive you are when you are detached. If you find yourself becoming too swept up in the vibration the movie is creating, pause the film, get up and move around or turn aside, fold your arms over your belly, and breathe until you can regain your sense of detachment. Finally, see if you can predict the outcome of the films from this more observant state of mind. It's fun and a great way to strengthen your intuitive channel.

Woo-Woo Wisdom

Don't be an energy sponge.

PART III

GOOD VIBRATIONS

CHOOSE YOUR WORDS WELL

Words are powerful energies that, once released, can create the conditions and circumstances of your life like magic wands. Every word you utter has a particular vibration, tone, and intention that attracts its equivalent on the earthly plane.

Words can be used to sow seeds of destruction or germinate gorgeous flowering experiences. What you say to yourself, and others has power, and if you want to live an extraordinary life, one that is guided by your spirit and goes with the flow, harness that power by using truthful, kind, and generous words spoken peacefully and harmoniously.

My spiritual teachers taught me the importance and power of words early in my apprenticeship. I learned that we are all Divine Beings, co-creators with the Universe, and that our life is built through our words. Nothing we say is ever lost or impotent—in fact, each utterance is powerful beyond belief and commands the Universe to obey. As far as the Universe is concerned, what we say is law because the Universe takes everything we say as truth and strives to make it so.

Have you ever called in sick to work because you wanted a free day, only to find yourself feeling under the weather before the day ended? Or have you ever made up an excuse to avoid dealing with someone, only to have it blow up in your face? I certainly have. Once when I was a teenager, I canceled a date with a guy I didn't really want to go out with by telling him that I had to babysit. Out of guilt, I told him several times that I was sorry and wished I could see him. As soon as I got off the phone, I joined my girlfriends ice skating downtown. I was on my third twirl around the rink when I found myself nose-to-nose with the very guy I'd just broken my date with. "Babysitting, huh?" he snarled at me before skating off. Feeling stupid and embarrassed, I couldn't help but think that I had it coming, because I did say that I really wished I could see him. . . . I guess the Universe just thought that I meant it.

Be mindful not only of what you say but of how you say it, because the Universe is built on sound and intention. The more focused and peaceful your words are, the higher your intention is, and the better your creation can be. Conversely, too many harsh, dissonant, and angry words—even if you believe that they represent your true feelings—have a destructive impact on yourself and others.

This was a hard lesson for my client Jennie to learn. She'd gone to a therapist who encouraged her to find her voice and speak her truth. With this therapist's coaching, Jennie began telling everybody exactly what she felt in precisely the way she felt it. She lashed out at her husband, telling him that she didn't like his hair, his breath, his taste in clothes, or his manners. She then told her in-laws she didn't like them. Gaining momentum and feeling proud of herself, she told her boss that his ideas were old-fashioned and that she wanted more money. Believing that she was becoming more empowered, Jennie was stunned when she lost her job, her husband moved out, and her son went to live with her in-laws. She'd been honest, so she couldn't understand why her life hadn't improved. After all, her therapist had spent two years convincing Jennie that being truthful was the only way to be happy. Unfortunately, when she told everyone what she felt, they left her behind.

The problem for the Jennies of the world is that they neglect to discern between truth and opinion. Opinions that come from your ego, the "me against you" perspective that makes others wrong, and you right, remember? Genuine truth, spoken from your spirit, never attacks anyone. Instead, it fosters understanding and mutual respect, and seeks to heal, not attack. Communicating in this way is an art and a discipline, and it releases powerful vibrations that bridge hearts, build trust, attract support, and create healing. Moreover, this kind of truth has a magical potency, for it allows you to speak your deepest desires into being.

The Universe is organized to support your true Self, and the more clearly you can communicate with it, the better it can. But unfortunately, when we speak out of confusion, anger, blame, or victimization, those sour notes and mixed messages send the Universe in circles, wanting to help but unable to do so.

My client Madelyn constantly complained about how impossible her ex-husband Bob was. According to her, he caused her endless troubles and made her life miserable. It had been 10 years since their divorce, and Bob rarely called her, lived in another city, and was remarried. As far as I could tell, psychically, he hardly ever thought about her at all. It inevitably turned into a fight whenever they did speak because Madelyn, unable to find closure or accept that their marriage was over, was constantly carping at Bob, which made them both angry and defensive. Even though he'd moved on with his life, she was still stuck in a struggle with him. She felt left behind, and her inability to accept this and tone down her anger so she could begin healing left her trapped in a painful, lonely place.

People avoided Madelyn because she was so negative, and although she gained a little pity each time she spoke to someone, she didn't achieve the freedom she needed to get on with her life. She occasionally mentioned a desire to find someone new to love, but it was more like a commercial break in the Madelyn-and-her-ex-husband saga than a genuine, focused desire. The Universe could only work with what she asked for, so it gave her more and more trouble with Bob and never introduced another man into her life. Until she stopped talking so bitterly about Bob and started speaking lovingly about herself, she would continue to push life away.

Eventually, she came to understand this. But it took a while. Slowly, Madelyn is finally focusing on her own life and learning to speak with kindness, love, and affection for her spirit, which she needed all along.

Ask yourself how well you're communicating your desires. If words are the building blocks of your life, you can't just hurl negative and debasing words out there and expect the Taj Mahal in return.

In addition, careless and profane speech is debilitating over time to a sensitive, intuitive being because it creates a dissonant, negative vibration. Swearing excessively or using vulgar language, especially in place of actual words, disturbs the soul. Although it may seem harmless, using this kind of language erodes your light body and seriously lowers your vibration. Now, I'm not saying that you need to be as pure as the driven snow. We all know that an enthusiastic expletive is sometimes precisely the truth about how we feel and what we mean. I'm talking about regularly and carelessly using profanity without putting any effort into communicating effectively. The Universe can only work with what you give it and how you give it.

All words are potent, but words spoken with love are positively irresistible. They're as powerful as magic spells and draw the world to your front door. For example, I once had a client who had struggled with obesity most of her life. She'd managed to lose only a few pounds, despite careful dieting and daily exercise. She constantly talked about "losing my fat," even though she really wasn't losing anything. Then one day, she changed her words. She began to enthusiastically say that she was "reclaiming my beauty." This more inspiring way of expressing her goal excited and motivated her, and she lost 10 pounds the first week. She loved her "beauty project" and moved toward it effortlessly. She also learned to love her size and stopped rejecting her body, ushering in the peace and self-acceptance she longed for all along.

Be conscientious about the words you use and the ones you hear. This gives you power. Know that words set the stage for coming attractions, so if you hear gossip, disengage; if someone is critical, be silent. Walking away from negative conversation not only keeps your vibration oscillating at a higher rate, but it also protects others from lowering their vibrations by removing their audience.

BE REAL

In addition to being conscious about the words you use and the vibration they broadcast, it is equally important to be truthful and authentic when speaking. This helps for all kinds of obvious reasons, but from the standpoint of tuning in to your intuition, telling the truth is crucial to creating inner calm and quiet so you can hear your inner voice. Not telling the truth, intentionally or by default, creates an inner cacophony of conflicting noisy vibrations. This is because the body only tells the truth, while the ego brain can say many untrue things, and the collision of these vibrations is intensely dissonant. So much of our inner noise comes from our own regret and frustration for not speaking up, not expressing what we really feel, or not communicating honestly from our heart. This creates such a conflicted frequency that our inner voice is drowned out and we can't hear it at all. This is perhaps the main reason why so many people have trouble sensing their intuition. They can't get past the static to tune in to their inner guidance.

I understand why people don't express themselves honestly. Many of us were trained and conditioned as children not to be honest by those who held power over us. Who among us didn't hear endless admonitions to "be nice," or "Don't say that," or "Shhhh, that's not polite" when we pointed out truth as kids? With this, we were taught to abandon ourselves so we could belong and be cared for. The price we pay for this abandonment is feeling confused. We've been conditioned to ignore our inner truth and seek outer approval to be accepted in the world. While we may not have had power to speak our truth as dependent children, we do now as sovereign adults. It may not feel easy, and your inner child may still feel scared, but the minute you break free of this fear and articulate your true feelings, you reclaim your spirit's power. When you speak from the heart—your true Self—with courage, conviction, and calm, any psychic hold from the past is broken and you quickly reconnect to your inner voice and get back into a harmonious flow with your spirit.

It takes courage to speak your truth because it may be risky, but in the end, this is far better than abandoning yourself. The key is to be calm and clear and at least be truthful with yourself if nothing else. If speaking your truth to others presents danger-ous consequences, keep your honest thoughts to yourself but then make plans to leave.

Being truthful doesn't mean cramming your point of view down other people's throats. It means expressing your true feel-ings instead of ignoring them. Stop agreeing to or going along with what doesn't work for you and start communicating what you need or what works for you as best you can in all situations, even if it makes you anxious or uncomfortable at first.

To do this, slow down, check in with yourself, and connect with what truly does feel in alignment with your spirit before you speak. Then breathe in deeply, center yourself, and give it a calm, grounded go.

My client Jeanne was a veterinarian in an animal hospital that was understaffed to begin with, but her schedule doubled when a colleague took a maternity leave, and the hospital didn't replace her with another surgeon as it should have.

Being a team player, Jeanne agreed to cover for the absent doc-tor for a few months even though it created tremendous pressure on her and made keeping commitments to her own family almost impossible. Then, out of the blue, the doctor decided to extend her leave for three more months.

The hospital director called Jeanne in and told her she had to keep her extended schedule for three more months. He didn't ask Jeanne if she would be willing to do this. He just said it was what she had to do. Jeanne was angered by the assumption that the animal hospital could keep piling work on her without her permission or agreement. The hospital needed another vet, and they were stretching Jeanne to the limits instead of hiring one.

Everything in Jeanne was screaming, *NO! Not fair! Not good for you!* as the director told what he wanted her to do as if she had no say in the matter. She wrestled with her lifelong conditioning of being told to be a "good girl" and "do as you are told." Finally, she took a deep breath, and quietly said, "No, I cannot do that. I cannot take on more work. It would be harmful to myself and my family, and I wouldn't do a good job for the patients." The director was surprised and said, "Excuse me?" Again, calmly but resolutely, Jeanne took a deep breath, dug her heels into the ground for support, and quietly but firmly said, "I cannot take on more hours." Then she was silent. She didn't feel the need to explain and intuitively sensed it would only take away from her resolve and power if she did. They stared at one another in silence for what seemed like an eternity, but in fact was probably only 30 seconds or so. Then, the director responded, "Okay." And that was that.

Jeanne turned around and left his office feeling jubilant and fully aligned with her spirit. It was the first time she had spoken up at work and said what she wanted without backing down. She was so pleased with herself that she nearly felt like laughing. On her way back to her office, her mind was calm, and she felt connected to her true Self, her spirit.

Being your true Self—communicating who you are, what works for you, and what doesn't—takes practice, but believe me, it's the best decision you will ever make in your life. Your best life is an authentic one, not one that shapeshifts on demand to please others at your own expense. Standing up for yourself does not require ranting, raging, yelling, or worse. However, it does require deciding to be true to who you are and saying so with straightforward, kind, unwavering words. This is an incredibly empowering choice. It may be scary at first, but it becomes easier and easier with practice, until before you know it, you simply cannot live another way.

BE LOVING

The best way to maintain an extraordinary life is to make every thought and word you use or listen to as loving and nurturing as possible. Make it a personal value to speak truthfully, using the best words, speaking honestly from the heart and with respect for yourself and others. There's no more direct way than this—there are no shortcuts, bypasses, or exceptions. Instead of mumbling "Fine" when someone asks you how you are, check in and express your genuine feeling. You don't need to complain; just be authentic. When greeting someone, say, "It is such a pleasure to see you. How is your spirit today?" rather than, "I'm sick of this weather." It helps to express gratitude for something rather than feel sorry for yourself. Be authentic and kind with others by first being kind and respectful to yourself. The energy you communicate either seeks to be honest, loving, elevating, loving, or creative, or it doesn't. And if it doesn't, you'll disconnect with your inner guidance and miss out.

Practice authentic, loving communication at every opportunity until it becomes second nature. The more honest, mindful, and kind words you use, the quicker you'll feel your vibes waking up. You'll feel lighter, freer, more empowered, and liberated from inner chaos. Your chest will expand, your shoulders will straighten, your heart will open, and you'll feel present. Your mental chatter will quiet down, and a softer, sweeter but more powerful tone will take over. Your inner voice will speak up, leaving you feeling more peaceful, far more creative, clearly and confidently aligned with who you are, and guided to where you need to go.

Woo-Woo Workout

Pay attention to what you say and what you listen to. Use your words well and notice how other people's words affect you. Don't participate in inflammatory conversations, no matter how justified, because they will throw you offtrack. It's tempting to get dragged into the ego game of "me against you," but it's a standoff that never ends. Don't go there. Remember that you're intimately connected with everyone else in the world, so when you attack another person, you attack yourself. Regardless of whether our ego understands this, it is nevertheless true.

Speak thoughtfully, truthfully, confidently, and with self-control, and use loving words of acceptance, conviction, and humor. Rehearse kind words if you must, especially if this isn't your usual style. If expressing yourself in person is too difficult, express yourself by writing honest, nurturing words that aren't defensive, attacking, or accusatory. You have the right to be who you are and being anything less than that will never make you happy.

Be cautious with text conversations. They are not intended to be used in place of heart-to-heart communication, so don't hide behind them or get dragged into them. Limit your text messages to three sentences. Anything else is best said on the phone or in person or written in an actual letter and mailed.

Do feel free to send heartfelt e-mails, letters, and cards. This is a great way to let people know you care about them. Don't let it end there, however. Practice saying what you mean effectively and kindly, even if it is not your regular habit. With practice, it will soon feel like the real you. Pay particular attention to avoid using unconscious yet destructive expressions in a mindless way, such as "To die for," "I'd kill to," "How lame," "I'm sick of this," "I can't afford to," and "I hate that!" Expand your vocabulary to include accurate, beautiful, sensual, inspiring, thought-provoking, mysterious, and compelling words—words that express the beauty of your marvelous spirit. Get a word-a-day calendar or a dictionary and learn new words to better serve your intentions. Every day, add one new word to your vocabulary and use it three times that day. Then go to bed each night by saying five positive things aloud to yourself using your beautiful new language.

Woo-Woo Wisdom

Your words have power.

PROTECT
YOUR SPIRIT

One of the most practical benefits of listening to your vibes is the ability to recognize and protect yourself from negative energy before it hurts you. This begins with recognizing negative vibes in your body, acknowledging negative energy instead of denying it, uncovering the source if you can, dissipating it or distancing yourself from it quickly, and transforming negative energy into positive energy whenever possible. It works best if you do it in steps.

Step #1. Identify how a bad vibe feels in your body. Pay attention to how you physically sense bad vibes, such as when someone is lying or misleading you, or when something does not feel right, as in a business deal. In much the same way that recognizing cold symptoms early allows you to treat them before they develop into something more serious, the ability to detect negativity before it overtakes you can spare you enormous problems and potential harm.

Your body registers the bad vibe before your brain does. It senses the discordant energy and sends you a signal. Maybe it's a tightening in your chest. Perhaps you feel a heavy, crushing feeling around your gut. Maybe the hairs stand up on your arms or the back of your neck. Maybe you just experience a vague sense of dread or discomfort. These signs can be subtle and easy to miss unless you pay attention, although some people feel bad vibes quite strongly. Whether subtle or intense, the key is to recognize these signals quickly. Once you consciously acknowledge these warnings for what they are, you won't be able to ignore them ever again.

The first hint I get of a bad vibe is that my breathing feels slightly restricted and becomes shallower, and my upper chest and throat tighten. I often sense a heavy pressure on the back of my head or a sinking feeling in my heart. If the vibe is really terrible or dangerous, I may even start to feel panicky. These feelings signal that negativity is moving in, like a storm, so I need to move out fast.

I ask my clients to describe how they sense bad vibes to make them more aware of this when it happens. Jeanne said, "Whenever I encounter bad vibes, I feel as though I'm 'smushed.'" Gary told me, "The minute I get bad vibes, I become impatient, even rude. Maybe this is my way of fighting them off." Others shared that their hearts race, their heads feel heavy, their hands tingle, or they become immobilized.

Pause right now and describe how you physically sense bad vibes. Try to be as specific as possible when describing what they feel like to you. Once you recognize how they feel in your body, you will pick up these signals faster so you can better protect yourself.

Step #2. Speak up loudly and acknowledge a bad vibe the *minute* you feel it. This shows others that you're fully alert and paying attention, no matter what. Start by simply saying aloud, "I have bad vibes," "Something's off—this doesn't feel right," or "Suddenly I don't feel well" the instant you feel negative energy, even if it's under your breath. Sometimes just announcing that you sense bad vibes in the air is enough to shut them down, especially if they're coming from secret psychic snipers. Some bad vibes are clearly apparent, like when your partner yells at you or a stranger menaces you with insulting hand gestures. However, the vibes from psychic snipers, those who secretly send you their poisonous arrows of negativity as they masquerade behind sweet facades and pleasantries, are more sinister. These types of bad vibes are easier to question or ignore, especially if you're inexperienced, unaccustomed to relying on your psychic radar, an overly trusting person by habit, or someone who just wants to be "nice."

My client Celine once met a woman who gave her slightly bad vibes but persisted in befriending her. Her new friend was flattering, invited her to fun events, and frequently bought her little presents. She was funny and, other than being boundary-challenged, did nothing overtly that smacked of danger. Yet every time Celine and this woman were together, Celine felt a bit uncomfortable. Still, Celine thought it wasn't nice to be on guard with such a sweet woman, so she played down her vibes. "I let my defenses down," Celine said with regret, sharing this story when she came to see me later. "Sure enough, before long, my new friend needed to borrow money, which I lent her. Then she asked me if she could stay with me because her roommate suddenly moved out and ended their lease—another red flag. I felt this was inappropriate, given that I didn't know her very well. However, I'm embarrassed to say that I agreed to it, knowing it was a mistake deep down. I just couldn't find a reason to say no. She stayed for three days. Then she skipped town, taking some of my jewelry and even some of my clothes with her. After that, I never saw her again. I wasn't surprised. I was just mad at myself for allowing it to happen. Getting over this is like getting over a horrible illness."

I felt compassion for Celine. She wanted to be kind and got taken advantage of. Yet she knew in her heart that this person was not to be trusted even if it was hard to see on the surface. (As my mother used to say, "A rotten egg is a rotten egg, even if it's decorated for Easter.")

Like Celine, you may question or even deny a bad vibe because you have no hard evidence to back up what you're feeling. Don't compromise your safety by falling into this trap. You do not need any other proof if you have bad vibes. If you sense that something is off, however difficult it may be to verify, trust your vibes and stay away. You may have to take a little heat for your suspicions, especially from five-sensory people who deny almost everything, but who cares?

I've spoken to many people who say that they don't want to admit when they feel bad vibes because it is so awkward and feels impolite. But that's just old conditioning that implies it's your responsibility to take care of someone else's ego over your well-being. It's not, and it never brings about good results. It only causes you to resent them and abandon yourself.

Love yourself by speaking up if bad vibes are affecting you. Bad vibes can hurt you as much as physical abuse, and you don't need to tolerate them. You can acknowledge a bad vibe without being rude. Just say, "This does not feel right for me," and nothing more. Often by simply exposing negative energy, it begins to back away because it feeds on darkness and secrecy and can't stand to be brought into the light.

DENIAL IS NO PROTECTION

Perhaps the biggest block to allowing your vibes to protect you is denial. Some people would rather not know if something bad was lying in wait for them. This may seem hard to understand, but it is so common it takes my breath away. Instead of being honest with ourselves, we choose to avoid the negative feeling. So we go along with the illusion, and then we suffer and feel victimized, even though deep in our hearts we knew something was wrong all along.

Betty booked a session with me because she had good news to share. She was excited to tell me about her new boyfriend, Mark, whom she'd recently met online. They had been chatting online for over a month before finally meeting in person just two weeks ago. She couldn't believe what a wonderful guy he was, especially since he'd suffered so much tragedy over the last 15 years. He told her that he'd lost his wife to breast cancer five years earlier and was just getting back into the dating world after a devastating grieving period. It was love at first Zoom call. He was handsome, warm, loved to dance, laughed easily, and wanted to spend all his time with Betty. She said she had such fun with him but added that he was "a bit intense and full-on." Then she smiled brightly again and said, "He's truly a nice guy!"

"*Intense* and *full-on* are not words that describe good vibes," I said, but continued to listen.

Betty argued, "Oh no, I don't mean it in a bad way. He's just a lot. I'm used to being single, and he wants to be with me all the time. I'm so flattered."

"Are you flattered, or do you feel smothered?" I continued.

She started to get annoyed with me. "Sonia, I'm giving you the wrong impression. He is a wonderful man. Look, we are engaged!" she gushed, and flashed a giant ring.

"Whoa," I said, "that's fast. And my goodness, that ring is impressive."

"Yes, I know." She nodded, a bit more subdued. "But really, it feels right," she insisted.

I looked her in the eye and said, "Right for who, Betty?"

"What do you mean?" she asked, playing dumb and ignoring the psychic alarms going off in the room.

"Just tell me how happy I am going to be, Sonia. And be happy for me," Betty snapped.

As much as I wanted to be happy for Betty, I wasn't. I was worried for her. Every word she said bounced off me like a wooden nickel and landed with a thud. This was not the real deal she was selling herself or me. It felt manipulative, pushy, controlling, and dishonest.

"Betty, I wish I had better vibes. I don't want to ruin your party, but I suggest you slow down, be true to yourself, and don't allow yourself to get swept away. You will regret it. If he is the perfect guy, he will slow down as well and let things unfold more gracefully."

Betty got angry then. "I cannot believe you're saying this. I know this is right for the first time in my life, and I'm getting married next week. I'm disappointed in you for not being happy for me." Betty stormed off. I felt upset that she was going ahead with her plans but let it go. She had made up her mind, so I prayed that her soul would learn what she needed to from this experience with the least amount of damage.

Betty married Mark as she said she would. I didn't hear from her for more than two years. When she finally came back, she said, "Why didn't you stop me from marrying Mark?"

"You didn't want to hear what I had to say, so I respected your wishes," I said.

"I wish you wouldn't have. I'm in the middle of a messy divorce now. It's a nightmare." Mark turned out to be a not-so-nice guy underneath all that sweetness. He was addicted to sleeping pills and up to his ears in debt after being fired from his job a year after they married. Betty was losing half of her assets to him because, drunk with romance, she refused a prenuptial agreement even though her friends tried to convince her to have one. "The worst was that my engagement ring was zirconium. It wasn't even a real diamond," she cried. "I was bamboozled all the way down the line."

That is when I challenged her.

"Really, Betty? You didn't have any bad vibes at all?"

Betty was silent, then admitted, "I did have bad vibes. I knew it was all wrong. I just wanted so badly to believe Mark and be swept away that I ignored them." She didn't have the happy ending she wanted. She had a train wreck and had seen it all coming.

Step #3. Identify where the negativity is coming from. Start by checking if it's coming from you. If you're tired, hungry, over-extended, rushed, or in any way unhappy or uncomfortable, don't be surprised if you're the one who's putting out bad vibes toward others (see Practice #2, page 9). Sometimes we're our own worst enemy, and simple physical neglect is all it takes to feel that the world is against us.

You may also be feeling negative vibes because you're being overly critical of yourself. If so, ease up! Change your focus and start to think more positively about yourself, others, and even the entire world. Negativity is infectious, but so is positive energy. Move to higher ground quickly by saturating yourself in as much positive energy as possible. Put out good vibes and ask others to do the same for you.

I have an outgoing message on my phone, for example, that says, "I'm not in right now. Leave a positive message and I'll call you back." It's incredible how many hang-ups I get with that message. It blocks a ton of bad vibes and negative downloads. The messages that do get left are so uplifting and wonderful and make my day.

When you can't identify the source of bad vibes and feel you need to, you might want to do some psychic sleuthing. To do this, ask your spirit to guide you, and then pose a lot of questions, beginning with, "Are these my bad vibes, or are they coming from someone else?" Next, work outward from there, asking, "Is this energy coming from my family, relatives, neighbors, friends, or co-workers?" Another way to uncover the source of bad vibes is to close your eyes and ask, "Who are you?" and then note who pops into your head. Following this, ask, "What do you want?" and listen to the answer you receive. This bit of detective work helps hone your bad vibe detector. Each time you seek more psychic evidence, your bad vibe radar will get a little sharper.

I went out to lunch with my friend Elena recently, when I noticed she didn't seem quite her bright Self. Being who I am, of course, I asked her what was up right away. "You seem off," I said.

"I am," she admitted. "I have been all morning. I have bad vibes, and it's bugging me."

"Do you know where they are coming from?" I asked.

"Now that I'm tuning in to them, I think they're coming from the new woman, Josephine, my company just hired. I don't know why, but I feel like she didn't like me for some reason, and I can feel her energy affecting me more than I want it to. This feeling started during an office meeting yesterday morning and has been with me ever since. I didn't want to admit this because it makes me anxious and uncomfortable, but now that I say it aloud, I know it's true."

"What do you think is best to do with her bad vibes?" I asked. She thought a little longer.

"You know, nothing. I'm going to send them back. They don't belong to me, and I don't need to do a thing. She can figure this out on her own." Once Elena identified the culprit, she relaxed. By acknowledging the source of her bad vibes, they ceased to negatively affect her. Deciding not to take them on as hers was a good idea. After that, we had a great lunch and fun the rest of the day.

FREEZE!

Sometimes, no matter how hard we try, we can't be sure where negativity is coming from. The good news is that with practice, this will change. The more you train your mind to pay attention, the more astute you'll become, especially regarding psychic protection. In the meantime, you can create a psychic shield of protection against negative vibes simply by saying, "Freeze!" as long as you really mean it.

My friend LuAnn taught me to take this even further by getting a glass jar with a lid and putting a piece of paper in it that says *I freeze all negativity, known or unknown, moving toward me as of now.* Fill the jar with water and blue food coloring for added protection and freeze it. I once worked with a very unhappy assistant who continually projected her negative energy my way. I wanted to fire her, but I lacked confidence at the time, so I "froze" her instead. She quit the next day, and we were both relieved.

Freezing bad vibes always works miracles for me because the ritual amplifies my intention. Whenever you set an intention and genuinely mean it, it becomes potent. The glass, the food coloring, the writing, and the freezer involve all my senses and pull in my imagination, which is the single greatest tool of intention we have. I have a client who once shared that she used an ice cube tray to freeze the negativity coming her way, writing down the source of every bad vibe, one by one, placing each in one of the little cube sections, then freezing the entire tray. "I laugh the entire time I'm doing this," she shared. "I don't know if it's the laughter or the freezing, or both, but it works every time."

You can also stop bad vibes in their tracks by saying aloud to their source, known or unknown, "To the light! I'm not willing to receive them. They're not mine." I say this immediately whenever I feel bad vibes buzzing around my head. Sending negative energy back to a higher frequency keeps it from attaching to me and transforms it on the way.

Step #4. Surround yourself in a shield of protection. If you feel negativity coming your way, check to see if you feel in danger. If yes, walk away, and mentally cover yourself in a loving shield of white-light protection. Send all bad vibes to the light and don't look back.

Don't be afraid of other people's negative energy. It may be unpleasant, even nasty, but if you refuse to fear it, you take its power away. Just as you would from a barking dog, walk away slowly, look the negativity on the eye, and project that you are in charge, connected to your spirit, and unafraid. Your spirit is more powerful than any ego.

Check in with your heart. Is this bad vibe something you can address with calm, loving communication? If yes, and it won't put you in harm's way, you can try to improve things by asking the source of your bad vibes if they care to discuss what's going on. Call on Divine love to help you resolve the problem and transform the situation. If the bad vibes are between you and a good friend, a family member, or a close personal relationship, then loving, honest communication often works well. If they are from someone you don't know or may even dislike, send the negative situation and its source to the light and let go.

Negativity is often born out of misunderstandings that can be turned around easily if you approach someone with a loving and open heart. Bad vibes are usually no more serious than bad breath, and they can be quickly cured if you get to the cause. Identify the offending problem and address it with loving communication as soon as you can. Say, "I feel confusion or negativity between us. Is there anything I've done to offend you? Is there anything you need from me that I am unaware of? I'd like to clear the energy between us, and I need your help." This creates an opportunity for everyone to express their unmet needs safely. Sometimes bad vibes are only misunderstandings that get out of hand. Addressing the "bad vibes elephant in the room" with a genuine desire to relieve them is often all that is needed to improve things.

The best protection against negative energy is to surround yourself and others with unconditional love and acceptance. More often than not, underneath a person's negative vibes is an unconscious need for love and reassurance. The negativity they put out is just a very poor way to ask for it. Knowing this, you can be proactive and send people good vibes and lots of love in advance. Doing this changes the vibe before you run into negativity.

By recognizing that every event and experience in your life, good or bad, is an invitation for your soul to grow and love more, you generate less of your own bad vibes and react less to the bad vibes coming your way. No matter what or who the source is, applying love first always works best to clear bad vibes.

Step #5. Finally, remind yourself that sometimes a bad vibe is just a bad vibe. Maybe someone is having a bad day and you accidentally walked into their line of fire. I suggest that you not take anyone's negative energy personally, even if it's directed at you. Bad vibes are just missed opportunities to love, understand, and communicate effectively. So pray for healing—then promptly leave. As you do so, surround yourself with the most loving and kind thoughts possible. Send caring thoughts to all approaching hostile forces—because they need it.

The simple act of distancing yourself from negativity breaks the connection, clears the air, gets you grounded, and helps you drop your defenses. It opens your heart and leads you to a higher perspective. This is especially true when you find yourself in a heated argument. Leaving is best done with grace, sensitivity, and discretion. If you can quietly leave a toxic situation, get out as fast as you can. If the negative vibe is focused on you, but you can't escape quickly or discreetly, simply say, "I need to walk and think. We can get back to this after we're both more grounded." Then go.

When you distance yourself, it helps to use your judgment wisely regarding where you go and with whom. If something doesn't feel right to you, trust your vibes, and stay away. Don't bother asking why something is off—you don't need to understand negative energy to know it's toxic. After all, when it comes to protecting yourself, you're in charge. No one else can do it better than you. Part of living a higher life involves paying attention to everything you feel and responding accordingly.

And remember: we're all connected, so the more good vibes you give out to others, the fewer bad vibes you will encounter.

Woo-Woo Workout

Protect yourself energetically by:

1. Paying attention to your body and listening if you feel a bad vibe

2. Acknowledging negative energy quickly and out loud

3. Seeing if you can identify where the bad vibes are coming from and get away if necessary

4. Changing the negative into the positive with loving communication

5. Doing what you can to send the rest to the light

Finally, after you've done that, consciously create good vibes. Recognize who and what feels good. Always pay close attention to the energy around you. Remember not to take any negative vibration or energy personally—simply refuse to be harmed by someone else's missed opportunity to love. Instead, shield yourself with positive, loving energy to stop any unpleasant energy in its tracks. And know that if the vibes you're receiving are bad, you can always walk away or freeze them.

Woo-Woo Wisdom

Send good vibes, and get away from bad ones.

TUNE IN

Once you start to trust your vibes, you begin to realize that we are more than physical beings who are separate from one another and limited to physical space and time. Instead, you begin to understand that we are spiritual beings, and whether our ego knows it or not, we are psychically connected and communicate with one another on different energetic levels—sharing thoughts, feelings, ideas, beliefs, and information all the time. This is known as telepathy. Telepathy works just like a radio station does, only it sends and receives frequencies on nonphysical bandwidths.

We have two main telepathic channels, the head (the barking-dog ego) and the heart (the spirit). The head channel broadcasts ego-to-ego. When we telepathically connect on this channel, we send and receive our ego's thoughts, ideas, beliefs, and feelings. Depending on how evolved your ego is, these broadcasts can be either beneficial or not. An example of a beneficial exchange is when two scientists on opposite sides of the earth have the same scientific insight at the same time, without directly speaking to one another. In this case, both scientists tuned in to the same energetic broadcast simultaneously, downloading the same information and applying it to help humanity. A low-level exchange is when people of one race suggest people of another race are all "the same" and not worth respecting. This kind of AM talk radio "blah blah" perpetuates negative thoughts, beliefs, and feelings that create more separation and suspicion between people and keep us trapped in fear. These low-level broadcasts drift into people's heads and take hold, often without the person even realizing what is happening. People who are unfocused, disconnected, addicted, or struggling in other ways can be vulnerable to being hijacked by low-level mass telepathy. The next thing they know, these low-level downloads fill their heads with all kinds of negative beliefs, fearful ideas, and nasty convictions and projections that are not born out of their direct experience but only psychic hearsay. This is an example of what I referred to earlier as psychic riffraff. Sadly, people are tuning into telepathic riffraff at an exponential rate right now, and it's having devastating effects on our society and our planet.

This kind of telepathic exchange is a downer, leaving you feeling stressed, anxious, scared of "other" people who are not like you, and powerless. It adds nothing to the quality of life or the improvement of your relationships. The best way to avoid low-level telepathy is to turn off that channel by focusing on what and who you love. Doing this shifts your focus to your spirit and automatically tunes you in to your higher telepathic channel, the heart. The telepathy of the heart does not broadcast spirit-to-spirit. It is a much higher frequency, one where we connect with one another from our highest, most authentic, Divine selves. This telepathic rapport affirms that we are always connected through love to those who are on the same higher frequency and who are here to love and help us spiritually throughout our lives.

Thankfully, heart-chakra telepathy is also occurring exponentially. More and more of us are spontaneously opening our heart chakras and reconnecting to the Divine spirit within ourselves and with one another, bringing more and more love to the planet. Heart chakra telepathy is one of the sweet delights of life. It transforms life into a magical experience in a million little ways that make a big difference to our outlook.

One simple example of heart-chakra telepathy is thinking of a dear old friend from high school, only to spontaneously run into that very person later that day. Or thinking of a song you love two seconds before it comes on the radio. Or wishing you had some chocolate, only to turn a corner and run onto a gorgeous chocolate shop that just opened a few days earlier. All are wonderful surprises. This kind of telepathy is the reason for synchronicities, those seemingly random encounters of being in the right place at the right time. Heart-chakra telepathy leaves us feeling connected, loved, surprised, affirmed, supported, and in the right place to receive blessings of all kinds, or what is called "in the flow."

The most common example of heart-chakra telepathic rapport is the kind that exists between family members. When I was growing up, my mother only had to go out on the front porch and "beam" us home to summon the family to supper. We felt her vibe, and we came running. Since I've heard the same story from many of my clients, I believe that this is a universal experience. I am sure that the power of Mom is one of the strongest telepathic lines between people; after all, we come from our mothers, so this makes sense.

This mother-child telepathic rapport can last throughout one's entire lifetime and can be reassuring, useful, and practical as well. For example, I was in London last month, visiting my daughter Sabrina and her family. On the last morning, before I took the train back to Paris, where I live, I made a last-minute dental appointment because I accidentally chipped my tooth the night before and needed to get it repaired fast. Luckily I got an appointment right away with a good dentist who could do the repair late in the morning. I briefly hesitated to take the appointment because it left little time for me to get back to Sabrina's apartment, gather my bags, and get to the station on time for my train. But since I wanted my tooth fixed right away and didn't know a good dentist for this kind of repair in Paris, I went for it.

After finishing packing my bags for the trip home, I rushed out the door in a hurry, saying good-bye to my daughter and granddaughter, who were on their way to their two-hour daily stroll through Regent's Park, a vast, gorgeous park near their home in central London. Then I fast walked in the opposite direction across the park to the dentist, making it right on time.

While sitting in the dental chair, I suddenly realized that I had forgotten to take my phone and keys with me before I ran out the door. As a result, I had no way to contact my daughter to let her know she needed to come back to let me in so I could get my stuff before I left. If I didn't get hold of her, I would miss my train.

Staying calm, I started to telepathically message Sabrina that I needed to meet her at home. After my quick repair, I intended to take a taxi but felt compelled to walk back through Regent's Park. Since I had no key, there was no point in arriving immediately because I knew my daughter and granddaughter would still be out.

Still telepathically messaging her as I walked, I suddenly had an overwhelming urge to sit down on a bench, so I did. Thirty seconds later, Sarina came strolling down the lane with the baby carriage, saw me, and yelled, "Mom!" I laughed out loud because it was so perfect. When she asked what I was doing sitting on the bench, I told her what had happened. She started to laugh as well, saying, "I got your message, because I was walking in the other direction but felt the need to turn around and come this way a few seconds ago."

Telepathy saved my day and made the ending even better than the original plan. We enjoyed a pleasant stroll home, which gave me a chance to see my granddaughter once more and say a proper unrushed good-bye to both, grab my bag, phone, and keys, and get to the train station with a half hour to spare. Such are the benefits of an excellent telepathic heart-chakra connection with someone you love.

Telepathy ordinarily works because we mentally tune in to the same vibratory frequency we send out, and we primarily tune in to the frequencies that we focus on or care about. It's a simple case of like attracting like: If we dwell on fear, we're going to draw the same to us. If, on the other hand, we focus on the positive, that, too, will be telepathically relayed to our field of consciousness by others.

I have a habitually negative friend who absolutely obsesses over how obnoxious, rude, and careless others are. Every time he turns on the radio, he inevitably hears a news account of another person gone mad. He's more than once found himself in the middle of intense situations, such as on the highway when a woman tried to run him off the road, and in a movie theater, when a man nearly punched him out after he asked him to stop talking during the show. In fact, my friend has had more unpleasant encounters with strangers than anyone I've ever known. What's worse is that they're not limited to his waking hours—he's also tormented in his dreams, having twice-weekly nightmares in which shadowy figures are out to kill him. These energies are so powerful that he sometimes feels their presence in his room. He insists that negativity is taking over the world, which is true. But it isn't taking over the world, it's only taking over *his* world.

On the other hand, I have a dear friend, Bill, who refuses to dwell on or express anything negative as a matter of personal spiritual discipline. Instead, he contemplates peaceful thoughts and shares them wherever he goes. In return, he's the regular recipient of invitations, letters of appreciation, small gifts, and warm, loving, cheerful greetings from everyone he meets. Moreover, he elicits the friendliest responses from even the most cantankerous people. It's as if his telepathic broadcast is music to everyone's psychic ears. Not only does he succeed in keeping the frequency of his vibration robust and very high, but the thoughts that flow into his field of awareness continue to be creative, humorous, and affectionate.

Sadly, these days it's all too easy to drift downward like my pessimistic friend: We tend to be fascinated and even mesmerized by dark images. From violent movies and video games to even the news and social media, death and destruction seem to appeal to a worldwide audience that considers such things entertaining. Perhaps because a part of us feels dead and disconnected from life, this fascination with horror, violence, and evil images fills that void and makes us feel alive in some perverted way.

I'm not saying that a good horror or action movie isn't entertaining now and then, but feeding your psyche a relentless diet of negativity and darkness poisons the mind and sends the spirit running for higher ground. These images create fear, which leads to disease, depression, despair, and destruction, creating a telepathic cancer that eats away at our spirit. This is the worst form of psychic terrorism.

Unfortunately, negative frequencies have increased exponentially in the past 20 years due to talk radio, cable television, social media, and the Internet. It's not that life itself is more negative, because there has never been more light and love on the planet than there is today. However, these mass media and Internet broadcasts are manipulating the mental airwaves, obscuring the light, and making it more challenging to avoid being sucked into the harmful undertow.

The worst example in world history of negative telepathic manipulation is that of Nazi Germany, where usually reasonable people were telepathically infected with submissiveness and hate and, in the process, went along with the idea of exterminating an entire race of people. It seemed that we'd eradicated this type of behavior, but we're now facing the same mass telepathic relay of destruction in radical, terrorist, and white supremist groups. So again, we're seeing usually sane people turn into monsters.

The best way to prevent being telepathically hijacked by lower-level energy is to be focused on what you love and spend time in your heart and spirit, sending out love to everyone and everything. The more you immerse yourself in love, the higher the frequency your spirit will broadcast in the world. When your spirit is uplifted, you will be more attuned to the positive telepathic heart chakra in the psychic airwaves. Moreover, by focusing on uplifting, heart-based, and loving energies, you'll telepathically attract others with these vibrations into your life, creating a self-reinforcing cycle of positive vibes.

I have a client, Eve, who is one of the most heart-centered, loving people I've ever met, despite having had one of the most traumatic childhoods possible. She grew up in the gangland projects of Detroit and was regularly beaten and nearly killed by her alcoholic stepfather. Removed from her home because of his attacks, she was also separated from her brothers, whom she loved dearly, and put in a foster home that felt worse than living with her family. As soon as she turned 14, she ran away and has lived on her own ever since. Despite having every reason in the world to close her heart and tune in to the lower ego's channel, Eve refused. Instead, she's kept her heart open and her focus on love, and has devoted her time to healing others. First she became a nurse, then a midwife, and finally a physician's assistant. Single until her late forties, Eve encountered the love of her life, a doctor from Switzerland who came to work on a fellowship in Michigan, by pure telepathic connection. They met at a Stevie Wonder concert in Detroit in 1981. They both went alone and ended up with seats next to one another. They danced all night long and had the time of their lives. "I wasn't going to go," Eve said, "but I had this strong pull that I had to be there, so I listened and forced myself to get ready. Wow, am I ever glad I did!"

This is a beautiful case of heart-chakra telepathic rapport bringing two souls together. They were on the same heart-centered wavelength. They married and eventually moved to Switzerland, where Eve lives in one of the most gorgeous hamlets in the world. Her life there is peaceful and safe, and she is deeply loved.

"I cannot believe my good fortune," she said last time we spoke. Now she and her husband are retired, devoting themselves to sailing and eco-farming. Eve is also learning to make her own healing flower essences from flowers that grow on their property. "My life is a fairy tale," she sighed. "Again, I cannot believe how wonderful it turned out to be." Given her relentlessly loving and positive broadcast, I can.

Choosing to focus on love is not merely some Pollyanna "stick your head in the sand" philosophy to avoid the real world, as those who are addicted to darkness and despair would suggest. Rather, it is a rebuttal to all those who want to control us and have us submit to their negative projections. Mentally choosing to focus on love is a powerful weapon against the darkest of telepathic oppressors. Take, for example, Mohandas Gandhi, who liberated India telepathically by transmitting his unwavering conviction of peace. His focus was so powerful and his broadcast to his fellow countrymen was so grounded in love and nonviolence that all India united and gained their freedom without arms.

Each of us receives all sorts of telepathic telegrams every single day. Which ones will you accept? Those that broadcast and affirm vibrations of healing and light? Or those that create hysteria and darkness? Everything you dwell on adds to humanity's collective telepathic pool. While you may not be responsible for all the contamination out there, you are responsible for the pollution you personally add. I've never seen such negativity, paranoia, and misinformation being broadcasted as I've seen on message boards, cable news programs, the Internet, and social media in the past few years. If a person lacks a connection to their spirit, they are vulnerable to being mentally hijacked by these low-level telepathic predators. Once this occurs, they start channeling groupthink and have fewer of their own original thoughts.

As you know, the ego's primary stance is "me against you," so life is reduced to battling to be right and proving that everyone who disagrees with you is a threat that must be eliminated. This is how you know you are stuck in the ego and disconnected from the spirit. As I've said earlier, the ego is consumed with survival, so anyone who doesn't share your point of view becomes an enemy.

I don't care to enter this divisive telepathic realm or address it further in this book because the more you focus on it, the more it pulls you in. That's how it works, like a super-powered vacuum sucking you into its grip. Instead, I want to invite you to experience the higher telepathic channel broadcast from the heart. This is the telepathic channel of creative ideas that heal and unify the world, take care of our planet, solve our shared problems, and search for ways to ease pain and suffering. This is the channel of art, music, inspirational breakthroughs in healing, solutions for reducing fossil fuel pollution, ways to turn our trash into nonpolluting fuel and clean our seas, among other higher-hearted interests. It is also the channel that will transform your personal life into an extraordinarily beautiful one, filled with blessings, gorgeous connections, and more love than you ever knew existed. You tap into this channel by tuning out everything else that steals you away from tuning in to your heart and beautiful spirit. And you do what you love with love every day.

The most significant difference you can make in healing the world is telepathically sending positive, light-filled thoughts while simultaneously rejecting messages of darkness and despair. You become a beacon of light to others when you follow your heart by broadcasting love and inspiration. And the more you convey light vibrations, the more they'll amplify, multiply, and return to you. Spiritual law says that you receive what you give times 10, so choose to put out bright, loving energy to the world. Despite appearances to the contrary, it will return. The more openhearted you are, the quicker the telepathic reception will be. Your heart chakra is the physical point in the body where high-frequency telepathic signals are relayed back and forth, so you can attract the most remarkable of circumstances, opportunities, and encounters with others by intending to beam love. Here's an example of what I mean.

When I lived in Chicago years ago, the license plate on my car was GDVIBES, meaning "good vibes," to broadcast a personal message of good energy wherever I went. People got it, and with that plate on my periwinkle-blue VW Bug, driving in Chicago was a beautiful, uplifting experience. People smiled, waved, honked, let me in, allowed me to pass, gave me parking spaces, and beamed good vibes back to me. I no longer own a car, but I still broadcast good vibes wherever I go—and I get the same results.

Telepathy is the most accessible of our six-sensory skills: Everyone is mentally talking to everyone else all the time, and everyone is tuning in. You're in telepathic chat rooms every second, whether you know it or not. If you pay attention to what crosses your mind, you'll see what I mean.

Woo-Woo Workout

Pay special attention to what pops into your mind this week. Avoid exposing yourself to negative, depressing, violent, or destructive images. Turn off the television, radio, smartphone, and computer, and avoid the news for the entire week. No matter what they report, it doesn't serve you if it's demoralizing and invokes fear. While it is important to know what is happening in the world, it's equally important to take breaks from it all. It is also important to be discerning when choosing your news source. There is a difference between accurate information and biased, toxic, and inflaming opinion.

Zero in on what you say and listen to mentally. Recognize the correlation between what you broadcast and what comes back to you. What kinds of thoughts are you in the habit of thinking? Are you seized with fearful notions? Are you invaded by negative images? Do you receive jealous, angry, petty, insecure messages that drain you and leave you feeling unloved and unloving? If so, consciously change the channel. Go to your heart. Mentally and verbally focus on higher things, and send out loving, peaceful messages to those around you. Call people and tell them you love them and why. When in conversation, talk about the things you love and make you feel happy. Avoid and leave conversations that drift downward into negativity. *Nothing* good will come your way if you stay. See your mind as an FM radio station that receives and broadcasts only heart-centered high vibrations and frequencies.

Say prayers and read poetry. Put down images of destruction and pick up art books. Listen to classical music and engage in positive conversations. Turn your mind over to humor, laughter, and joyful music.

Note the difference in the quality of thoughts that drift into your awareness as you mentally elevate your airwaves. Also, see if what floats into your awareness adds to the quality of your life. It's pretty simple: If you want inspiration, think inspiring thoughts. If you want to heal, broadcast healing thoughts. If you want to be creative, broadcast creative thoughts. If you want love, broadcast loving thoughts. And if you want to live in a higher way, think higher thoughts.

Woo-Woo Wisdom

Choose a higher frequency.

PIVOT

If you want your vibes to guide you, then it's up to you to be as guidable as possible. That means when your vibes suggest you make a change in your plans, you do so quickly and with no mental resistance. One way to do so is to practice becoming flexible in your thinking and actions—in other words, rather than fight, argue, or resist your vibes, consider them blessed messengers and gifts, and pivot with them the minute they ask you to. Because your spirit guides you from moment to moment, it will often suggest that you abandon your original plans and redirect your course of action quickly because conditions have changed. If you stop to question your vibes or seek an explanation, you might miss your moment and no longer have the opening to continue in the flow.

In 2001, when I lived in Chicago and had recently published my first book, *The Psychic Pathway,* Deepak Chopra came to speak at the then-largest New Age bookstore, Transitions. It was a huge deal and the event sold out in a matter of only two days. To my surprise and delight, the owners, friends of mine, called and asked if I'd like to be introduced to Dr. Chopra. One of the perks of this event was a private VIP champagne reception to which a small number of people could buy a pricey ticket and meet him in person before he spoke. I was told that I would be invited to this reception as well.

That night, the line to meet Dr. Chopra was 25 deep throughout the entire reception, and I was both disappointed and not in the mood to wait. Feeling guided to meet and mingle with the other guests, many of whom were local Chicago celebrities, I began to look around the room. One of these guests I spoke with was Dr. Chopra's publicist, a man named William. We had a great chat, and I shared my views on how important a flexible attitude and body are to living an intuitive life. He told me that Phil Jackson, the famous coach of the Los Angeles Lakers and a personal friend of his, once said to him, "Don't watch their heads; watch their hips. Their hips flow with the ball. That's how you'll know what's coming next."

I smiled. "I believe that's what makes a champion player in any field," I said. "In fact, it's the key to living an extraordinary life, period. When you sense and flow with the energy and don't let your head get in the way, you win in life."

On my way home from the event, I realized that meeting William had been the gift of the night. Learning that Phil Jackson, one of the greatest basketball coaches of all time and a huge sports celebrity, shared my view on the importance of being spontaneous and flexible was even more exciting that shaking Dr. Chopra's hand.

That is precisely what trusting your vibes involves, and why I was led to this party. It was not to meet Dr. Chopra, but to connect and have this conversation with William because it helped me become crystal clear about what living an extraordinary life involves. Going with the flow of your vibes and not trying to control them but rather *trust* them. In other words, as the saying goes, "Let the spirit move you." Just make sure you are movable.

This basically means when making any plan as you travel through life, be fully willing and able to quickly pivot at any moment if signaled to do so. Just as your car's GPS system might start out sending you in one direction but redirect you in an instant if the circumstances along the route change, so, too, will your vibes signal you to change direction if obstacles arise. The whole point of having a GPS system is to keep you flowing in the direction you want to go without interruption or getting lost or stuck in traffic. The same holds true for your inner guidance system. It wants to keep you flowing in the direction of your highest good in the most efficient way possible, free from trouble and trauma. Your vibes, your inner GPS, tune in to more than your ego and five senses can. It is invaluable if you use it.

This lesson hit home for me one snowy November afternoon several years ago. I was on my way to pick up my daughters from school when, with one block to go, I suddenly felt an urge to drive in the opposite direction. Perplexed but trusting that the Universe was at work, I turned the car around and followed still another impulse to turn left three blocks later. As I came to a stop sign, a barefoot toddler wearing only a diaper ran in front of my car and continued across the street. There was no adult in sight, so I parked the car and ran after her. Thankfully, I managed to grab the baby just before she was about to run through another intersection. *So this is why I had to turn around and drive this way,* I thought. *The Universe needed me to save this child.*

With the child tucked under my coat, I started walking. I followed my vibes, looking for signs of where she had escaped from. After a few minutes of wandering around, I was drawn to an open door and knew I had found the place, so I rang the bell. A young woman answered the door, and when she saw me standing with the child, she screamed, "Oh my God!" I explained what had happened, and she told me that had no idea the baby was missing. Overwhelmed with shock and gratitude, she couldn't thank me enough.

By the time I went to pick up my daughters, I was 35 minutes late. At first, they were furious, but then they were happy when they learned I'd saved the little girl.

This story is a perfect example of the importance of being spontaneous, flexible, and following your vibes, even when they ask you to do something that makes no immediate logical sense. Had I resisted the impulse to drive in that direction, who knows what would have happened to that child? Because I was willing to be flexible and follow my vibes, the angels used me that day. In fact, the more spontaneous and flexible you are, the better a candidate you become for spirit to move through you and use you. My teacher Charlie once said that whenever he left the house, he had notions about where he was headed, but he was never sure if he'd get there because spirit might lead him elsewhere. I admired his willingness to follow his vibes, which led him to situations that blessed and graced his life every day.

Following his example, I'm entirely open to trusting my vibes and being flexible, especially when traveling. Of course, I make plans, but I always leave them a little loose, just in case I'm led to something better. This kind of trust sends control freaks up the wall, but I find it incredibly exciting. It almost feels like a game I play with the Universe, and it has opened hundreds of doors for which I could never have prepared. For instance, I waited to make a hotel reservation until the very last minute on a trip to London. I called a discount broker who said he only had one room available for less than $100 a night, a bargain in London. Everyone had warned me of the difficulty of finding a reasonably priced, decent hotel room in the city without an advance reservation, but I ignored them and trusted that it would work out.

When I arrived at the hotel, I was greeted politely by the desk clerk, who seemed perplexed when he looked up my reservation. He disappeared into the back room for several minutes, then returned and said, "I'm sorry, madam. We are overbooked. I just gave the last available room to the person before you. But don't worry—we're sending you to one of our other hotels where they can gladly accommodate you for the same rate."

"Would you mind telling me which hotel?" I inquired.

He smiled and said, "It's Le Meridien Waldorf on the Strand, near Covent Garden. I think you'll approve, as it's the best location in London." In addition to giving me a five-star hotel room at the same rate as my three-star reservation, they even paid to send me over in a taxi. My flexible, hang-loose approach had certainly paid off handsomely!

I recognize that this kind of confident trust may be a bit much if you're used to planning things in advance. I don't recommend that you be as daring or open as I am, but I do think that if you want to live in a higher way, it's necessary to always leave room for your sixth sense to get in there and influence things. Then pivot when asked to and go with the flow when it does show up.

A client recently experimented with being flexible when she wandered into a neighborhood that she'd always avoided. A few blocks into her walk, she happened upon a secondhand shop she hadn't known about. Inside, she found a beautiful old Venetian glass mirror that was the exact size and style she'd been searching for for several months, at a price that was a steal. She was thrilled and grateful for this gift from the Universe. So now she makes it a habit to take an intuitively guided walk into new territory at least once a week, searching for treasure.

The best reason for listening to your vibes is to allow the Universe to lead you to the best outcomes, and they are usually better than the ones you had in mind. If you're a rigid and controlling Tin Man, stiff and inflexible, it's time to get out the mental oilcan and seriously loosen up. Being flexible means getting out of your head and stopping your fearful ego from controlling the show and stopping the flow in your life, with its belief that you must know everything in advance. Instead, let your spirit lead you directly to things in the quickest, easiest, and often most delightful way ever. It can and wants to if only you agree. The more you open your heart and listen to your spirit, the more you will be guided to the best things in life.

People with rigid attitudes block the opportunity to let their spirit guide them. They miss opportunities simply because they are unwilling to make room for a better idea from the Universe. When you feel this tendency, remember that you are spirit and allow your spirit to lead. It directs you to the best opportunities, while your ego backs you into a corner or leads you to dead ends. The more you let go of your attachment to ideas about how things "should" be, the more your intuition can get in there and show you a better way. It's not that you shouldn't set intentions or establish personal goals, because you absolutely must. Nor am I telling you to become an aimless wanderer, because that will only lead you in circles. What I'm advising is that you decide what you want while at the same time leaving room for your spirit and the Universe to help you achieve it.

My client Lucy lamented her unwillingness to go into business with a high school buddy. Lucy needed to remain in her job five more years to become eligible for early retirement, but she loathed her job. "Everything in me said that I should quit and work with my friend in her software company," she said. "I loved the idea, I loved working with her, and I loved what she wanted me to do. My vibes were loud and clear, but my mind refused to trust them. Even though I hated my job, I was so attached to my five-year plan that I said no. Now, 18 months later, she's taking her company public and has earned millions. And here I sit, stuck in the same old familiar position, still hating my life. I really missed my chance, even though she offered it to me five times."

Sadly, Lucy missed her opportunity, as do most people who are unwilling to follow their gut. A willingness and readiness to release plans and go with the *feel* of the moment is essential to intuitive living. As one very successful client once told me, "I don't think—I *feel*. And I follow my feelings wherever they lead me. That's why I do so well."

How open are you to being spontaneous and following your intuition, even if it may mean changing plans? Do you tend to rigidly adhere to the same old routines and thoughts without ever allowing your intuitive genius to intercept and make a few suggestions? Are you so committed to sticking to the plan that you never let your soul lead? If so, you're following the ego's rules, which, as you know by now, always leads to the same old predictable conclusion.

Following your vibes is a lot like dancing. You may know the steps, but you won't succeed unless you're willing to move with the music. The Universe has a pulse and rhythm of its own, and it wants to carry you with it—so if you dance with spirit, just remember to allow it to lead the dance.

Woo-Woo Workout

Let's practice becoming looser and less rigid by doing gentle bending and stretching before starting your day. Begin by raising your arms slowly over your head, gently rolling your neck, raising, and lowering your shoulders, shifting your ribs, and rotating your wrists and ankles. Then, ease into this exercise, doing a little more stretching each day.

As I mentioned earlier, an excellent way to practice developing flexibility is to loosen your hips. An easy way to do this is to get a Hula-Hoop and twirl it around for a few minutes. If you don't have a Hula-Hoop, you can simulate the motion of the plastic circle revolving around your middle.

Follow your physical-flexibility exercises with some mental-flexibility stretches. Invite your intuition to take over by asking your spirit what it wants to do. If it wants to speak up, speak up; if it wants to be quiet, be quiet; if it wants to go on an adventure, go. Say yes to all your intuitive impulses and be curious about where they'll lead you. Take a new route to work, wear something completely different from your usual outfit, consider a new pair of glasses, or get a new haircut just for the sake of discovering a new you. Be curious and surrender to your soul's lead by trying a new restaurant, exploring a hidden neighborhood, or going for an open-ended walk or drive. Turn on some exciting music and dance—move, shake, twist, and bend just because you can.

One of my teachers once suggested that if I wanted to take full advantage of my intuition, I had to act like Gumby, the plastic toy that can easily bend and stretch. If you have any children under the age of five, watch them for a couple of minutes and notice how flexible and spontaneous they are, not hesitating for a moment to change a plan, an idea, or a direction. Follow their example.

Woo-Woo Wisdom

Go with the flow.

LIGHTEN UP

To live an intuitive life, it helps to clear away everything that prevents you from tuning in to higher vibrations—that is, everything that takes up space or energy but doesn't contribute to your life. This includes unwanted possessions, unfinished business, excess commitments, negative thinking, judgments, mental projections, resentments from the past, and conflicts in the present.

Let's start with your physical stuff. Like psychic pollution, useless stuff creates dead, toxic energy that drags you down. As a six-sensory person, it is essential to keep your atmosphere clear, both internally and externally. Scrutinize everything in and around you and ascertain whether these things add to or detract from your clear energy. The clearer you are, the more you'll be able to keep the psychic airwaves of your life free of energetic obstructions and open to higher transmissions.

Just as you would never agree to spend time in a toxic-waste dump, neither should you agree to live or work in a psychically polluted atmosphere. Although you can't see dead energy, it still takes a toll—even seemingly harmless stuff can block good energy from entering your life.

An example of this occurred to me years ago. I was looking for something to wear to a teaching engagement and tried on a dress that I hadn't worn for several years. Even though it was nice enough, it didn't feel quite right. My then-12-year-old daughter,

Sabrina, walked in, looked at me, and said, "Mom, you're not thinking of wearing that, are you?"

"Yes," I said. "Why not? It's a nice dress."

"It's okay, but it's not you."

She was absolutely right—that dress wasn't me. Even trying it on made me feel drab and lifeless, so I gave it away. You wouldn't think that simply giving away a dress could make much of a difference in the world, but it actually started a chain reaction that led to my clearing my entire closet of clothes that weren't the "real me" anymore. By the time I'd finished, I had emptied my closet of 12 bags of clothes! As I sent the last bag out the door, I was more inspired than ever and was back in the flow of life. I was suddenly more energized than I'd been in months and emerged from the writing slump I'd been in for a long time.

Sabrina is a grown woman now and still lets me know when something is not for me. A few months back, I went to Harrods, the most famous department store in London, and one of my favorite places. I love shoes, so made a beeline to the shoe floor to see what was new. While strolling around, I noticed pair after pair of white army boots on display, each designer featuring their own version, clearly letting me know this was the "It" fashion boot of the season. I wasn't sure what to think of them. Then, while eyeing a pair made by an Italian designer named Fendi, a handsome young Italian salesman whooshed upon me, gushing, "Aren't those the coolest boots you have *ever* seen?"

"Well," I answered, smiling at his enthusiasm, "they are certainly different. They look a little intense, though, don't you think?"

"*Oh my God,* not at all!" he shot back. "Come on! They are so chic and would look so hot on you! You must try them on," he insisted, picking up one of the boots and holding it up gently as if it were a priceless Fabergé egg. How could I possibly say no to him?

Long story short, I succumbed, and before I knew what hit me, I was strolling out of Harrods with those white boots, not sure whether I was beyond ridiculous or too cool for school. Strutting into Sabrina's apartment later that afternoon sporting my neon-white trucks on my feet, I hoped her reaction would make me feel better than the silly way I actually did feel. Two feet inside the door, she saw what were on my feet and gasped. *"No!* Mom, take them off and return them right now!" Again, my fashion-police daughter called it like it is. "Those boots are awful. What were you thinking?"

"They are the hottest boot of the season," I replied, trying to defend my apparent lapse of sanity.

"They look like a cross between a nurse and a clown shoe!"

She was so offended by them, I burst out laughing.

"They are awful, aren't they?" I admitted.

"Beyond . . !" She rolled her eyes.

I took them off and put on my Adidas instead. These were not the power boots I had fantasized them to be. If anything, they undermined me. Having such silly, heavy shoes on my feet did nothing to lighten my vibe. They did the opposite, leaving me feeling so self-conscious they tripped me up.

Now, I am not suggesting that your shoes should be light-weight by any means, but they should make you feel light on your feet. After all, I just suggested you be ready to pivot when the vibe moved you to do so. In other words, what you wear, including on your feet, is important. Clothes energetically affect you and can influence how receptive and responsive you are. If you're buried underneath drab clothing or dragged down by uncomfortable or all-too-wrong shoes, how do you think that affects your overall perception of the world around you? Clothing and shoes that leave you feeling lackluster, self-conscious, constricted, in pain, or uncomfortably exposed diminish your awareness and block the flow of energy from your spirit, causing you to miss important messages and clues coming your way.

The boots went back. My Italian salesman was very gracious about the return. I told him they were simply too heavy. "It's hard to be quick on my feet in big white army boots!"

"Oh, really?" he answered. "I never thought about that before. You might be right."

My mother used to say, "You are a Divine and Holy spirit, so dress your spirit well." As I shared earlier, she made and wore the most beautiful clothing every single day of her life. She lived to be 90 and only recently passed away. Until then, she was as healthy as they come, and she attributed her strong life force and well-being to the high amount of light in her body, which she insisted was enhanced by what she wore on her body. I've come to agree. We don't need to become fashion victims, like I was with those absurd boots. We only need to find clothing that enhances the light within and makes us shine. Our bodies, after all, are our intuition receivers. If they are draped in clothing that makes us feel happy and confident, and supported by shoes that feel good on our feet, our receivers will be in top form.

CLEAR YOUR PHYSICAL ENVIRONMENT

Clearing away negative, heavy energy restores the flow in your life and gets things moving in a higher direction. The Chinese art of feng shui is based on the principle of keeping the energy in your in your environment light and balanced so that your life flows freely. Just as you can "feng shui" your office or home, I encourage you to "feng shui" your entire physical atmosphere. Pay attention to how things affect you. Get rid of anything that doesn't feel good, serve, or uplift you. Don't be sentimental—no matter how priceless an item may be, nothing is worth keeping if it doesn't leave you with a positive, light feeling. If it irritates you, reminds you of something or someone who makes your heart close, or if it distracts you from recognizing the subtle energy of the moment, give it away. Trust your intuition, not your intellect, when making these decisions.

Years ago, my sister gave me a Salvador Dalí painting that was quite valuable. I was both impressed and excited to own such a sophisticated piece of art . . . but the painting got on my nerves. Although Dalí is a great artist, the painting depressed me; nevertheless, for 10 years, I considered myself lucky to have such a fine work of art in my home.

One day I looked at the painting and wanted to scream. At that moment, I knew the Dalí had to go, so I took it down and put it in the closet. That made me feel much better, but it wasn't enough. Knowing that the painting sat in my closet still bothered me and took up too much of my attention. I thought about it every time I walked by that closet, as though it were being held hostage in the dark. Having had enough of this distracting energy, I finally sold the Dalí at a yard sale. I was so relieved to see it go that I couldn't believe I had kept it so long. I later sheepishly admitted to my sister what I'd done. She laughed and said, "I don't blame you. I hated that painting, too—that's why I gave it to you!"

KEEP IT SIMPLE

Trusting your vibes is easier when you have a clear, uncluttered, environment so that energy isn't blocked or leaves you feeling stuck in the past. Don't hold on to things for sentimental reasons because you "might need it one day," or for any reason other than it brings you good vibes. Holding on to things for any other reason will just bog you down and keep you stuck. Instead, ruthlessly go through your stuff and get rid of everything that doesn't feel positive. And remember that as long as we hold on to things, they hold on to us.

I have a client named Ellen whose divorce settlement left her an exceedingly wealthy woman. With her millions, she bought several properties in Texas. She filled them with priceless works of art, enormous expensive crystals, antique singing bowls from Tibet and Thailand, healing stones, and massive amounts of jewelry, luxury furniture, and designer clothing. No matter how much she acquired, however, nothing made her happy. Instead, she only felt worse and worse. Trying to fill the emptiness she felt since her divorce, she got involved with a man who cheated her out of so much money Ellen couldn't even speak about it. Now she was buried under a mountain of things, a heartache the size of Texas, a dwindling fortune, and a spirit that was dying.

"I don't know what to do. I can't keep up my properties, and they are falling apart. I have so many cars, speedboats, and Jet Skis I never use, it's pathetic. They sit behind my houses, taking up space and draining my life force. I don't even know how I will sell it all. I'm so exhausted, and it's too much work. It's a vicious cycle.

"And," she continued, "I cannot sell my houses until I get rid of the stuff inside. I feel so overwhelmed and I'm afraid I'll never get out from under all of this stuff," she sobbed.

"Ellen," I advised her, "forget selling your stuff. Just let it go. Donate everything and then sell the houses."

"What do you mean, donate it? This stuff is worth too much money to donate."

"Not really," I answered. "It's only worth what it's worth to someone else. If it's killing your spirit, it's not worth anything at all. If you ask your spirit and the Universe to help you lighten this load, they will. But only if you mean it."

Ellen was taken aback by the thought of giving all of her possessions away and resisted for some time. But the longer she held on, the worse she felt. Finally, one day she called and asked, "How do I get rid of this stuff? I'm over it."

"If you donate it, the Universe will help you more than you know." I suggested she call a local chapter of the Boys & Girls Clubs of America and see if they might want her boats, Jet Skis, and even her cars. Her spirit took over, pushed her ego aside, and she called that afternoon. Not only was the local club she chose overjoyed with her donation, but they took tools from her shed, a lawn mower, and a bunch of other junk she needed to get rid of as well. They came and collected all these things the following weekend, giving her a considerable tax deduction on top of it all. Once the stuff was sold and cleared out, Ellen felt drawn to speak to a young Realtor whose energy she liked, even though her friends and brother advised her to go with a more experienced agent in the area. He was such a wonderful, eager guy that Ellen was moved to give him the listings for all three properties she wanted to sell at once. He was beside himself with excitement and promised she would never regret going with him. Four days later, the Realtor called Ellen and said he had great news. He found a buyer for all three properties, a developer who was new to the area. Even better, the guy said he would take her properties as is, so she didn't even have to do any repair work, a significant worry of Ellen's. It was nothing short of a miracle.

Once she decided to let go, Ellen went from buried alive to home free in less than six weeks. Ellen liquidated in a flash and had enough money to live comfortably and simply for the rest of her life. The best part was that the Realtor's wife was an eBay specialist and offered to inventory and resell all of Ellen's now-unwanted designer clothing and shoes for a small commission. Ellen was ready to move on in every way, clothing and all, so she was grateful for this offer and considered it, too, a minor miracle. The burden of dealing with unloading her wardrobe was lifted in one fell swoop as all of it disappeared into a rental van the following week. Last we spoke, Ellen was contemplating moving to Costa Rica. Whether she went or not, at least she was now free of her past and could move on to a sweeter, simpler, lighter life.

CLEAR OUT PEOPLE TOO

Perhaps the most difficult thing to do if you want to be in the flow with your vibes is to rid your life of people who hold you back, stand in your way, bring you down, don't get you, or dim your light. This is the most challenging clearing of all but will bring the greatest benefits.

I had a client, Sophie, a talented writer and artist, who discovered this firsthand. Sophie had a friend named Julie, whom she had known since high school. Julie was also a writer and artist, though not as talented or successful as Sophie. Whenever they got together, Julie was forever comparing herself to Sophie, causing Sophie to feel as though she needed to hide her successes and downplay the good things in her life for the sake of keeping Julie's jealous ego from sniping at her. Eventually, however, Sophie could no longer tolerate Julie's negative energy and distanced herself from her once and for all.

Choosing to cut Julie out of her life was liberating and long overdue. "I betrayed myself every single time I saw her," Sophie said. "I didn't dare share anything good that was happening in my life because Julie was never happy for me. Finally, I realized I didn't have to have her in my life just because she had been around for so long. Once I admitted that to myself, my heart breathed a sigh of relief. I came into integrity with myself. No more playing small for anyone!"

Soon after, Sophie made a new friend, Rochelle, a talented musician with a tremendously generous heart and spirit. The two of them hit it off immediately. Rochelle celebrated Sophie in ways Julie never did. She was happy for Sophie's success and wasn't threatened by her. Rochelle was in her spirit, not her ego. They were soul-to-soul friends and helped one another in all ways. Both women went on to enjoy great careers and a great friendship for years. None of that would have happened had Sophie kept spending time with Julie.

If there are people in your life who are intimidated by your light because they are stuck in their egos, I suggest you cut the connection and move on. These kinds of people will never want *you* to rise because they know *they* are not rising at all. If anything, they are on a downward trajectory.

Many beautiful, talented, bright-light people have energy suckers attached to them. I have a friend named Mara who said there is a Yiddish word for such people: *farbissina*. It's a person who brings you down, so you stay at their level. There are no rewards for hanging out with farbissinas. Yet there are high costs. It's never safe to be in a relationship of any kind with a person who cannot get past their petty ego and connect to their spirit.

Be honest about the people in your life and let the farbissinas go. When you do, your life will take off. People who match your vibration will step in and take their place so fast you will be amazed.

GET RID OF EMOTIONAL HOOKS

When letting go of people, be sure to let go of the things they gave you, too, especially if those items carry the same negative energy as the person themselves. A friend had a psychic revelation regarding an expensive coral necklace that her ex-boyfriend had given her. She'd had a very painful, unhealthy relationship with this man, yet everyone advised her to "keep the jewelry and forget the jerk"; if anything, he owed her that much. But psychically, it didn't work that way—even stuffed in her drawer, the necklace's vibrations left my friend sad, tormented, and unhappy. One day she opened the drawer and saw the necklace, and her spirit plummeted. She took the necklace out of the drawer. "This thing is a downer, like he was," she said. She finally realized that it caused her to feel drained and sad, and decided to donate it to a nearby Salvation Army.

"It was like lifting hooks off my back," she told me later. Her heart instantly soared, and once out of the necklace's grip, she was even moved to have kind thoughts about her ex-boyfriend.

The importance of releasing old energy and keeping things light and simple can't be overstated. And it shouldn't be limited to the physical plane—we can become just as bogged down by old attitudes, negative thoughts and beliefs, heavy and melodramatic emotions, and even old relationships. These are the energy suckers that interfere with your ability to hear your spirit. Clearing them out may be more challenging than clearing your physical space, but it can be done.

In working with people one-on-one daily for nearly 35 years, I can unequivocally state that unless you remove all kinds of psychic debris, your journey will most likely stop right here. In other words, you can't move one inch closer to trusting your vibes if you let your ego tenaciously cling to your hurt feelings, resentments, and projections.

If you need support, be honest and humble enough to seek expert help to do this energetic clearing. The ego is too vain to admit that it needs anything, but the spirit rejoices in gaining support. If you're stuck, seek the help of healers, teachers, and guides of every sort. Clearing the past may require an entire team of assistants. You may need a therapist, a support group, a faith leader, a financial counselor, a coach, a lawyer, a personal trainer, an art teacher, a babysitter, an exercise buddy, or even a new hairdresser.

Now, most people would probably tell me that they can't afford this kind of support. But I say that if your life is being stolen and your spirit is dying, you can't afford not to seek help. Most support services are free or at a reasonable cost. For example, 12-step meetings are free; community services offer counseling and support groups for as little as $10; massage-therapy schools seek bodies to work on all the time; teenage babysitters are always looking for work; and for an exercise buddy, ask a friend. These services become affordable when you value them.

Note that I do not order you to "snap out of it," which is a popular approach by some motivational speakers. In working intimately with thousands of vulnerable, wounded, and overtaxed people for many years, I've never seen this approach bring about deep healing with any of my clients. However, what *does* work is for them to get under it, through it, above it, and into it until they learn how to love themselves and forgive other people. I believe in patience as we seek to dig out from under our "human experiences." No amount of yelling will work, but being determined to dig out will.

To sum up, if you want to reach out for something new, first let go of what's in your hand. Let go of what's in the closet, under the bed, and in your mind. Release your grip on anything that doesn't serve your spirit. You need to free your attention to hear your intuition, but if you're swaddled in stuff, you'll miss it. What's worth holding on to that would cost you that? Our planet can no longer afford to support those who insist on wallowing in the muck of old and negative vibrations. We're here to have a joyous life experience, not to dwell on the past.

Woo-Woo Workout

Begin to methodically clear out everything and everyone in your life that no longer uplifts your spirit. Start by emptying out your wallet or purse, and then move systematically outward through your desk, car, office, closets and cupboards, garage and basement, or any other space where negative energy may dwell. Keep nothing that doesn't leave you with a feeling of light, positive energy. Be ruthless in your assessment of whether you should keep something—and when you do eliminate it, be quick about it. Don't second-guess yourself.

As soon as your physical space is clear, you'll have to address the energy suckers. Take an inventory of where you're stuck, and don't get discouraged. Notice all the negative attitudes, resentments, dramas, and old vendettas you carry and write them down.

Once you recognize how much psychic dead weight you carry around, take one step toward relieving yourself of it by seeking help. If you have addictions, contact a 12-step group in your area—there are groups for those who abuse alcohol, drugs, money, and sex and those who live with or are in a relationship with addicted people.

Perhaps you can use the support of a life coach, intuitive healer, or therapist. Ask your doctor or friends for a referral and try several professionals until you find one who resonates with your soul. If the prospect of talking to someone makes you uncomfortable, know that it's completely normal. However, the minute you're around a true healer, this will end immediately. If you resist, remember that that impulse is your ego trying to keep you from becoming connected to your heart because it doesn't want to raise the quality of your life. Refusing to get support is death to your spirit, so listen to your spirit and reach out. You aren't weak or broken—you're human, as we all are, and you need support, as we all do.

Seeking out soul supporters was the best decision I ever made. They strengthened my ability to live in my heart, love my life, like who I am, and have compassion for others. We're all students and teachers, and we need one another to learn.

Start small but be diligent in your search for healing—and be patient. I know that clearing the past can feel like a vast and endless task at times, but even a few sessions with a talented healer or teacher, along with a focused effort, can free you considerably. At this point, the important thing is to decide to plunge in and not worry about how long it will take. The work of healing our past is called karma, and on a soul level, this work may take a lifetime or two, so don't rush it. Your peace won't begin after you heal, but when you *agree to heal*.

GREEN FIRE

My favorite clearing ritual for opening the way to a higher vibration on all levels is to make what I call green fire. Green fire cleanses the atmosphere, leaving it in a pristine state, and invites a fresh start. It's a powerful ritual to officially signal the beginning of a new season in your life. Some five-sensory people think rituals are pagan and ridiculous—I prefer to see them as artful and creative, as they speak to our nonintellectual side.

To perform a green-fire ritual, start by writing down all the things that you want to release mentally and emotionally.

Next, grab some foil, a box of Epsom salt, a bottle of rubbing alcohol, a deep pot, and a match. Line the bottom of the pot with foil to protect it, fill it with two cups of Epsom salt, and pour no more than an ounce or two of rubbing alcohol over the salt to fully cover it. Place the pot on a protective plate in the middle of the floor of the main room of your home, apart from anything that can catch on fire. If you have a fireplace, put it there.

When you light the mixture, ask your spirit, angels, and guides to help you release all old and negative vibrations, leaving your environment free and clear of any unwanted energy.

Take the list of things you want to release and place it in the fire. It usually takes about 10 to 15 minutes for the fire to burn out, so remain with it. Whenever I burn green fire, I like to drum out the old energy as well. If you have a drum, you might want to do this; you can always make one with another pot if you don't.

Making loud noises helps dissipate negative energy, so feel free to make loud sounds, grunts, or chants. Laughing is another excellent cleanser, and this ritual does make one laugh. You can also ring a bell while burning the fire, or even shout at the energies in your home. A simple "Get out!" does the job, and it's fun and cathartic.

A green-fire ritual is extremely potent and effective and should only be done with clear intention. I do it every three or four months, or whenever I feel a little blocked, just to clear and renew my spirit. It's a beautiful ritual to finish this week's psychic purge. Notice how much lighter and more conscious you feel after cleansing your energetic space.

Woo-Woo Wisdom

Clear the decks.

Bonus: Clear Your Space Meditation

As a bonus, here is a link to a meditation to energetically clear your space.

Visit https://www.hayhouse.com/downloads and enter the Product ID **9592** and Download Code **audio**.

CHANGE YOUR STORY

As I've mentioned previously, an extraordinary life comes with tuning in to spirit and following our vibes. However, if we get bogged down in the lower frequencies of our ego, we simply cannot do this. This makes it necessary to let go of any limiting misperception that we are our experiences alone. If we mistake who we are, Divine spirit, for our experiences, we get stuck on this lower ego channel and lose our power to create. If we recognize our past for what it is, however, lessons for our souls to grow, we remain connected to our spirit and become resilient, resourceful, creative, and truly unlimited. That is the Divine plan.

Steve Jobs, inventor and world game-changer, had a terrible beginning. He was an unwanted child, given up for adoption, and deeply rejected by his family of origin. His past provided his ego plenty of reasons to fail, feeling unwanted and unloved in the most critical formative years of his life. Nevertheless, Steve Jobs did not allow his past to limit him in any way, becoming one of the most creative people in the world. He invented Mac computers, iPhones, and started Apple instead. He, along with his partner Steve Wozniak, changed the face of technology forever, making it accessible to millions. His past didn't hold him back.

Louise Hay, the founder of Hay House, the celebrated publisher of almost all my books, and the woman credited with single-handedly bringing self-help to the world, was born into poverty and violence. And yet she transformed her past adversity into power and prosperity by teaching millions of people how to heal in her groundbreaking book *You Can Heal Your Life*. She was influenced by her past but never limited by it.

One of my favorite singers today, Adele, is one of the most prolific musicians globally, selling over 120 million records to date. She was raised in south London by a single mother and an alcoholic father. Hers was far from an ideal past, and school was very problematic for her; she often played truant. Still, she reached dizzying heights of success at a young age. Her past didn't limit her possibilities. Instead, she used it to create an extraordinary present.

This is what happens when we view the past from the perspective of spirit as opposed to ego. The spirit helps us create the best with the raw material we are given, making our lives and the world we live in a better place, just as Steve, Louise, and Adele did.

On the other hand, the ego tears us down, makes us doubt ourselves, fails to see the world's goodness, and keeps us stuck and small, and feeling like powerless victims. Our ego cuts us off from our spirit, our vibes, and our creativity, along with the love and support they bring. The ego simply cannot tune in to a higher creative frequency, just as an AM radio cannot tune in to the Internet. Instead, the ego broadcasts a distorted reality that tells us that we are nothing but our experiences. It tells us that if our experiences are unfortunate, we are also unfortunate—which is just *not* true!

As powerful, painful, and impactful as our experiences have been, we must see them for what they are: opportunities for our souls to learn. Our lessons shape who we are but do not define or limit who we are.

We are Divine Beings, eternal students, and we are not limited by our past experiences nor those of previous generations. Our experiences are our teachers and help us grow as souls. We learn by our experiences, by creating empowering stories that help make sense out of our lives, yet we must remember that any version of reality we create or have handed down to us is only part of our true story, never the whole story. Our spirit fills in the rest. We can hugely benefit from our past if we use it to catapult forward to create better, more empowered, creative, authentic experiences ahead.

MY STORY

When I was younger, I saw myself as the daughter of a war refugee and Holocaust survivor because my mom's story was so epic. The things she went through and survived boggled my imagination and broke my heart. Even though her journey was compelling, it was also excruciatingly horrific and painful. Somehow along the way, as a sensitive child, I attached my identity to her story, placing a dark veil of sorrow on my heart. Maybe because I was named after her or because I intuitively felt her pain, I became more focused on her well-being than on my own. I felt compelled to protect her even though she never asked me to do that. I chose to do this all by myself. I was so horrified by stories of her wartime experiences that I felt the need to somehow try to make up for her past trauma. The more focused I was on my mother's story, the less I was connected to who I was—to my path, my lessons, and my purpose. The world she had survived rattled in my bones. I failed to see her journey as *her* soul's lesson, not mine. My feelings were mainly unconscious until a boyfriend pointed it out to me. He said, "You focus so much on your mom, but she seems okay to me. Why are you so worried about her all the time?"

He was right. She was living in the moment and was more or less okay. That is when I knew I needed to let go of her story and move on. She already lived in hell and survived. What was the point of my continuing this when it did neither of us any good?

Still, I was compelled to see firsthand where she came from, what she had gone through all those years ago. On my parents' fiftieth wedding anniversary, my older sister, Cuky, her husband, Buddy, and I took them back to Dingolfing, Germany, where they met and had been married. It was an emotional trip for everyone, with both moments of hilarity and tears as they recounted the past. At one point, Cuky and I asked to see the work camp my mom had been sentenced to before meeting my father. We approached the gate in silence, holding our breath, all of us feeling the tension and fear she must have felt way back then as a terrified child when all of a sudden, my mom looked down at her feet and gasped.

"Paul," she said, turning to my father in total surprise, "Look! There are flowers here!"

Shocked to see such beauty sprouting up from the rocky path leading to her horrible memories, she stopped walking, looked at us, and said, "There is no point in going backward. I see what I needed to see. There is beauty here now, and that is all that matters. Let's go."

And so, we turned around and left, not once looking back. That decision brought closure and release from her past, both for her and also for us, her children. She didn't deny the past, nor did we. We honored her experience. We just didn't let the story end there.

This tendency to carry on the story of our parents and let it define and limit us is not uncommon. I knew a guy named Alan from Iowa, the oldest son in a large Irish Catholic family. Part of his family story and identity was that during the great Irish famine of 1845, his family was on the brink of starving to death from extreme poverty. His great-grandfather and his entire family of 10 siblings and their parents found a way to board a ship to America to escape the famine and start again. Unfortunately, they all became terribly sick. Since they were weak to begin with, the journey proved too brutal to survive. They all died except for Alan's great-grandfather. He survived. His family's experience was an incredibly tragic, awful, heartbreaking story.

The "starving family" story was repeated for generations to come. "It became their identity," Alan said. "No matter how good life got, how much things improved in our family lineage, since my grandfather's fateful journey in 1850, the family remains eternally devastated and impoverished. Though my family today lives a comfortable, if modest, life, they are still starving and impoverished in their minds. If anyone in my family actually said they wanted to prosper, or—God forbid—did, the rest of the family would look down upon them, saying absurd things like, 'Who do they think they are?'"

Alan continued. "My family taught me that I was a poor Irish kid. We all were, and I was to be proud of it. To aspire to more was arrogant and betrayed my heritage. We weren't those phony, awful 'rich' people. We were better than them. And I wasn't allowed to forget it."

Alan said when he tried to better himself by going to college, his family laughed at him. When he traveled to see the world, his family said he was getting "airs." "I couldn't belong to my family and improve my lot in life. I had to pick. It was one or the other. As long as I stayed in my small town and lived near them, I had to be 'cheap and poor.' I couldn't take it anymore. To belong with them, I had to betray myself."

He ultimately decided to leave and moved to Montana. Still, the identity followed him. "I don't want to be, but I am still as suspicious, cheap, and resentful as they are, even though I physically left them behind years ago. This identity followed me. I can't escape."

I suggested Alan stop seeing himself through his family story as someone incapable of prospering or rising higher in life and start recognizing his true spirit. His spirit wanted him to go to college, see the world, start his own business, and live a more expansive life. It was his true Self, and he was faithful to this. His ego story told him it was a lie, that he wasn't allowed to be more. I reminded him that his grandfather had had a similar spirit. He went on to survive and eventually moved to Australia and made a fortune in gold. This other ignored story of his grandfather's resilient spirit lived on in him. His grandfather didn't allow himself to be trapped in the devastating, disempowered version of the story the family told, and Alan didn't have to be either.

A light went on in Alan's s eyes that day. I reminded Alan that he didn't need to share this version of the family story to belong to the family. He belonged no matter what. Maybe his soul came to change the family story into a more victorious one.

WHAT'S YOUR LESSON?

You don't have to remain stuck in a disempowering version of your or your family's past. To get free, do a little digging. Ask yourself what lessons your past and your family's history bring with them. What have you learned from all you've been through? What might you still need to learn?

Surprisingly, the moment you sincerely ask these questions, your spirit offers answers. After all, this is the whole point and purpose of being here. Whether it's your own story, your family's mythology, or the world's history, discover then take the gifts the past brings with it and use them to create a better future. This doesn't mean we cannot feel the pain of the past or must get over it as if turning off a lousy TV show—not at all, nor can we. Our past lives in our bones. It has value and commands respect. We come from a human lineage rife with mistakes, loss, tragedy, and pain. This cannot be avoided because life is temporary, and loss is an inevitable part of it.

We can, however, transform our pain into power. We can take these experiences and weave a new chapter—one that allows us to move freely forward, learn from the mistakes, and find the gifts they brought to live a more conscious, empowered, fulfilling way today. In all of this, please don't ever deny or minimize your personal history. It is rich with gifts and blessings, even if buried under a rubble of tremendous pain and heartache. Don't allow your past to keep you small. It is not what we encounter, but rather what we do with what we experience that truly matters. Keep from the past what serves you, grieve what needs to be grieved, heal what needs to be healed, love what needs to be loved, and learn what needs to be learned. Let go of the rest.

Take your time, and be kind and patient as you sift through your life. Get support to liberate yourself from what hangs on. And use your imagination, connect with your spirit, trust your vibes, and when you are ready, know you can and will move ahead to create your future the way you want.

WHY THIS STORY?

It takes a lot of energy to carry a heavy history with you all the time, and it clouds your connection to the Divine. Honor the story you've lived and the one inherited from your family. Your soul picked this family and this classroom, and even if it makes no sense at times, this experience was the way your soul chose to learn things this time around. I know I picked my family to begin my soul mission from the earliest age. All the necessary pieces for stepping into my life as an intuitive guide and teacher fell into place without trying. I never had a moment when I was uncertain about my future. I always knew what I was here to do and why. That is what I learned from my family story, and that is the gift it offered, and I decided to keep it. Leaving the trauma and drama behind left me with a quieter, calmer, more peaceful mind, and a clean slate as far as who I chose to be. I could do anything I wanted and would not be limited by anyone or anything.

Freeing yourself of the past is easier said than done. Life experiences get stamped into your bones and brain. But you have complete power over how you choose to interpret these experiences and what you will do with them. You can absolutely have compassion and respect for the difficulties you and your family have faced, as life is tough and can be pretty brutal at times. Viewing your life's experiences as one your soul chose to grow, on the other hand, can transform these same experiences into gifts of opportunity, resilience, creativity, courage, and love.

Seeing your history as a personally designed soul classroom changes your perspective and gives you power. Knowing you chose the path you've walked makes it easier to see the value it holds. This doesn't mean that you're to blame for the circumstances you've encountered—not at all. It only means that on a soul level, the path you've walked is one that suited your soul's desire to grow in the ways you wanted to.

My path introduced me to a family that valued six senses and laid the foundation for my purpose in life. At the same time, ours was a dysfunctional family like any other. There were too many kids to get our needs met, not enough money to feel secure, and too much drama to be anything but calm. I cannot count the times in my past I felt as if I was lost in the shuffle and had no parents to take care of me. As a teenager, I experienced physical and sexual assaults, one at gunpoint, and had family members who struggled with addiction and mental illness. In other words, a typical family life. It was not a walk in the park at any time. But I had the flashlight of my vibes to lead the way when it got dark. I chose then, and now, to focus on the gifts of my past rather than the parts that felt like the night of the living dead.

I learned from Dr. Tully at age 14 that viewing our lives as our own design is the only way to be fully empowered. Thank goodness I believed him. It turned out to be true. No one is immune from the pain and drama of being human, but we can keep ourselves from being victimized by life if we remember we are spirit, not ego.

The ego asks life, "Why is this happening to me?" while the spirit asks, "Why is this happening, and what can I learn from it?"

Transcending the limiting ego version of who you are and connecting with your empowered spirit when times are difficult takes imagination, intention, and help from others. It's part of our soul's work to learn to live an empowered, authentic life and not merely be a prerecorded tape replaying the past mistakes of others. Breaking free of victimization and becoming free of the past is one of the most significant challenges all humans face, some far more than others, to be sure. Still, we can all succeed if and when we decide we will. Overcoming our life circumstances and experiences is something we know we are here to do on a soul level. This is why we go to therapy, see energy healers, consult psychics, meditate, read books, take master classes and online workshops, go to retreats, seek out shamans, and more. We need all the help we can get. And it's vital to seek—and receive—all the help you need. Set the intention to transcend the ego and the past, and you will.

LET GO OF EVERYONE'S STORY

It is essential to free ourselves of our limiting history and stop casting limiting stories onto others as well. I learned this lesson in a humbling way 40 years ago, when I lived in Chicago and met with clients in person in my home. One day a young man came to see me for a reading. He dreamed of getting into the University of Chicago, a long shot for sure, but he was determined. He lived in what was at the time a low-income housing development called Cabrini Green, which had a lot of crime and gang-related activity. It was a scary and sad place to live.

I was genuinely impressed with this talented and ambitious kid. I saw he would achieve his dream and get accepted to the school, long shot or otherwise. Wanting to help him because he was so refreshing, I told him that he didn't have to pay me at the end of our session. It was my gift. Rather than accept the offer, he got annoyed with me and said, "No. You are only offering because of where I live. You have no idea who I really am and what I can afford. I can pay like anyone else. I know you mean well, you see me as someone who needs financial help, and I don't."

He was right. I did project my limiting interpretation on him, and it was presumptuousness. He taught me such a big lesson that day that I thanked him and told him I should pay him for the invaluable lesson he just taught me. He paused and thought about it. Then smiled and said, "Actually, you should." So we laughed and called it a wash. We have stayed connected ever since. He fulfilled his dreams and became a highly successful engineer who eventually started his own software gaming company. I learned never to assume you know anyone entirely, so keep your stories to yourself.

THE MORAL OF THIS STORY

Honor and love your history. It is rich with gifts and blessings, even if buried under a pile of pain. See others as spirit, with compassion and respect, but not as victims alone, even if their lives have victimized them in terrible ways. Honor the spirit in others even if they don't. Then, when any one of us is ready to grow, we can create and live a new and exciting chapter in our lives— one that expresses our brilliant spirit in all its glory. It's why we are here.

If you slip and find yourself looking backward, stop by saying aloud, "That's the old story of me. It's not who I am or who I want to be today." See how your vibration lights up with this decision and how much easier it is to hear your guides, spirit helpers, and angels once it's made.

Look forward to expressing who you really are as a Divine spirit while experiencing the love, support, and even miracles that are part of your unfolding, extraordinary new you.

Woo-Woo Workout

It's time to focus on the past. If possible, write down your life story as thoroughly and dramatically as possible, and then share it with as many people as will listen, telling it again and again. Observe how you embellish the story each time you tell it and notice the reactions you get. If you are alone, read it aloud to yourself, or if you have a pet, to them.

Pay keen attention to any payoffs you get from replaying this past drama. Do you feel sorry for yourself? Do you feel brave, courageous, or heroic? Or do you feel small, crushed, or victimized? Notice how truthful your story is each time you tell it. Does it accurately reflect who you are and who you want to be today? Do you acknowledge the gifts it brought you? Do you feel light and loved? Are you guided by your spirit, spirit helpers, and angels?

Finally, after telling your story every day for a week, let it go. Start imagining your next chapter rather than looking backward, knowing the best in life is yet to come.

Woo-Woo Wisdom

Create an extraordinary story.

PART IV

PSYCHIC SIT-UPS

WRITE YOUR
VIBES DOWN

Your vibes are useless if you don't trust them. Most people I've met want to trust their spirit, but they don't because their barking-ego dog is afraid to. Over and over, I hear, "What if I make a mistake?" "What if my vibes are wrong?" or "What if something awful happens because my intuition is off? What if my vibes lead me off a cliff?"

These are possible scenarios, of course, yet if you are actually tuning into your vibes and not your head, these catastrophes will never occur. Trusting your vibes is a risk you'll eventually have to take if you want to grow into your own power. If you ask me, it is far riskier and unsafe to ignore your vibes and follow your fearful ego. I can't think of a single example of a person's fearful ego giving good advice or leading them to a positive outcome. But I can think of countless times when letting the fearful ego lead a person's life brought about the worst results possible.

Standing on your own two psychic feet feels like a big and often scary decision, but it doesn't have to be the blind leap that your ego will try to convince you it is. You can learn to trust your intuition in the same way you learn to trust anything else in life: through experience. What you're really doing when trusting your vibes is taking full responsibility for your life. You're allowing your spirit to be the boss instead of surrendering your power over others and letting them control you, like a sheep being led to the slaughter.

Trusting your vibes is an awakening process in which your spirit partners with your body, your ego steps aside and learns, and together they move you directly and swiftly out of harm's way and straight into your very best life. As in any partnership, trust and confidence develop naturally over time, as you get to know one another and make successful decisions together. In other words, the more you allow your spirit to lead your body to success, the more trust will evolve on its own.

The best way I know to enter this partnership with your spirit is to get a small pocket notebook that you can carry with you at all times. Every time you get a hunch, gut feeling, "Aha!" moment, hit, sense, vibe, or any other nudge from your intuition, jot it down in your notebook. Don't let your ego censor, judge, discriminate, interfere, or in any way edit the information or feelings you receive. Don't worry if your vibes feel silly, irrelevant, irrational, or stupid, or if you think that your vibes are nothing more than your imagination. Write it all down anyway. At this point, you don't have to follow your vibes. Just record them instead of ignoring them and see if they prove to be valuable. In a short while, you will see that every single vibe you felt made sense eventually in one way or another.

You won't have to trust me either; you'll have evidence. If you record your vibes faithfully for three weeks, all your doubts will start to shrink and give way to confidence because you will have collected solid, undeniable evidence that your sixth sense is worth trusting.

TAKE A MOMENT TO GET CLEAR

Sadly, even if they want to trust their vibes, many of my clients and students struggle to recognize, let alone describe their vibes, because they habitually "stuff them." Writing vibes down helps stop this. For example, my student Barry said, "I used to automatically strangle my vibes before I even knew what they were. If I felt uneasy, rather than take my hunch as a warning, I'd immediately go in the opposite direction, telling myself that I was crazy—everything was fine. Then I'd pick up my phone and start mindlessly scrolling on social media to dull the feeling. Inevitably, my uneasiness would turn out to be an accurate warning of things to come, but because I ignored it, it did me no good. This hindsight drove me crazy.

"However, once I began writing down my intuitive flashes, I stopped stuffing my vibes and got more and more dialed in. The more I wrote, the clearer and more specific my vibes became. What started out as a vague description, like 'Bad feeling about Gary . . .' turned into a full-blown clear picture of what was bothering me—'Gary is lying to me about the amount of money he has to invest and wasting my time on this deal . . .'—once I put pen to paper. Within a few weeks of starting to record my vibes in my notebook, I could describe exactly what I intuitively felt."

My other client Kyle told me that writing down his vibes helped his intuition really take off: "The more I wrote, the more vibes I had. Soon I was getting intuitive hits on things all day long. I had vibes on so many things that I had previously ignored until I began my journal. It's like I opened up the fountain of truth. I was able to tune in and get a good intuitive read on everything. Writing opened the front door to my intuition, and I walked into another world. I know what to do now in every matter. I only wished I had started this so much sooner. It could have spared me from making so many bad decisions."

Another client, Georgia, reported, "I began briefly noting my vibes in a rushed general way, but the more I wrote, the more my vibes became clear and specific. Moreover, I noticed I started having powerful vibes on things I've always been interested in, like the stock market. This had been a hobby of mine for years, but never something I allowed myself to take seriously. The stock predictions I wrote in my vibes journal were on-target for three weeks. I didn't invest any money, but I sure wish I had. That is going to change going forward, now that I have this clear way of tuning in."

Each written message from your spirit provides evidence that vibes are trustworthy and builds confidence on which to go forward. You'll no longer just have a vague feeling to trust—you'll have solid verification that your vibes are legitimate guides that you can count on.

Keeping a journal also tells your subconscious mind that you value your intuition now, so turn up the volume. This is a game-changer when it comes to sensing your vibes. Every time you write something down, you validate it, even if what you are writing down doesn't make immediate sense to your logical brain. It trains your mind not to dismiss or ignore these subtle messengers but instead make a note of them and expect them to make sense *eventually*. It doesn't take long for your ego to get the message and to cooperate in every way.

If you've been trained to ignore your spirit, writing your vibes down on paper, on a computer, or on your smartphone will "untrain" you. In doing this your intuition is reinstated to its proper place as leader and you will reestablish this empowering connection to your true Self. Fortunately, our spirit never stops broadcasting its light on our path. It is our ego that stops noticing or tunes out the broadcast. When you write down your vibes, your inner receiver tunes right back in. I've made this suggestion to students worldwide for more than 40 years, so I have tons of evidence that it works.

My client George took my advice and began writing his vibes down. One day, quite spontaneously, he wrote in his vibes journal, "I need to quit my job and go into business with my brother right away. I am going to get fired soon." He was pretty surprised by this note because, while quitting his job had crossed his mind, it never occurred to him to go into business with his brother or that he would get fired. That was an intuitive revelation he hadn't expected. Still, he didn't quit his job as warned. He ignored the message. Sure enough, he got fired a week later. He couldn't believe that he walked right into the very situation about which he was forewarned. When he came for a reading, he said, "I was clearly guided to leave my job, but my ego wouldn't accept it. While I am happy to be done with that place, it just stinks that getting fired is now part of my work record. It hasn't helped me get a new job, that's for sure.

"My brother and I have talked about starting a home renovation company for years, and my vibes said now is the time to do it. I'm not going to make the same mistake twice. I will never ignore my vibes again!"

George and his brother did start their business. Their first year was slow, but the second year the pandemic hit, and the entire world seemed to leave cities and move to small towns. George's business went through the roof. They hired 14 people in less than six months and still could barely keep up with the demand for their services.

All I could say was, "Well done, George. It only takes listening to one clear vibe from your spirit to change your life."

PLAN B

Having taught people to trust their vibes for as long as I have, I know that many people, no matter how persuasive I try to be, will simply not write down their vibes despite how valuable this practice is. The reasons they don't are many: "I forget." "I don't like writing." "I'm too lazy." So for that reason, I have formulated a plan B for you guys.

As with my suggestion to write down every vibe you get, do the same but instead record every vibe you get using your phone's voice memo app. In many ways, this is an even more powerful tool because when you name it, you claim it. The minute you verbally acknowledge your vibes, your body registers this and turns up the volume. Also, when you verbally recognize and record a vibe, you have the added benefit of hearing the sound of your voice when honoring your true Self. When you recognize genuine intuitive guidance, you both speak from the heart and feel it in the heart. When expressing fearful thoughts, wishful thinking, or your ego faking you out, your voice comes from your head and ego. It doesn't feel the same at all. It has no resonance in your heart whatsoever. You can clearly feel the big difference between these two channels. Real vibes ring true throughout your entire body. False ego alarms clang around like sour notes and slide right off your body moments later. They don't stick, like vibes will. Your body is hard-wired to be intuitive, so you will not confuse the two. Your ego can talk you into believing what isn't true, but in the end, your body will never lie.

At this early phase of trusting your vibes, remember that you don't have to follow them. I'm only suggesting you hear them out and express them. You don't have to trust them yet. However, after a few weeks of missed opportunities, you won't want to ignore them.

INSPIRATIONAL WRITING

The best way to realize how powerful your spirit is is to get to know it. Each day at more or less the same time, make an appointment with your spirit and write consistently for a few minutes. In my experience, both morning and right before bed work well. It doesn't matter what time of day you chat with your spirit as long as you do it regularly.

Once you sit down to write, imagine you are having an active conversation with your spirit. It knows you better than anyone. It knows your soul's goals. It calms your turbulent emotions, quiets your drama, and guides you to a higher frequency while at the same time reassuring your frightened ego that everything will be okay while loving you fully and unconditionally, forever.

When writing to your spirit, feel free to discuss any subject you wish. Start by simply sharing what is on your mind. Don't edit a thing. Put it all down on paper and hold nothing back.

Once that is done, ask your spirit for assistance on how to best move forward.

Next, imagine your spirit answering. Write quickly and don't stop and think about what you are writing. Don't lift the pen off the paper. If using a computer, don't lift your fingers off the keys or stop to read or spellcheck the text. Just continue to let the words fly out of you until you feel it's done.

Your spirit will respond immediately. This is known as inspirational writing. Once you have completed the response from spirit, put the pen down or sit back from the computer and close your eyes for a few moments. Feel the presence of your spirit and the love flowing into you. Then, open your eyes and read what was written. It may be eye-opening and make tremendous sense. Or it may not at the moment. My experience has shown me that 99 percent of the time, inspirational writing gives you the answers you seek right away. The other 1 percent of the time, it will make sense soon enough. In all cases, you will feel a deep and strong connection to your spirit.

Take what you've written to heart. If you are genuinely open to receiving guidance, inspirational writing will provide it every time.

AUTOMATIC WRITING

If you keep up your inspirational writing practice, it will soon evolve into automatic writing. This occurs when you sit down to write, and the pen or computer keys take off by themselves. The words flow directly from your spirit and not from your ego. In this case, the messages usually flow one way and do not respond to your questions or concerns, although they do address them. Automatic writing is not like the psychic e-mail exchange of inspirational writing. These messages are downloaded and sent to you without you asking questions. They often come from your teacher guides who want to help you accelerate your soul's growth and increase the amount of light in your body. You will always be surprised by what you uncover when writing automatically, and it will be evident that what you've written did not come from your ego. It may not sound like your voice at all. Another thing that you will often notice with automatic writing is that it is often far more beautiful, organized, and flawless than your own prose. You feel as if someone else is writing *through* you, not just to you.

The writing is sometimes old-fashioned or formal but always refined and coherent and leaves you feeling calm, grounded, and uplifted. Authentic automatic writing will never leave you feeling threatened or afraid, but it can leave you feeling in awe. Automatic writing adjusts your view because it comes from a higher perspective than your own. Where you were confused before, you now become clear. Automatic writing feels as if you've just downloaded a profound lesson from the wisest teacher in the Universe. Because you have.

With both inspirational and automatic writing, you feel deeply reassured, knowing that you have help readily available behind the scenes. You aren't just making up stuff to feel better—there really are higher forces at work on your behalf, and they're doing a great job of connecting with you. Even your ego will be impressed because the writing that comes through as you connect with your spirit provides the evidence that your inner voice is trustworthy and will take care of you. As a bonus, when you practice intuitive writing skills, your intuitive abilities will considerably sharpen, and your ego will relax and quit controlling your life. If anything, it will be happy to be off the job of running the show. After all, your ego isn't your enemy—it really is trying to help you, although it isn't capable of doing a very good job. It is simply not your Higher Self. It's just a helper. The idea here is for your ego to step aside and allow your intuition to take the lead while helping in every way to make it easier.

With each vibe journal notation, your intuitive radar will become sharper, more accurate, and even more entertaining. It's empowering to look back at what you've written and realize how brilliant your intuition really is. Each entry, like a newly discovered pearl of wisdom, will have great value, if for nothing else than to remind you of how magnificent your artful soul really is.

Woo-Woo Workout

I find it best to have two journals: one for the road and one that you keep at home. The one for the road can be small, while the one at home can be more substantial.

Carry the little one with you everywhere, and record everything your vibes relay to you. If you hate writing, go to plan B and record your vibes using a voice memo app. Speak freely; acknowledge every vibe you have, and don't censor yourself. You never know if something that doesn't make sense now will have meaning later.

Try both inspirational and automatic writing every day at a time when you can consistently devote 15 minutes to the effort. Use your big vibe journal for this, as well. If you are using a computer, create a "vibe journal" folder and keep your installments in this one place.

Woo-Woo Wisdom

Make a note of it.

PRAY

The hotline that connects you to your spirit is prayer, which is simply the practice of communicating on an intimate, heart-to-heart level with your Creator. When you pray, you ask your ego to step aside and surrender your personal energy to a Higher Power. Prayer is basic training for anyone who wants to stay faithful to their intuitive voice and live in a higher way. It not only opens you up to receiving assistance from a Higher Power, but it also relieves you of the stress of figuring things out for yourself. One of the hallmarks of intuitive living is the absence of worry over how things will work out. Prayer involves simply leaving it up to God.

Prayer immediately raises your personal vibration, ushers more light into your body, and opens your heart center—all of which activate your intuition and connect you with your spirit. In study after study, research has shown that prayer has a healing effect on the physical and emotional body, calming anxieties, soothing nerves, and easing tension. It has even been known to relieve high blood pressure, lift depression, and cure sickness. As it heals, calms, strengthens, balances, and restores order, prayer also attracts solutions that we could never imagine were possible—in other words, miracles.

There's no one way to pray. Since it's such an intimate connection with your spirit, the right way is however you intuitively feel moved to do so. For example, I know people who wouldn't dream of beginning a day without reciting the rosary aloud, while others kneel in devout silence. I have friends who pray by walking, while others go to a synagogue, mosque, or church. Some people I know pray formally, while others simply chat with God in their minds. I have neighbors who gather around the dinner table on the Sabbath, while others commune in drum circles, chanting, dancing, and even sweating. I pray in all these ways and more—in fact, from the time I open my eyes until I fall asleep, I'm praying because I don't like being disconnected from God.

The other day I logged on to the Internet, and much to my dismay, something was wrong with my computer, so I couldn't establish the connection I wanted. I felt frustrated at being unable to access this vast resource when I really needed to. Well, praying is very similar to logging on to the Internet, only better. When you pray, you spiritually log on to Divine Wisdom, the ultimate resource for support and guidance.

I often ask people if they pray. Almost everyone answers that they do, but when I ask how often, they tell me "now and then" or "in an emergency." These individuals all have various reasons for not praying, and some are even rather noble. Some say they don't want to bother God. Others claim that they save their prayers for important matters. Some people have told me that they don't pray simply because they forget to.

Like everything else that connects us to our spirit, prayer is most effective when practiced, meaning that you should pray whenever you think of it until it becomes automatic. In other words, pray when you wake up in the morning, while you take a shower, before you drink your morning coffee, and as you drive to work. Pray for the easiest and best way to get through your day. Pray for success in your projects and for patience when those around you get on your nerves. Pray for forgiveness and an open heart. Pray for creative inspiration and for better health. Pray to release the past and open your mind and heart to a better future. Pray for the willingness to let go of the old and reach out for something new.

These are just some suggestions to get you started. But you get the idea—you can and should pray for everything you can think of.

When I was in the fifth grade, my teacher, Sister Mary Joan of Arc, had us create a personal collection of our favorite prayers. I loved my first homemade prayer book, and I've been making them ever since. Every time I read or hear a prayer that I love or that speaks to me in some meaningful way, I write it in my prayer book. I've also included devotions that I've written myself. My prayer book has become a tremendously important and intimate part of my spiritual and intuitive practice. It has such a beautiful vibration that simply holding it brings me a deep sense of peace and inner tranquility—it feels holy, and it is. Just having my prayer book near me serves as a great source of inspiration and protection, so I take it wherever I go.

Even though I've kept a personal prayer book for more than 50 years, I've rarely mentioned it to anyone else. Lately, however, I've felt a need to tell others about this powerful practice so that they can create one for themselves. Look at the popularity of Bruce Wilkinson's book *The Prayer of Jabez*. If a prayer as impersonal as one written by someone you've never heard of can be so powerful, can you imagine how potent a book of personal, familiar, intimate, and treasured prayers could be? The intentions within such a book will take on grace and power of their own as they're accumulated over the years, and I assure you, the vibration is extremely powerful.

Several of my loved ones also keep prayer books. For example, my friend LuAnn has a collection of special devotions to Mother Mary, while my friend Julia has a prayer pot that she uses to ask for miracles—and it has come in very handy. More than 35 years ago, one of my mother's clients gave birth to a baby boy who was born brain-dead. Needless to say, the woman was beside herself and the entire family was devastated. My mother went to her prayer book and began to pray for this child even though he was placed on life support and wasn't given a chance to live. A week later, the doctors suggested that the child be removed from life support so that nature could take its course. All the while, my mother prayed for a miracle and didn't allow herself to consider anything less. The baby was unhooked and expected to die; instead, he took a big breath and lived. And to everyone's amazement, he suffered no brain damage. A year later, he was even the subject of a *Denver Post* story called "The Miracle Baby." Does prayer work? I'd say yes, without question.

Whenever I'm asked how we know if our prayers are heard, I always answer, "By the peace of mind that follows." For example, I've known my client Susan for more than 10 years. I've watched her struggle with finding and keeping job after job as a writer for television, as well as searching for the perfect partner and harmonious family relationships. Yet no matter how much I assured her that all would be well, she never believed me.

Finally, I suggested that instead of trying to control everything, she try praying. I could psychically see that her vibration was resonating at an extremely harmful level. Her fear and desperation was draining the life force out of her. By praying, she could shift the energy to a higher level and get some immediate relief.

Susan reacted to my suggestion by laughing. When I asked her why she responded in this way, she answered, "Because my mother was a religious fanatic and she always forced prayer on me. So I rebelled and haven't prayed since I left home at seventeen. It just sounds so odd to me to pray."

"Did praying help your mother?" I inquired.

Susan was quiet for a moment and then said, "You know, I'd have to say that it did. When I was growing up, we went through some tough times, yet she always managed to pull through, saying that prayer saved her. So maybe she was right."

By the time our conversation ended, Susan was feeling much better. Simply thinking about praying helped ease her anxiety, and she had yet to begin. That's how powerful prayer is.

Prayer also prepares me for my intuitive readings. I use the same ones every time: "Divine Father, Holy Mother, use me," "God, please take this out of my hands and place it in yours," and "Thank you." All three make my life very simple because they allow me to be open and receptive to Divine direction, and they offer up my appreciation for my gifts.

I don't suggest that you follow any "rules of praying"; instead, just pray when you feel like it, about anything you feel like, and in whatever way you feel like. Don't worry if you're doing it right—the Universe knows better than you what you need. The point is not so much what you pray for or how you pray, but that through the act of praying, you allow the Divine spirit to enter your heart. The beauty of prayer is that God straightens things out and the solution God provides to our problem is always better than anything we could have asked for or imagined ourselves. So pray to strengthen your intuition and help you expand into a more soulful, guided, six-sensory being. And if your psychic workout relies heavily on prayer, you'll immediately feel the expansion in your own consciousness, as well as the relief and the peace of mind prayer can bring.

WHEN ALL ELSE FAILS . . . PRAY

Sometimes we need to pray for a miracle. These are situations when you see absolutely no way forward and appearances point to a dead end. To pray for a miracle, you must have absolutely no ego resistance or interference. In other words, create an inner state of mind that *completely* surrenders the problem over to the Universe to resolve on your behalf and be 100 percent receptive to Divine intervention to successfully bringing about the desired outcome. It is also important that you pray with the understanding that if what you ask for goes against Divine Will and your soul plan, those will take priority over your request. Therefore, when praying for a miracle, it's important to include in your prayer that even though this is what you desire, if God has a better plan, thy will be done. This is especially important when praying for healing when death seems imminent. We simply don't know what that soul's plan is, so we can ask for a miracle and leave it with God and that soul to work out the highest ending. Also, when praying for a miracle, you cannot be selfish and focus only on your self-interest over the best interest of all concerned. By that I mean you cannot pray, for example, that the married man you love leave his wife and children for you. What you can do, however, is pray that this relationship evolves in the most loving manner and in the best interest of all the people involved. It may be in your best interest that your relationship end because the man is a cheater. Or it might be better for all concerned that he leave his marriage because they are both unhappy and their children suffer for this. We simply cannot know what's in the best interest of all concerned. So we give that part to God.

Four years ago, my daughter Sabrina married an Egyptian man who was getting his biomedical engineering Ph.D. from Imperial College in London. While there, he was on a student visa set to expire before the end of June. At the end of April, he turned in his dissertation for review and approval to complete his education and graduate. All he needed was for his reviewer to sign off on it and return it before the end of June so he could extend his visa for another three years and he and my daughter could continue to live in the U.K. and plan their next phase of their life. Since my son-in-law turned in the paper nearly 10 weeks before the deadline, he was confident that he had all the time in the world to get it back and renew his visa with no problem.

Things didn't go as planned, however. The professor reviewing his paper officially had three whole months to review the document and decided he would use that entire time, even though he knew full well that my son-in-law's visa would expire. By the time my son-in-law discovered that the professor would not be completing the review in time, he and Sabrina had less than a week to pack up and leave the country. It was the last thing they expected and put them in a panic. My son-in-law appealed to the college and was told they could do nothing. He called 10 immigration attorneys who also told him there was nothing he could do. Unless his paper was returned in time and their visas could be renewed before the expiration date, they would have to leave. With only days left before his visa was set to expire, we prayed for a miracle.

After we prayed, Sabrina got the vibe to once again Google emergency immigration attorneys. This time she landed upon the name of an attorney whom she e-mailed immediately. When they got her on the phone, Sabrina's husband explained the crisis and how bizarre it was to have a professor sabotage a Ph.D. student like this, and the attorney listened.

Then, to my daughter and her husband's surprise, she said there was a tiny loophole in the immigration law that said a person has a legal right to an education, and since his education was ongoing until his dissertation was approved, he still was considered a student. So he could apply to the immigration board, get a hearing, and see what happens. If nothing else, it would buy them the time they had run out of to make other plans.

By now Sabrina's husband had only 20 hours left before the deadline to apply for a hearing on his case. If the application was sent and accepted in time, they would be allowed to legally stay in the country with expired visas. This was the miracle they had prayed for.

They worked all day to fill out the long and complicated form and turned it in with only four hours to spare. An hour before the deadline, they received a notice that it had been accepted and he would receive word about a hearing date in the next eight weeks. The professor reviewing my son-in-law's paper only had seven more weeks to review it, so it would be returned before the hearing. At that point, my son-in-law could apply for renewal before the hearing, get their visas renewed by the university, and they could continue on with their plans to build a life in London.

That this attorney popped up on Sabrina's radar and knew of a loophole when 10 other immigration attorneys said there was no possible solution for their situation, and how it all fell in place on time, was indeed the miracle we prayed for. My son-in-law received an approved dissertation two weeks later and they renewed their visas without a problem.

Prayer works when you have no resistance to a miracle.

PRAY WITH CONFIDENCE

Pray with confidence that your prayer will be heard and answered in ways you do not have to figure out. Trust that you will be shown the answer one way. Pray, then let it go. You don't have to endlessly pray, plead, or beg. Pray with certainty that you are loved and that the Universe will give you the miracle you need. Then you just need to step aside and surrender your will to the Divine Will and allow it.

I have the simplest prayer that covers all of this, which I have prayed every morning since I was a child. It has brought about countless miracles. The prayer is simply:

Divine spirit within me
Aligned with the power of God
Move me this day
Move my mind, heart, my body, and feet
In the direction of my highest good and the good of all
Amen and so it is

Woo-Woo Workout

Pray the instant you wake up. You may want to start by thanking your Creator for giving you another day on this beautiful planet, or if you have any pressing concerns, ask for assistance, protection, and blessings throughout the day. During the day, pray whenever you think of it. Pray for your family, friends, neighbors, and co-workers. Pray for your enemies. Pray for the world. Pray for everything that concerns you, for all that gives you a reason to doubt. And pray in gratitude for all your blessings. Finally, pray to remember to pray.

Creating Your Personal Prayer Book

Why not create a prayer book of your own? Begin by selecting an attractive journal with blank pages, then simply write down all the prayers you hear, read, or write yourself that bring you peace, speak to your heart and soul, and uplift your spirit in any way. Because ritual is such an essential part of many prayers, you may want to integrate it into your prayer book by writing with a specific pen, one that makes the entries especially meaningful and sacred.

You might also want to print your prayers in a distinctive manner—perhaps you'll feel moved to draw something sacred or place a holy card or talisman in your book for inspiration. This is your personal collection, so trust your spirit to move you to create your prayer book in whatever way speaks to you best.

I carry my prayer book with me all the time, especially when I travel. I suggest that you do the same. These days, this might be precisely when you'll need it most. Creating your own prayer book is a beautiful way to develop the practice of prayer and the habit of keeping your heart open to spiritual guidance.

Woo-Woo Wisdom

Ask for help.

SEEK HIGHER
FREQUENCIES

By activating your intuition, you become more sensitive overall. Sounds will amplify, everything you touch will take on a heightened feel, what you see may appear brighter and affect you more profoundly. You may even develop a keen sense of smell—all because your psychic channel elevates your awareness of your energy body, your aura.

Your aura is the energy field surrounding your physical body, and it's usually up to 12 layers in thickness. When your aura is sensitized, all your senses go up an octave to perceive energy in the higher dimensions. This means that your vision may expand to the higher octave of clairvoyance, your hearing may extend to the higher octave of clairaudience, and your sense of touch may extend to the higher octave of clairsentience. (Your sense of smell and taste may also become more acute, and although there's no specific term for it, you may get "a nose for things," or find that something leaves "a bad taste in your mouth.")

Like setting up a satellite dish on the roof, when you clear your psychic pathway, a lot more energy floods through your senses as more awareness comes in. The result can be pretty overwhelming in the early stages. For example, one woman told me that her intuitive awakening "was like nuclear power suddenly coursing through a toaster." She was left feeling fried, especially when she was in very loud, intense situations.

"Things that didn't bother me before do now," said my student Gary. "It's like I've just woken up. For instance, I can no longer go to bars. I just can't stand the noise, the smoke, and the feeling."

Carmen, another student, explained, "I've always been sensitive to what I hear, but after I began to use my intuition, I found that I couldn't listen to office gossip anymore. I wasn't taking a moral high ground—I just couldn't stand the way it made me feel."

As your sixth sense improves, you'll become more sensitive to the quality of vibrations around you and their effect on you, which is a part of being psychically attuned. Living an intuitive life compels you to be more selective about what you tune in to, just as you would be when watching satellite TV. In other words, just because you can pick up 1,000 more shows doesn't mean that you'd want to watch them.

"The more my intuition opened up," said my client Donna, "the more I felt on a deeper level what was true and what wasn't. It's hard to explain, but I could tell by how it rang or resonated in my body; it felt dissonant and irritating when people lied. I couldn't listen."

A long time ago, I worked with Detective J. J. Bittenbinder, who had a show in Chicago called *Tough Target* in which he taught people to use their vibes for protection against crime. He called his sixth sense his "BS sensor." He said each of us has an inner psychic-truth barometer that guides us and, once activated, acts like radar. It scans for trouble and danger and leads us away from it. The signal is subtle, though, so we must increase our awareness to avoid missing the signs. As my client Adam told me, "After taking your intuition class, it became really annoying to listen to someone lying to me because my own 'BS sensor' sounded off like an alarm." I knew what he meant. It is so irritating to your intuitive ears to hear someone lie—it's often so internally dissonant and flowing in the opposite direction of the truth that it feels as though the person is running their nails across a blackboard.

As your vibes fine-tune, you may also have a sudden overwhelming craving for silence. This is because you may be on vibration overload. Too many dissonant vibrations may be crashing about in your body. Silence regulates the rush of these vibrations as they pulse through your aura. Silence is like shutting the floodgates. Your attention is turning away from the physical world and your ego; instead, you're expanding your awareness upward and outward toward your spirit. Unless you have enough internal silence, you won't be able to hear your inner voice or your guides, so the yearning for silence is a sign that your natural channel is opening to spiritual assistance. This explains why mystics usually seek quiet—it connects them to God.

"I'm so desperate for quiet," said my client Anne, "that sometimes I run to the garage and sit in my car for ten minutes. With three boys under the age of five, that's the only place I can find some peace."

As you begin to sharpen your own sixth sense, you may also develop a strong reaction to what you see. As your sensitivity to vibration increases, so too will your desire for beauty over ugly images. And if you don't get exposed to enough of the earth's loveliness, you'll probably start to crave it. For example, the more sensitive I became over the years, the more I needed to get out of the city and into nature. This soothed my nerves and helped me shake off the energy of my clients. Joshua, a student of mine, realized a similar craving for beauty, but it manifested differently for him: "Suddenly, all I wanted to do was paint," he told me. "I spent hours and hours doing watercolors, and the more I did it, the more it fed my soul."

Intuition increases the more we immerse ourselves in beautiful, calm, peaceful, grounded energy—the kind you find in nature. In cities, which I love, by the way, you are bombarded by energy coming at you in all directions. The noise, the activity, the thousands of people moving about, all on their phones, doing their thing while you try to do yours can short-circuit your intuitive channels if you don't pay attention. This is what I call "having a psychic meltdown." A meltdown is more than a barking-dog fit. It's a system crash, when your entire body is saturated with bad vibes and cannot take it anymore. So you lose your temper, run out of patience, lash out, cry, and throw a fit, basically sending everyone running in the opposite direction. This is precisely what you want to happen because you need to be alone and shut down all your sensory channels to reset. The problem is that doing it this way is embarrassing, not to mention further depletes your energy because it takes a lot to throw a tantrum.

Meltdowns often catch us off guard, and unless we are highly self-aware, we don't see them coming because we lose touch with our bodies. They sneak up on us, usually while we're trying to multitask under intense pressure, such as when we're driving in harsh conditions with a car full of kids, all screaming for something at once or working under pressure to meet a deadline while the people around you won't stop vying for your attention with requests of their own or trying to do too many errands in too short a time without eating lunch and you can't find a parking space and are on the verge of missing an important business phone call. You know what I mean. Overload. The tantrum is an energetic purge so your system can reset. I call this the "everyone out of the pool now!" maneuver. It works, but it's not the best way to reset because you look and sound like a maniac. You need a grown-up version of a child's time-out, only you are getting it the wrong way by acting out of control.

It's better to recognize a meltdown coming on and quietly remove yourself, saying, "I need a break. I'm flooded. I'll be back shortly after I reset." Then put yourself in time out, shutting off all stimulation and being quiet. Turn off the phone, close your eyes (and the blinds if you can), sit or lie down, and breathe calmly with one hand on your belly and the other on your heart until you re-regulate. This takes about 15 minutes. Once you are grounded and calm again, you can reenter the group as a sane person.

Skills for avoiding a meltdown are threefold: preparation, awareness, and pace.

Let's start with preparation. Meltdowns usually happen if you aren't properly grounded with enough water, food, and rest, which I mentioned at the beginning of this book. Breakfast, lunch, and dinner with enough protein throughout the day are necessary to fuel you. It's not optional. Drink plenty of water as well so you are hydrated and get enough sleep so your nerves aren't crispy critters.

Pay attention to your environment and avoid places and situations that rankle your nervous system. It can't take high tension vibrations for long periods. Listen to classical music instead of angry or dissonant news channels. Better yet, go outside and listen to the birds chirping. Wear comfortable clothing and shoes so you feel good in your skin. Breathe deeply instead of holding your breath. Look ahead to where you are going and move in the most peaceful direction. In other words, pay attention to vibrations and move with awareness toward calm, harmonious vibrations and far away from tense and disturbing ones to the best of your ability.

And finally, pace yourself. This is simple. Go forward at a calm, steady pace. Do not rush. Do not overload your schedule. Nothing causes a meltdown faster than going too fast or trying to do too much. Your sensitive system isn't designed for this. Slow down. If you cannot slow your pace, at least slow your breathing. If you feel a meltdown coming on, stop what you're doing altogether. Breathe for a full minute or two. Then restart, going slower. Rushing collapses your system. Give yourself plenty of time to do whatever you need to do. If you rush, you'll miss the vibes. Leave early for appointments. Schedule in buffer time for unexpected delays between appointments. Leave time to breathe, rest, and regroup between meetings. And if at all possible, give yourself a scheduled time-out every day. Five minutes should be enough time to allow you to take account of the vibes around you, integrate the day's input, do a vibe check so you proceed in alignment with your spirit, and make intuitively informed choices instead of knee-jerk reactions. You don't need a meltdown to get time alone. Let those around you know you need a short break. It regulates your vibration and keeps you grounded, aware, and alert. This is the best way to tune into vibes and save face in public.

FEED YOUR SPIRIT

As six-sensories, we need to feed our spirits as surely as we must feed our bodies. By this, I mean giving our spirit the nourishment it needs to feel happy and content. Two things are fundamental to feeding your spirit. One of these elements is beauty. Beauty sends harmonious, uplifting vibrations to every cell in our bodies. When in a beautiful environment or when observing beauty, we begin to entrain this energy. That is why people feel so relaxed and rejuvenated when in nature. The greener and more colorful the nature, the better. The real deal is best, but even nature scenes calm the nervous system and improve your intuition. One way to feed your spirit is to be in nature or surround yourself with nature scenes on your computer and phone screen or as art on your wall. Notice how calming to your spirit nature is. You feel it right away.

Our perception of beauty is up to our individual nature, but most people who expand into higher awareness agree beauty is not optional. It is necessary. For example, Steve, a Chicago Police Department detective who spent all his time dismantling street gangs, was rapidly awakening his sixth sense and noticed that it was affecting him quite a bit. "My work demanded that I use my nose for trouble," he said, "and eventually it seemed that my nose for other things kicked in, too. I began to have a sixth sense about everything, so I took your class to develop it. After that, a funny thing happened—all I wanted to do was visit art museums, something I'd never even thought of before. My buddies laughed at me, saying I was going fancy on them, but now I have a few of them going with me, and they enjoy it as well. Now they get it."

Melanie, a high school teacher in Baltimore, was wiped out most days after work, which was intense, as she often dealt with kids coming from difficult home conditions. She loved her work, but it was a far cry from a beautiful experience. Every day on her way home from school, she strolled through one of the city's beautiful botanical gardens. "It was like a massage for my spirit.

It cleared the day and soothed my soul. This stop on the way home fed my spirit more than anything."

Gary went horseback riding for an hour once a week to feed his spirit. He had a favorite horse, Bucket, at the local riding stable. This weekly hour with Bucket fed his spirit and calmed his body completely. "I received some of my best intuitive hits shortly after my riding lesson when I was grooming Bucket after the ride," he said.

The second thing that feeds your spirit is being creative. We are born to create, and when we create beauty, we thoroughly nourish our spirits. We are all able to create something. We can create art, music, paintings, sketches, clothing, and dances. We can also create on a simpler scale. We can create a beautiful meal, a flower arrangement, or a new hairdo, for example. We can re-arrange the furniture and create a new ambience in our homes. We can create gardens, songs, poems, stories, gatherings of people. If you think about it, everything we do is creative. We just need to do it beautifully and with care to feed our spirits.

I have a dear friend named Karl who dresses beautifully in an ironed shirt, blazer, and pocket scarf no matter what. Even when he's in casual attire, which is not often, his clothes are still freshly ironed, and he looks like a million bucks. When I see him, I always feel moved to say, "Wow, you look so beautiful," because he does. By taking the time and making the effort to look his best, he feeds both his spirit and the spirits of those who see him. It's thoughtful. Make yourself a work of art. Express your creativity and dress with style. Style your hair and makeup with care and pizazz. Present yourself to the world as beautifully as you can to feed your spirit and the spirit of others.

Live your life with awareness and express beauty and cre-ativity in all ways. You don't have to be an artist to live artfully. Just do what you must but with style. Looking back, I appreciate that whenever our family went on our weekly family outing to the mountains in my father's 1965 Cadillac, before we set foot in the car, my father washed and cleaned it inside and out until it shined. We never entered a dirty vehicle. His cars were always beautiful. They lasted forever because of his loving care. Keeping his cars beautiful fed his spirit.

What feeds your spirit? Make a list of the things that lift you up, bring out your creativity, and help you add more beauty to the planet. For example, both of my daughters make beautiful meals and serve them with tremendous love. Two of my sisters create fabulous home interiors for people. My brother Neil, who lives in Harrisburg, beautifully restores antique furniture. His creations are stunning, and his spirit is fully nourished by his work. My son-in-law creates beautiful energy. He is calm, always polite, easygoing, helpful, cheerful, patient, and generous. Being around him is a lovely experience. He created a company and an app called NUKI, Nutrition for Kids, to quickly guide new parents in preventing and treating children with food allergies. It's a beautiful creation and helps many overwhelmed new parents and their infants and children suffering from digestive pain to find relief.

Feeding our spirit is not difficult. It's just doing what we love to do and doing it with love. This comes naturally to us. Our egos convince us to do what we truly loathe at times because we need "to survive," which is always the ego's primary focus. When we feed the spirit within, we move far beyond surviving and into thriving. The things that feed our spirit are those that bring the best out in us and turn up our inner light.

AVOID BLACK HOLES

Once your intuitive sensibilities wake up, things that disturb and drain the spirit become intolerable, such as violence, chaos, and even too much concrete. If you do become overexposed, you'll instantly start to gravitate toward more healing things and places. The ego numbs our senses, so when our sixth sense wakes up, so do our sensibilities. We realize that we need harmony and beauty and can't tolerate gross violence on a gratuitous level because it's dissonant to our spirit.

The soul's need for beauty has affected my clients in different ways. When Larry awakened his spirit, he started reacting to ugly things he once paid no attention to, such as the graffiti in his neighborhood. He organized a massive community graffiti-busting campaign because he couldn't stand the vibration it emitted.

The more her sixth sense kicked, the less my client Linda could watch violent TV shows or movies. "Until now, I thought things like that didn't affect me," she said. "I'm stunned that I didn't realize it did, because now when I see this kind of stuff, my energy immediately drains out of my body. I'm not in favor of censoring TV or movies; I just regulate what I watch because it affects me. It's as though the volume has been turned up and now I'm aware that I'm being bombarded with bad vibes. So I'm careful to be more protective of myself."

As you move into a more intentional six-sensory life, you'll become aware of how delicate and sensitive a soul you are. The more you evolve, the more you'll recognize what upsets your internal psychic equilibrium. As a client Louise explained, "Before I started listening to my spirit, I was very careless and sloppy about what I wore, often grabbing any old thing and not really caring how I looked. But after I began to live an intuitively awakened life, I became very picky about what I put on. It's not a fashion thing, either—it's an energy thing. Once I began feeling more aware, I no longer wanted to wear certain fabrics like polyester because the vibes were uncomfortable. Instead, I wanted clothes made of natural fibers, which felt good on my skin and comforted me."

Another client Tom said, "After I started to pay attention to my vibes, I couldn't wear a tie anymore. It just wasn't me, and I couldn't stand it. So I had to take it off! Thank God my work didn't require me to wear one, because the vibration was too restricting."

Another client, Kate, noted, "Once I started listening to my spirit, I couldn't wear dark colors—they were too depressing. So I wore only white or pastels and I felt much better. It just felt necessary to my soul."

Bob, one of my regular students, said the opposite: "Suddenly I craved wearing dark greens and browns—and no more suits. I had to have cashmere sweaters because they felt right. They calmed me."

Don't worry—awakening your intuition won't make you eccentric, suddenly needing the right shoe, the suitable fabric, and the right color. Instead, it simply makes you more discerning and self-aware. Of course, you've always required beauty, nature, solitude, balance, and harmonious sounds, sights, and textures—but now you'll realize that without such things, you're diminished.

Living a six-sensory life makes you more sensitive, which is why empaths and intuitives are called sensitives. As you become more psychically aware and more faithful to what feeds and what drains your spirit, your choices will shift more to respecting and preserving your inner peace. You'll be able to honestly determine whether or not what's happening feels good. If it doesn't, you'll be motivated and brave enough to step away even if it feels awkward.

So, in the name of self-love, listen to your vibes and feed your spirit with creativity, love, and time to yourself. Many of my students have shared that they mindlessly committed to invitations and requests without checking in with their vibes. Since becoming intuitively awakened, their priorities have changed dramatically. So if something is beautiful for you, don't hesitate to follow it. If something offends you, distance yourself from it. Visit nature often and bring it into your home with natural plants and fresh flowers. Settle down. Go within, fill up with beauty and calm, and protect this vibe when around others.

Woo-Woo Workout

Listen to what your senses tell you and what they ask for. Pay attention to your environment and the sights, sounds, and feel of those things in it. If you feel dissonant energy or vibrations, or if something feels like a downer, tune it out, turn it off, or move away. Feed your spirit daily doses of beauty. Bring fresh flowers and plants into your home and office. Play classical music. Open the windows. Let in the sunshine.

Also, keep your nose sharp. If something doesn't smell right, don't ask questions, just trust the message you're receiving. Stay away. Be aware of smells and how they affect you. Try using aromatherapy, scented candles, perfumes, and incense, and see if they raise or lower your vibration. Take the time to give all your senses a break. Sit in silence in a quiet, dark space, and rest. Then listen for your guides, focus inward, and fill the well of your spirit.

Woo-Woo Wisdom

Feed your spirit.

PART V

CREATING YOUR PSYCHIC SUPPORT SYSTEM

FIND YOUR PEOPLE

One of the most frequent comments I hear from clients is, "I wish I had your gift and could listen to my spirit like you do. It would make my life so much easier."

True, I do have a gift—in fact, I have several. But I'm probably most grateful for the gift of my psychic soul mates, who, like me, are six-sensory beings who talk to spirit, are aware of life on the Other Side, and listen to their vibes. Being surrounded by such loving and believing eyes and ears has made trusting my vibes much easier than alone. It's hard to learn to trust your vibes if you have to hide them from the people around you, so it's important to seek out kindred spirits to build your confidence.

I was very fortunate to grow up in a home where my intuition was accepted and encouraged, and I was allowed to express and develop it without any danger of being laughed at or dismissed as crazy. It was also wonderful to have a six-sensory mother. She set the tone in our home, enabling me to stretch my intuitive capabilities freely in a spirit of creativity and play. Not only did my mother encourage me to recognize and respect my intuitive vibes, but my brothers and sisters were also great sounding boards for testing my sixth sense without being self-conscious or doubtful. They did the same with me. As a family, we spoke "spirit." We all had vibes and we counted on one another to help us better tune in to follow them.

I honed my intuitive skills at home the way other kids practiced the piano. I shared my vibes every day as if I were playing psychic scales. Sometimes my vibes were sharp, while other times they were off—but with daily practice, they got more acute, more consistent, and more reliable. This atmosphere was the very incubator I needed for my sixth sense to develop into the powerful guiding force it is for me today. Without this practice at home, I never would have gained the confidence or good habits I needed to listen to and trust my inner voice the way I do now. Sharing my sixth sense with my family strengthened my vibes until I became more and more comfortable using it as a primary compass in my life.

Many of my clients and students have told me that it was difficult or nearly impossible for them to express their intuitive feelings safely because they were told not to by people who didn't get it. These stories affirm my conviction that being surrounded by kindred spirits is essential to developing a solid intuitive channel. All the intuitive people I know hang out with at least one or two other six-sensory individuals. Nothing helps you trust your vibes more than being around other intuitive people who do the same. Those who, like me, grew up with positive reinforcement are understandably much more at ease with their intuition than those who have had only five sensory people to relate to for most of their lives.

I've heard countless horror stories over the years from people who grew up in a five-sensory world where they wouldn't have dared to openly express or share their intuitive feelings for fear of being ridiculed, perceived as crazy, or worse. If that was the atmosphere you were raised in, it doesn't have to be that way now. It's time to let yourself relax into your heightened awareness by cultivating relationships that offer genuine support, encouragement, and enthusiasm for your intuitive insights as well as share their own.

If you felt like the ugly duckling, a six-sensory living in a five-sensory family who didn't fully fit it growing up, just know you are like the swan in the fairy tale who simply grows and evolves differently than the ducks. You are simply more perceptive and aware of energy than your family members are. I sometimes describe the experience of being a six-sensory in a five-sensory world as being the high-powered zoom lens video camera in a world of disposable ones from the drugstore.

What you can see through your sophisticated lens versus what they can see through their basic plastic lens is incomparable. When you say you see the fly on the wall three rooms over when you look through your lens and they can't even see the wall in front of them through theirs, they naturally think you are making things up and are a bit weird. This discrepancy in perception cuts off all options for creating something exciting together. In other words, we need people who get us, share our depth of perception, and especially people who will co-create with us. We need our community.

Your life will change for the better when you realize this and create the connections your spirit needs. We intuitives all need a grounded and interested six-sensory support system with which to share our psychic vibes. It's easy to believe that you're "the lone ranger in psychic land" (as a favorite client calls it)—that is, if you let anyone know about your gifts, they'll shoot you on sight. However, the consciousness-raising industry is one of the largest moneymakers in the world, selling billions of dollars' worth of books, online courses, and seminars on the sixth sense and related spiritual pursuits every year. Happily, the world is evolving. More and more people everywhere are spontaneously activating their sixth sense these days. It's fun to watch, like popcorn popping. One person's activation sets off another's and another's. We need our sixth sense now more than ever, so this global activation is happening before our eyes.

In reality, millions of people are six-sensory, but the silly thing is that many of these millions are still in hiding. So many people are in the intuitive closet that it must be getting pretty crowded in there. If you come out of hiding and reveal your intuitive interests to others a little more—or at least turn on the light and see how many other people are secretly pursuing spiritual and intuitive growth these days—you'll be on your way to finding lots of support from the most unexpected places.

When I did public workshops and readings, people showed up in the hundreds, even thousands, and many of them claimed to be skeptics—yet there they were. Some of these skeptics even sat in the front row. I knew they weren't really skeptical of their own intuition; rather, they were unsure that it was safe to let the world know they're intuitive and trusted their vibes. The questions they asked were more about finding support than validating their inner guidance. I believe that in the very near future, this bias against intuition will end. The emerging perception is no longer, "This is too 'woo-woo.'" The new perception is, "How do I make my 'woo-woo' channel work better?"

Don't automatically assume the people around you will negatively judge you if you let them know you use six senses to make your decisions. More likely they will be interested and full of questions.

I once read for a client named Carl who said that he thought he had strong vibes, but lamented his lack of psychic support, especially at work. "I'm six-sensory and highly sensitive," he said, "but I work with Neanderthals who are so insensitive and unconscious that it's scary. I wouldn't dare let them know my interests, or they'd laugh me out of the office."

I invited Carl to a workshop so that he could meet other six-sensory people and perhaps make friends. He was stunned to see two of his co-workers there—but I wasn't. After all, we tend to presume to know what others are like, and we're often wrong. It's best to keep an open mind and assume nothing as we seek intuitive support. In the Dark Ages, six-sensory people did have to hide and sneak around for fear of being misunderstood and attacked. Fortunately, people are slowly evolving, so woo-woo is becoming less and less dismissed, and more pursued. Because you are reading this now, you are part of the progress. Of course, some people still don't get it, and may never, but happily, more and more are starting to.

If you feel that you can strengthen your vibes on your own without any support, you're kidding yourself. Empaths and intuitives especially need supportive people to help us remain true to ourselves. We can easily get lost in other people's energy and become drained, overwhelmed, and confused. I encourage you to actively seek out your soul supporters (those other six-sensory people who are listening to their spirit) as part of your effort to strengthen your inner channel. Find people you can connect with, who will listen to you, respect your vibes, and keep them safe and protected from negative judgment, including your own—in other words, your team. These people do exist, and you need to connect with and invite them into your life as fast as possible. Intuitive people are most comfortable with kindred spirits—we don't do as well alone. As I like to say, even Jesus Christ picked 12 helpers before he went to work. So let's use him as a role model and begin to seek our own supporting cast.

When seeking support, don't let your ego sabotage you by confiding your intuitive feelings to those who clearly won't be supportive. Be discerning when sharing your vibes or seeking soul supporters. If you approach another six-sensory person, or at least another person attuned to their spirit, you'll be fine, but if you confide in someone who's stuck in their head, over-identified with their ego, or disconnected from their spirit, your words will likely fall on deaf ears.

Exercise a little common sense here. You probably already realize that most five-sensory people don't get it and may be dismissive when it comes to acknowledging vibes, so do your detective work first. For example, when I was a teenager, I had a good friend named Vicky. Vicky had an extremely sharp spirit and had very accurate vibes. Yet every time she shared her vibes with her mother, she would get flustered and say, "Stop, Vicky! You're scaring me." This reaction annoyed Vicky to no end because she wanted her mother to listen to and appreciate her insights and not shut her down.

Once, the three of us were in a car together when Vicky suddenly said, "Mom, slow down. I feel that a cop is in the area, and you're speeding." As always, her hopelessly limited five-sensory mother overreacted: "Vicky," she snapped, harshly, "don't say things like that. You sound weird." And she didn't slow down.

Two blocks later, a cop pulled out of the shadows, flagged down Vicky's mom, and gave her a ticket for speeding. Rather than admit that she'd made a mistake, Vicky's mom blamed Vicky for the ticket. I couldn't believe it, and neither could Vicky. It made no sense.

I later mentioned to Vicky that maybe she shouldn't share her vibes so freely with her mom because she was so scared by her limited ego perceptions that she couldn't understand them and never would. I suggested that Vicky share her vibes with my family because we'd get it and would listen.

From that day on, Vicky stopped sharing her vibes with her mom and adopted my family as her spiritual support team. The more we listened, the more comfortable she became being a six-sensory person and the more fun she had. By the time Vicky entered college, her spirit was her guide—she even used it to guide others by doing intuitive readings later on in her life.

If you look into your own family, you have a fifty-fifty shot that you may find at least one ally. It's worth the effort to check into it because family support is the best there is. But start with those in the family who've already shown interest; under no circumstances try to convert someone. We all awaken to higher awareness at our own pace, and no one can hurry anyone else along. If a five-sensory person doesn't get it, don't take it personally. Just move on. Seek support, not sabotage, and never argue about it.

If there's no one you can relate to at home, look further. Is there anyone at work who shares your interests? You can test the waters by asking your co-workers if they listen to or believe in intuition. I know this seems risky, but don't assume the worst—intuition is an exciting and intriguing subject for more and more people than ever before.

See if any friends or neighbors share your interest. Raise the topic of intuition casually in conversation and see what happens. It's my experience that those interested are *really* interested and love to share, so it won't take much to get them to step up. You can also find team players in places where intuitive people tend to gravitate, such as spiritual bookstores, workshops, lectures, or progressive churches where following your intuition is encouraged and supported.

All you really need is one or two sympathetic kindred spirits to talk to from time to time. That's all. I'm not advising you to join a cult or an exclusive, secretive, or controlling group. That's not support—that's creepy, so please stay away!

Once you find your six-sensory friends, check in with them often, for at least a few minutes a week. Freely share and respectfully listen to one another's intuitive feelings. Just listening helps more than you know—that's the best support anyone can give or receive because it affirms each other's intuition when the outside world may not.

One final note: I've found that one of the quickest and most efficient ways to find intuitive friends is to simply pray for them to show up. Ask the Universe to connect you with kindred spirits and intuitive soul mates, and it will happen. When you're ready and willing to receive support, it shows up, and usually quite quickly.

Finally, because having support is such an important part of strengthening your intuition and trusting your vibes, I've created a six-sensory community myself. It's called the Good Vibes Tribe. I invite you to join us today. In this community, you will meet kindred spirits from all over the world who offer tremendous encouragement and support. Among the many gifts you get as a tribe member, in addition to the fantastic and dynamic creative, loving tribe members, are many free online courses and meditations to strengthen your sixth sense. The tribe works these courses together, which they love. I'm very involved in the tribe and address the group every single day, offering a tip, a tool, and encouragement as you move into your fabulous woo-woo life. You will find all the information on how to join the Good Vibes Tribe on the home page of my website: www.soniachoquette.com.

Woo-Woo Workout

Try to find some psychic soul mates. Maybe you have a few already—if so, establish check-in times with them when you can share your vibes. If you aren't sure who your fellow six-sensories are, do a little detective work. You can even read this book in public, like at a coffee shop or on the train on the way to work. You could also try laying it on your coffee table or desk and observing the reactions it receives. If someone shows interest in the subject of intuition and vibes, explore a little further. It won't take long to discover whether you've found someone who can be supportive. On the other hand, if someone is disinterested, don't take it personally—they simply aren't ready. Don't take their comments or behavior personally. Smile, change the subject as gently and diplomatically as possible, and quietly withdraw.

Also, always pray for support and then be open to receiving it. Happily, evolution is prevailing, and six-sensory people are emerging in droves. These days it's becoming less and less difficult to connect with such kindred spirits if you really want to.

Woo-Woo Wisdom

Gain support.

TALK SHOP

One of the most outstanding traits of six-sensory people is their ability to comfortably acknowledge and express their vibes, no matter whom they interact with. Sharing our vibes with others— starting with our trusted spiritual support team, and then the world at large—takes us a long way toward living an extraordinary life and improving the lives of those around us.

Five-sensory people don't talk about vibes because their ego says vibes are not logical and should be completely ignored. This prevents their intuition from developing. But we six-sensory people love to talk about our intuitive experiences, and we have many colorful ways of doing so. For example, whenever my friend Julia feels her sixth sense tap her on the shoulder, she says, "I'm getting marching orders," or "My gut says . . . ," while Scott, a restaurateur and strong intuitive, says, "I'm getting that shoutout from the big boss above again." I often say, "My spirit tells me . . ." because when I feel vibrations, I know that my spirit is talking to me.

Talking about your vibes freely and without embarrassment or apology opens the door for more vibes to come into your life. Just like naming a baby when it's born, speaking enthusiastically about your intuition acknowledges it is alive and well in your life and you are happily letting the world know. You want people to know about your vibes, not to shock them or seek approval from them, but because you love to share what makes your life so extraordinary.

My client Jay confessed that he didn't know how to tell others about his vibes. "In my world, people just don't talk about these things. I want to share how great my intuitive flashes are and how they've helped me, but I worry about what people think. My vibes are the best thing in my life, and I want to talk about them because they help so much."

I believe anyone can be open to hearing about vibes if you talk about them in a way they can hear and doesn't make them uncomfortable. People are fascinated by vibes because we all have them, and they are so magical. If we are casual and easygoing, and let others know how much vibes make our life better, they will get on board. If you act like vibes are your personal *Twilight Zone*—weird, strange, or unsettling—however, people will run away.

No matter what you say, don't be too concerned with how people react. When you talk about your vibes some people may roll their eyes or laugh, but the truth is that they're doing this more because they aren't sure how to respond, not because they dismiss what you are saying. Most people wish they felt vibes like you do. More often than not, they will respond by opening up and telling you about some of their vibes as well.

I have a client who is a highly successful CEO in Illinois. Recently she received an award for Businesswoman of the Year. When she gave her acceptance speech to what she knew to be a highly conservative group of people, she finished by saying, "Above all, trust your intuition. It will lead you to your greatest successes in life, as it has mine."

Instead of getting the silent treatment, which she feared, she was surprised and delighted to receive a standing ovation. "Apparently, the conservative business world is more ready to hear this than I imagined," she said.

I answered, "They listened because your business stands head and shoulders above the rest. These people want to know your secret. You gave them a gift by sharing it."

I think we do the world a service by being open about our vibes. It gives others permission to do the same. Not only does talking about our intuitive experiences validate them for us, but it opens the door for others to get connected with their vibes as well. It may also open up opportunities for creative collaboration.

I once told my sister Cuky about an intuitive dream I had about going to the ocean with a great group of people who were singing, healing, dancing, and having a wonderful time. As I was describing it to her, I got the strong feeling that it was a prophetic dream and that I'd be doing what I dreamed about very soon, even though I'm not a beach person. My sister then told me that she'd had a similar dream about doing a healing workshop in Hawaii. Our shared, combined dreams soon led us to create a powerful joint retreat, Translucent You, which we taught in Hawaii for over 10 years. The participants sang, danced, played musical instruments, and had fun in the ocean. They also received intuitive readings, had healing massage therapy sessions, and did artwork and visioning to heal their psychic wounds and reawaken their intuitive voice. Had my sister and I not shared our dreams, we never would have devised that profound healing work, and we would have missed the joy it brought to everyone involved.

The more you talk about your vibes, the more specific they become. Talking about your vibes helps you open your inner treasure chest. Sharing your intuitive feelings helps pull out hidden gems rolling around inside your heart. Spirit brings them to light and allows them to come to life.

Your sixth sense speaks to you in many ways—in symbols, pictures, metaphors, feelings, dreams, and even signs on the road. Your spirit has a language of its own, and the more freely you talk about your vibes, the more you come to know the language of your spirit. In talking with my students, I often hear, "It wasn't until I was describing my vibe to you just now that it dawned on me what it meant." You begin to pick up the messages sent to you in all sorts of creative ways.

VIBES SURPRISE YOU

When I do intuitive readings for clients, I often feel as if I'm following a trail of clues. Thoughts, feelings, and images pop up as I go, and I never know what I'm going to say until I say it. I'm usually just as surprised to hear some of my insights as my clients are. And when I investigate my own problems, I speak aloud, even if I'm alone. Vocalizing my inner world invites my intuition to jump in at any moment and offer solutions I hadn't thought of before. The more I openly ponder my challenges, the more quickly guidance comes.

For instance, I struggled over whether to take a trip to Menton, France, to see a dear friend Michele a few years ago. I intuitively felt it was important, yet, logically taking such a trip would be expensive, inconvenient, and conflict with my work commitments. Mulling my vibes over out loud, I heard myself suddenly saying, "I need to go. It'll be the last time I can visit Michele, and the hotel where I lived 40 years ago when I was a student there."

The hotel was a place I loved and held dear in my heart, and the possibility that it might soon be gone—even though no mention of that was ever made or had occurred to me—made me think about this very seriously. Mulling this over out loud helped me make up my mind. I made the reservation right then and changed the other commitments I had in place to accommodate the trip.

Three days later, I received a letter from my friend Michele saying that the hotel was being turned into condos, so if I wanted to see it again I needed to come fast. I wrote and said I already had my airline ticket and would arrive just in time to visit this sacred place before it was gone forever.

FIND *YOUR* WORDS

If you want to express your vibes to others, it helps to have the vocabulary to do so comfortably and without fear, restraint, hesitation, or self-consciousness. For example, I'm very comfortable using the word *psychic* when discussing my intuitive sense, but I know I am the exception. Most people cringe when they hear that word, which amuses me to no end. I think it is because the word cuts through everything like a knife, and implies, "I see you." What people don't know, however, is that what I see is beautiful, because I see the spirit in you. For many people, the word *psychic* still has so many superstitious or negative connotations that they don't feel comfortable using it at all. If that's true for you, don't worry. There are other words you can use.

It makes no difference what you call your sixth sense, as long as you call it something that works for you. Try using "my gut," "my instinct," "my radar," "my flash," "my vibes," or even "my wise and eternal wisdom," if you want to. As long as the words you choose express your sixth sense positively, you can continue to make room for it in your life.

Seasoned six-sensory people who follow their intuitive sense are enthusiastic and even proud of their insights. They love to describe how fabulous their vibes make their lives. On the other hand, people stuck halfway between the five- and six-sensory worlds have the urge to share their intuitive insights, but they hesitate because they often don't know how to explain their experiences.

They might say, "I had a weird feeling," "Something bizarre happened," or "I have this odd sensation." They use negative terms that water down their vibes or even give them an ominous spin. I give them an A for effort; however, if you want to comfortably use your vibes, you'll have to do better than that. Your intuition is gold, so it should be gathered with appreciation, then described positively and shared enthusiastically rather than with negative qualifiers. For example, try saying, "I just had a terrific inspiration," "I just had an incredible feeling that . . . ," or "My inner genius tells me . . . ," and see what response you get back from others and from your spirit. In my experience, the more I positively express my intuition, the more it rewards me with even more wisdom, so I get a double bonus.

As an added word of advice, please don't exaggerate either. I know you are enthusiastic, but if you blow things up too big, other people will be dismissive and roll their eyes with this as well. You don't want to attract their bad vibes and judgment if you can help it. I have a client who describes every single vibe she receives as *amazing*. One or two amazings are okay, but 10 in 5 minutes is hard to absorb and makes you wonder what drug she's on! Just speak about your inner voice with confidence and ease, which shows that you value it and view it as the most natural thing in the world, because it is. I've even seen a few grounded and confident six-sensory people win some die-hard five-sensory folks over to their intuitive way of living by simply describing their sixth sense with calm assurance.

After observing people struggle to describe their vibes for as long as I have, I've concluded that the best way to talk about your sixth sense is simply to say, "I always trust my vibes. It works for me," in the most matter-of-fact voice possible. Then smile. Enough said.

Woo-Woo Workout

Openly acknowledge your vibes, starting with your closest friends and then with people everywhere. Carefully choose the words and expressions you use to describe your intuition. Be clear, matter of fact, and confident, as if talking about the weather. Don't lay it on too thick or exaggerate. Just tell it as it is. Also, notice how others talk about their vibes, too, even if it's unconsciously, such as when your boss says, "I have a hunch that won't work," or when your spouse says, "I have a good feeling about that." Almost everyone has some words to describe their vibes because we all have them, even if we don't realize it.

Put a positive spin when sharing your intuitive feelings, such as saying, "I have a great idea" instead of "This feels weird." If you think of vibes as "pearls of wisdom" instead of "strange feelings," then it's easier to share those pearls with grace, humor, and style. Be creative when describing your intuition by using expressions that acknowledge your psychic sense without being provocative. You might want to avoid the word *psychic* when talking about your intuition in your board meeting or at church, for example, but if you say, "I had this brainstorm," "my sense is," "my gut reaction tells me," or "the spirit moved me," I can assure you that no one will even give it a second thought.

Remember: it helps to speak people's language. When you're around five-sensory people, use words they can hear and understand, and create connection, not distance. Be practical. Make a list of 20 ways to describe your vibes easily, comfortably, confidently, no matter who you are around.

It doesn't matter which words you use, as long as you talk about your vibes in a positive, appreciative, and enthusiastic way.

Woo-Woo Wisdom

Trust your vibes. It works.

FAKE IT 'TIL YOU MAKE IT

When my daughters were four and five years old, I took them to an outdoor shopping mall to enjoy a warm summer evening. First, we window-shopped, then we stopped for an ice-cream cone, and finally, we strolled to a children's play area in the center of the mall so they could play with the other kids.

As we sat down to eat our ice cream, I noticed a couple sitting across from us with their two-year-old. My older daughter, Sonia, impulsively stood (ice-cream cone still in hand), skipped around the perimeter of the play area, kicked up her heels, and then plopped down next to me. Not to be outdone, her sister, Sabrina, immediately leaped to her feet and did precisely what Sonia just did before returning to her seat next to her sister.

The toddler, fascinated by my daughters' every move, watched them very closely. Finally, after the girls sat down, the little boy turned to his father, who also had an ice-cream cone, and demanded that he hand it over, which he reluctantly did. Then, with the cone in his hand and eyeballing the girls all the while, the little boy attempted to skip around the play area just as he'd seen them do, managing to mimic them to a tee . . . for about five feet, at which point, he lost his balance, tripped, and buried his left eye in the cone.

It was a hilarious and poignant moment that clearly reminded me how much we learn from observing and imitating others. Our role models invite us into new experiences by their examples. Unfortunately, not many of us have had positive role models to follow when it comes to living an intuitive life. And while the general attitude toward intuitive living is evolving, we still need good teachers and role models to show us how to navigate the unseen world with ease and grace.

We can all agree that infomercial psychics and storefront spiritual advisors do not represent the six-sensory life. Like everything else five-sensory, they should be left in the Dark Ages. However, there are still people who are naive and vulnerable to believing that certain psychic people have "special powers." These snake-oil salesmen suggest if you pay them well, they can bend the Universe to your will while you sit back and do nothing. That won't happen. There's no shortcut to learning how to live a fully empowered, intuitive life. You can never hand over the reins of your life to anyone and expect a good outcome. However, with trustworthy mentors and teachers, you can learn from others without giving away your power.

Find inspiring, authentic, empowering, creative, supportive role models who demonstrate, moment to moment, what living in spirit and operating from the heart really entails—and then copy what they do. Many people are shaky-leg beginners when it comes to trusting their vibes and just need a little encouragement. They don't know how to incorporate their sixth sense into their lives with confidence and ease . . . *yet*.

Years ago, before author Julia Cameron was my friend, she began having consistent and unexplained psychic feelings, hunches, and inspirations. Uneasy and not wanting to look like a nut, she consulted a psychotherapist and confessed her anxiety at being so psychically aware: "I worry that I'll look like a freak, or people will think I'm crazy."

He listened to her for a while and then quite ingeniously said, "The problem isn't your naturally functioning sixth sense, Julia. The problem is that you have no positive role models to teach you how to use it and wear it publicly. Do you know anyone who is both openly intuitive and graceful? Someone who is comfortable with their psychic sense and is as normal as you or me? Someone who can show you how to benefit from this gift so that it will serve you?"

This question opened her up to a new possibility that had never occurred to her and eventually led her to me.

In working with Julia, I reflected on my own intuitive role models. First and foremost, as you know, was my mom, who was beautiful, sophisticated, brilliantly creative, and while a little intense and dramatic at times, used her vibes in the most practical ways. Then there were Dr. Tully and Charlie Goodman, my two elegant, well-traveled, educated, and articulate teachers whose intuition was artful, high-minded, and oriented toward healing and spiritual growth and bettering the planet. Other mentors included LuAnn Glatzmaier and Joan Smith, two creative, artistic, intelligent, spiritually centered, and worldly women who were highly educated, wrote books, counseled, taught, and created countless beautiful works of art. They were all my inspirations, and what I learned from them was empowering. I relied on these people as my intuitive and ethical foundation—I studied their work, replicated their views, and held to their high standards until I developed and strengthened my own intuitive integrity. I danced in their playgrounds until they became my own . . . and then I became the one to invite the new kids on the block to play with me.

Finding your own intuitive role models is becoming less complicated because more and more leaders are letting the world know their intuition is a primary guiding light in their lives. As I've noted, one is Oprah Winfrey, who attributes her extraordinary success and happiness in life to following her inner guidance. Other public figures include Richard Branson, Steve Jobs, Steven Spielberg, and David Lynch, not to mention Jonas Salk, Nikola Tesla, Frida Kahlo, and Niels Bohr. Every day we hear of another influential person attributing their massive success to using *all* of their senses to achieve their incredible breakthroughs. Thankfully, there is no lack of potential role models and teachers for intuitive living to choose from these days.

The key is to pick role models that are right for you. There are still plenty of charlatans who promise overnight success with little effort if you follow them. The storefront manipulators may now be found online. So be mindful of who you choose to learn from. Above all, use common sense. The subtle realm is still like the Wild West, and because this is such new territory for so many, you don't want to hitch your wagon to someone who takes you for a ride. If you feel pressured in even the tiniest way, walk away. A natural teacher or mentor has no need to do that. They already have enough to do living their own bright life. The ones who tug and pull and coerce are not teaching you to trust your vibes—they are asking you to ignore them.

To find a good role model, start by really noticing the people around you. Are there people who positively affect you? Do they listen to their heart, follow their vibes, and act without hesitation? The best teachers draw you to them by the process of attraction rather than promotion. They have good vibes and their lives work, so people are drawn to their light. Good teachers and guides won't have neon signs flashing, but they do shine. The light will be their aura and self-confidence, the sparkle of their great laugh and enthusiasm for life. People are naturally drawn to them because their energy feels so good.

People who live by their sixth sense don't seek approval. They have their own approval. They enjoy acceptance and often get it, but they don't need it. Like having a sophisticated ear for music or a developed eye for beauty, intuitive people have a talent for detecting high vibration, and they follow it.

Once you identify creative and courageous people who follow their heart, listen to their vibes, trust their feelings, speak their truth, and act on their intuition, model yourself after them. Like a karaoke singer entering the stage for the first time, sing their song with the same enthusiasm they do, even if it doesn't quite feel like your own. It will only feel this way in the beginning—with practice, intuitive living becomes so familiar and comfortable until you would never consider living another way. In other words, *fake it 'til you make it.*

My student Christine wanted to be a songwriter from the time she was a young girl. Complete songs would rush into her head, mostly before she fell asleep at night. She knew she was channeling music and told her parents. They laughed at the notion and said that just sounded weird. So Christine, not wanting her parents' disapproval, stopped telling them about her song downloads. But the songs didn't go away. That's when Christine quietly signed up for one of my workshops. While there, she met Jason, a talented intuitive composer who told her that he channeled more than songs. He channeled symphonies. Christine was stunned to learn that someone else received music the same way she did. Only Jason took it in his stride and was already having some success publishing his compositions while hers sat there. It was an eye-opener. Christine stopped acting as if her intuitive downloads were bizarre and started doing what Jason did, recording her songs and putting them out into the world. Jason's love of music, along with the way he worked and his enthusiasm for his inspiration, gave Chris permission to do the same. And his warm, easygoing spirit, which was so beautifully conveyed in his compositions, helped her relax into this new way of being. In short, Jason became Chris's intuitive role model. Following Jason's lead was precisely what Chris needed to do to claim her musical gift. "I'm following Jason's spirit, and it's working. He gives me the courage to put my songs in the world."

So if you want to have a creative, confident, extraordinary life, study and model every creative, intuitive person you meet and do what they do. This is how human beings learn—and how we spiritual beings express our authentic Self. Choose intuitive role models who inspire, create, and experience life with style, grace, integrity, and confidence. The best way to identify good intuitive role models is to search for people who love their life, a sure sign that they're using all their senses well. Ask them what their secret is, and then use it.

Being intuitive is an art that can be mastered in the same way you master anything—by being a good student and finding good teachers. Work alongside your mentors, practicing your art as you apprentice with inspiring role models. Eventually, like a journeyman stepping out on his own, let life be the next teacher and your mistakes be the exams. Then, gracefully, over time, with patience, persistence, and practice, you'll come to master being you. That's what the higher way of intuitive living leads to: becoming your fully enlightened, empowered self—not only the person that you want to be but also the person that God designed you to be.

As a final note, a real teacher always sets the student free. If you want to officially study with someone, check to see if that teacher empowers you to lead your life from your heart and spirit versus wanting you to follow them. The mentor-student dynamic should function like geese flying south for the winter. The strong one leads at the beginning, and the others follow, catching their wave. As they get stronger, the front one falls back and rides the wave while the one behind steps into the lead position. That way, everyone leads in the end. In looking for teachers and guides, consider if they will give you the tools to step into the lead position in your life or just keep you following behind. Your sixth sense is your best guide. Look for people who acknowledge and respect your vibes and encourage you to trust yourself as much as they trust themselves.

To get you started, I invite you to consider choosing me as your first intuitive mentor and believe me when I say, "You've got this!"

Woo-Woo Workout

Open your eyes, ears, and heart, and be on the lookout for your intuitive role models. Who is your intuitive hero? Who sings your song and plays in your creative playground? What about these people can you imitate? Don't limit yourself—find as many sources of inspiration as possible. Walk their walk, talk their talk, dance their dance, sing their song—emulate them in every way.

The more you do, the sooner you will be the master of your own inner journey.

Woo-Woo Wisdom

Find teachers, mentors, and role models.

GET HELP
FROM BEYOND

Just as we telepathically communicate with one another on the physical plane, so can we communicate with angels and spirit guides on a higher plane. Each of us has a very personal link with our spirit helpers at all times—all we have to do to receive their assistance is open our hearts.

If you want guidance from angelic forces, you can access it most quickly by praying for help. In addition to asking for general assistance, you can also seek the support of specific angels for help on particular projects. If, for instance, you're a musician or you want to undertake musical projects, you can pray to the angels of music to help you. If you're a writer, you can ask the angels of communication for assistance. If you're looking for a new home or renovating your current residence, the housing angels can help you. There are travel angels, healing angels, angels who protect the family, angels who can help you address any particular concern—indeed, there are angels for every need, and they're happy to be called upon to assist you.

I personally pray for help from my teaching, writing, and relationship angels, to name a few. And I'm still grateful to my cooking angel for getting me out of hot water a few summers ago. When I was married, my ex-husband, Patrick, was an excellent cook and took a lot of time and care to prepare meals, especially for guests.

On this particular day, he had invited some good friends over for dinner. He spent all day preparing a pork roast for barbecuing, then he placed it on the grill and told me to watch it for a few minutes while he went to pick up our daughter Sonia, who was nearby at a friend's house.

I sat next to the barbecue for about five minutes when the phone rang. It was my oldest and dearest friend, Sue, whom I hadn't spoken to in more than six years. Needless to say, I forgot about the roast until I heard a terrible scream from the backyard. It was Patrick, nearly hysterical, yelling, "The barbecue is on fire!" I immediately hung up the phone and ran out to see what was happening, only to discover him holding a large fork on which the roast was speared—in flames. (Apparently, the grease from the roast had collected and had set the meat on fire.)

Just as Patrick doused the flames, our guests arrived. Furious that I hadn't watched the roast after he had worked so hard to prepare it and feeling embarrassed that we now had nothing to serve, Patrick silently glared at me and went to answer the door. Desperate not to spend the evening in the shadow of his passive-aggressive wrath, I begged my angels for help.

Patrick stormed back with the guests and announced, as if tattling, "I might as well tell you that Sonia didn't watch the roast, so it caught on fire. So you can thank Sonia for the ruined dinner now that we now have nothing to eat."

"Wait," I said, praying like mad. "We're not sure the meat is ruined."

I insisted that he cut into the roast anyway. "Why bother? It's completely burned," Patrick sneered. But to everyone's amazement, the meat was seared to absolute perfection. It was the most delicious roast we've ever had—even Charlie Trotter, the most famous chef in Chicago at the time, couldn't have done a better job. The dinner was a smashing success, and I repeatedly thanked my cooking angels for saving the day. At the end of the meal, one of our dinner guests turned to me with a smile and a wink and said, "Since Patrick said you are responsible for the dinner, I must say it was one of the most delicious meals I've ever eaten." I smiled and answered, "I can't take any credit. It was the cooking angels who deserve our gratitude."

Every undertaking will unfold much more easily and with more peace and sweetness if you ask your angels to assist you. They're present and ready to help in every situation. I've never known an angel to let someone down in all my years of working with them. But your spiritual support team isn't limited to angels—saints, prophets, spirit guides, light beings, nature spirits, deities, and more are also available to help. If you've been raised Catholic, you're undoubtedly familiar with the various saints and their ability to assist us from the Other Side. My personal favorites are St. Joseph, the patron saint of houses; St. Anthony of Padua, the patron saint of finding things; St. Thérèse, "The Little Flower," the patron saint of love; St. Christopher, the patron saint of travel; St. Jude, the patron saint of hopeless causes; and, of course, my most beloved favorite—Mother Mary, the feminine face of God, who brings compassion and tenderness to all.

It doesn't matter if you seek support from a deity who resides outside of your spiritual tradition, for the higher powers don't make any distinctions. For example, my American client Sally routinely prays to the Indian goddess Kali, while my Christian friend Steven prays to Buddha for support. My Jewish friend Dan asks St. Anthony to help him find new accounts, and he's been amazed at the assistance he's received. One of my Catholic friends asks the spirit of the great white eagle in the Native American tradition to assist, and I regularly ask Gaia, Greek mythology's Divine Mother, to help me out.

To ask any spiritual force for aid, simply focus your heart on where you need assistance or are in pain, and then say, "Help." The Universe will give you access to all aspects of itself, so if you focus on receiving help in a particular area, you'll telepathically send that communication forward, attracting a resonating response in return. And if you specifically invoke the spiritual help of deities, these benevolent higher forces will respond.

Some people worry that asking angels, saints, or gods and goddesses for help is worshiping false gods. Don't worry—that's your ego talking again. There's nothing wrong with this; God exists in all forms and faces, and in all ways. But if you don't feel comfortable reaching out to and communicating with these many types of loving assistance, you don't have to. You can simply ask God to put helpers on the job without your knowing who's been assigned to it.

You may also get help from those you've known or heard about who have crossed over into spirit. People do this naturally, and many cultures make it part of their daily spiritual practice to invoke the wisdom and assistance of their ancestors. The spirit of the departed lives on and can still connect to us, so it makes sense that they're here to help us. You can also telepathically ask for help from those on the Other Side who, while they were alive, achieved great success in a particular area, such as art, music, medicine, and even government. For example, two very dear friends routinely ask for help on their musical projects from past composers such as Richard Rodgers and Oscar Hammerstein. I once knew a budding young artist who constantly struggled with painting techniques until he psychically sought the assistance of Michelangelo and Raphael to help him get the hang of it. I'm not sure they ever answered him, but I do know that he quit complaining and started to enjoy himself.

I have recurring dreams in which I'm being taught by three of my most important spirit guides—13th-century French Catholic bishops named De Leon, Lucerne, and Maurice—who instruct me in the church's secret doctrines and in the deeper meaning of the tarot. These nocturnal classes have helped me channel some of the most meaningful information I've ever received and are perhaps the most significant source of intuitive guidance in my work as a spiritual teacher.

Keep in mind that when you ask for guidance, you should always use common sense. Would you have trusted a particular individual's input before they passed? If not, don't trust it now. Low-level information can come from energetic vagabonds, lost souls eager to stow away or hitch a ride with you if you let them. You see, we don't automatically evolve into spiritual consciousness the minute we die. Whether in the body or not, we still have to grow, and we pick up after death where we left off in life.

My student Emily's husband drank and gambled himself into an early grave at 59. Shortly after he died, Emily came to my class seeking healing from the loss. Within weeks she began to feel his spirit communicating with her, which comforted her greatly because, despite his failings, she missed him terribly. Soon after, she started having dreams in which he advised her to gamble. Believing that he was trying to make up for his earthly mistakes, Emily trusted the dreams and did as he suggested. Within three months, she lost over $3,000.

Feeling distraught and confused, Emily came to see me. "How can this be happening to me again?" she cried.

"Your husband is just as addicted to gambling without a body as he was when he had one—and now he's using you."

Occasionally those who have abruptly passed out of their body can get confused and hang around on the earth plane for a while. Because they still identify largely with their human existence and don't fully realize they are now in spirit, they'll gladly offer their two-cents' worth if you're willing to listen. This is especially true of souls who were largely ignored in their earthly form. If you pay attention to them now, they're delighted—yet their input is almost always useless and can even be damaging. So if you ever feel that a soul is connecting to you but not contributing, simply command them into the light and ask their angels to come and get them.

Many beginner intuitive students who don't take the necessary steps to get grounded and be discerning end up with low-level spirits holding their attention and keeping them hostage to their endless and nonsensical ramblings. For example, a neighbor was contacted by a spirit guide who told her that she was an enlightened being. No offense, but this should have been her first clue that she was connecting to a spirit with questionable credentials. A high-vibration spirit guide never flatters and doesn't tell you you're special—after all, on a soul level, we're all the same, just at different levels of awakening.

My neighbor believed this nonsense and started to act as though she deserved special attention, even expecting others to pay homage to her. But, of course, there were no takers in her scheme. Her family and friends dropped her like a hot potato.

Confused about why no one would listen to her vibes, she came to me for advice. I told her that you can always tell if vibes are reliable by the results they bear. If they're from a higher plane, they'll bring about improvement and closeness to others. I washed her windshield of self-delusion, assuring her that although she was as important and lovable as we all are, there was nothing extraordinary about her.

My guides suggested that rather than pose as an enlightened being, she'd be better off doing some enlightened service, such as working in a soup kitchen, where the light she did have could shine upon others. Accepting my counsel, she turned in her turban, put on an apron, and began helping out at the local church's homeless lunch program.

We're all equal spiritual beings, interconnected and in various stages of unfolding consciousness. At our deepest level, we're one body and spirit. Any suggestion to the contrary isn't worth the time of day, so ignore it. If they haven't made the transition from ego to spirit, out-of-body beings will keep trying to get to you by appealing to your ego, even from the Other Side. So it's essential to be discerning when receiving guidance—you don't want to be distracted by psychic riffraff or drivel that flatters and offers no substantial assistance. Trustworthy guidance is balanced, sensible, and never tells you what to do. It simply provides supportive suggestions and leaves the decision up to you, respecting your freedom to make your own choices and mistakes. If the message you receive is frightening, overly flattering, or leaves you feeling uncomfortable, telepathically change the channel *immediately,* because it's definitely not from a Higher Source and is a waste of your time. Simply say, "I send you into the light. Be gone."

As a soul-based, intuitive person, you have access to support from the entire hierarchy of Universal Light beings, beginning with people who have crossed over, to your Creator. Use your ability to connect to Divine Wisdom to your advantage. When you feel weak or confused, ask for help, then listen to what comes through. Spirit is subtle, so pay close attention. When guidance does come through, see how it leaves you feeling: if it's from the light, it will leave you feeling that same way—light and energized.

If you want to know more about receiving help and support from angels and guides, please read my book *Ask Your Guides*. Here you will find everything you want to know about engaging this unlimited Divine support into your life.

Woo-Woo Workout

Ask your spirit for more assistance. Invite in all your spirit helpers. You have an entire psychic support system available to help you at all times. They will not interfere, so you must ask first. If you feel vulnerable, ask your guardian angels for protection. If you're working on a particular project, ask the angels in that area to assist you. If you want help from mentors from another age, invite them to help you. If you're missing someone who has crossed over to the Other Side, send them love, and if you want, ask for their support. But be sure to ask only for loving, helpful support, grounded in light and love from these benevolent forces. Carefully discern the quality of guidance you receive, and always thank your Divine Helpers for their loving assistance.

Woo-Woo Wisdom

Call in the troops.

CONNECT WITH YOUR DIVINE TEACHERS

The more we grow spiritually, the more help we receive from our spirit guides, and in particular our Divine Teachers, whose primary purpose is to help us evolve spiritually. These guides oversee our personal soul development and oversee the soul curriculum that each of us selected before we incarnated into this lifetime. These lessons reflect our individual soul ambitions and help us recognize our weaknesses so that we can overcome them and love more freely. They are the primary soul purpose of our lives.

The focus of my intuitive practice has been to help people recognize and understand their soul curriculum. I tune in to clients' past-life histories and look at their souls' evolution from lifetime to lifetime in the same way you might look at a student's progress report from kindergarten to college. I can see what lessons my clients are assigned but fail to learn, which causes them to suffer. I see this with the help of my teacher guides and those of my clients—together, they show me what the clients are here for and what they must focus on to grow and find peace of mind and a fulfilled sense of purpose. My spirit teachers work overtime because my personal soul curriculum is to help raise the awareness of others to Divine Guidance. This is why I use my intuitive abilities when I teach.

It's valuable to get in touch with your spirit teachers, for they'll influence you to become self-reflective and honest about your life and improve those areas that cause you difficulty. They'll also relay strong messages to help you grow spiritually—spirit teachers have been known to bring books to your attention or have you turn on radio and television programs that address your particular areas of weakness. They'll also connect you to people who can instruct you on the earthly plane.

As a spiritual teacher, it surprises me to see how resistant people are to learning new things. They don't want to know that their troubles may result from their own poor choices and could be alleviated or solved by learning; instead, they'd rather blame someone else—even evil spirits from the dark side. Yet the entire point of incarnating into a physical body is to evolve in a continuous classroom. The only way to finish the curriculum is to die, and even then, you'll just begin a new one. But right now, you're here in this life to learn as much as possible.

Spirit teachers work in very subtle but direct ways. They usually come in those moments when you feel you're hitting rock bottom. They get your attention by exposing you to relevant information—such as brochures, announcements, or invitations by strangers to lectures and workshops. They suggest that you turn on the radio or TV when someone you should hear is about to come on. A favorite maneuver of spirit teachers is to have a book fall off a shelf in a store or library and hit you on the head. For example, my client Catherine wanted to learn more about her psychic sense for years but never did. "One day, I went to Barnes & Noble," she told me, "because I had an overwhelming urge to read something new. I didn't know what I was looking for, so I was poking around the metaphysical section when suddenly a copy of your book *The Psychic Pathway* fell off the top shelf and hit me on my head.

"I was so surprised that I started laughing! Reading your book led me to your workshop, which led me to the study of energy medicine. Now I'm apprenticing to be a Reiki healer and an intuitive channel. Not only am I discovering that I have a gift for healing, but I've never been happier and more fulfilled in my life. When people ask me how I got into my field, I say it literally hit me over the head."

Another way a spirit teacher works is through messengers, people who suddenly step forward and make recommendations for learning for no apparent reason, even though it may be uncomfortable for them to do so. For instance, a spirit teacher must have enlisted the help of the woman standing next to an old friend in a grocery store line because she unexpectedly told him, "You must be a painter or a poet."

He laughed and replied, "No, I just want to be."

"Do you paint?"

"Yes, but not well and not often."

"Do you write poetry?"

"Sometimes, but I'm only an amateur."

"Then you are a painter and a poet," she remarked. "You just don't recognize it."

When my friend told me about that conversation, I said that his spirit teacher was talking through that lady: "She probably didn't know what came over her to say those things, but I've been saying them for years. So I guess your spirit teachers thought a stranger might have more impact."

He got the message and started painting again the next day—and was clearly happier for it.

My client Alice's spirit teachers took a similar approach with her. Struggling financially for as long as she could remember, Alice lived in a state of constant drama. She never thought about examining her life or imagining that it could be different; instead, she just lived from crisis to crisis. I told her that she needed to learn about money because she had been a servant in a past life who never had any money. One of her soul assignments was to make money instead of expecting others to support her.

I suggested that she find actual teachers to help her learn financial responsibility, but Alice wasn't interested—she thought that marrying a rich man was the solution. I told her I didn't want to burst her bubble, but I intuitively saw that this wasn't an option for her.

"So that's why I never date?" Alice asked as a light bulb went off in her head.

"Yes," I replied. "You've blocked that possibility in this lifetime so that you could grow. I'm sorry, but there's no sugar daddy in the picture for you."

Even though it may feel like a bitter pill, people are always relieved on some level when they hear the truth and what they must do to spiritually evolve.

The next day at lunch, as Alice was reciting her daily laundry list of financial complaints and struggles, a co-worker she barely knew blurted out, "Have you ever heard of Debtors Anonymous?"

Taken aback and remembering what I'd told her the day before, she said, "No, I haven't. What is it?"

"I'm not really sure," the person replied, "but I think it's a free program for teaching people like you how to handle money better."

Alice felt a little weirded out until she realized that her spirit teachers were on the scene inviting her to grow. So she inquired, "How do I find out where to contact them?"

"I don't know," her co-worker answered. "Try the Internet."

As Alice drove home that evening, she heard an interview on public radio featuring a famous actor. The latter was recounting his life, particularly his gambling problem and how he'd solved it. Alice hated to admit it, but she, too, had gambled quite a bit, so she listened intently as the actor explained how he'd cleaned up his act by, among other things, joining Debtors Anonymous. Now Alice had received the same message three times in 24 hours. Obviously, *someone* was trying to tell her something.

"Okay, I surrender," Alice said aloud. "I admit it. I need help." A deep feeling of peace quickly enveloped her, replacing the constant anxiety. The minute she got home, she went on the Internet and found a Debtors Anonymous group in her area. "It was a turning point," she later told me. "It was the first time I ever received a real education in financial responsibility. With the group's help, I stopped my out-of-control spending habits—and it didn't cost a penny! I'm so grateful that my guides gave me the kick in the pants I needed to get financially sober. I was desperately in denial and didn't even know it."

All people must grow in this lifetime—no one is exempt from learning. Anyone who thinks that being intuitive excuses them from self-examination and growth is delusional. Being intuitive means being responsive to energy, not being a know-it-all. We're all at different levels of evolution, and the more ambitious we are, the steeper the learning curve. I make it a practice to constantly learn new things from people who are more knowledgeable and accomplished in certain areas than I am. However, many years ago, I did feel that because I was intuitive, I should know all sorts of things without being taught. This put an enormous—and unnecessary—strain on me. When I began to listen to my spirit teachers, I discovered we are all perpetual students in this lifetime. I was relieved to know that being a student was not an indication of failure. It was the point of being here on earth. This is a school for all souls, and as long as we are alive, we are all students. Once I understood this, everything became more apparent, and new teachers presented themselves to me—and have ever since.

Several years ago, feeling particularly bogged down by too many responsibilities and not enough balance, I asked my spirit teachers for help. In response, I was guided to visit a counselor friend. "I know there must be something I need to learn to feel better. I just don't know what it is," I admitted to her. "Do you have any ideas?"

"I just heard about a workshop called the Hoffman Process," she said, handing me some literature. "It might be what you need—why don't you check it out?"

Just holding the brochure in my hand felt right. I knew that I had to go. Acting on pure instinct and guidance, I cleared my schedule for the next 10 days (which was no small feat) and was on my way 48 hours later. This proved to be one of the most profound healing classes I'd ever attended. It helped me clear the debris of self-sabotaging patterns I'd been stuck in for years and opened me up to even more profound intuitive channeling and healing. The way the workshop fell into my lap, timing and all, was a lifesaver. I knew that my spirit teachers had led me to this instruction as part of my spiritual growth.

I was so enriched by this experience that I've made it a personal practice to attend some type of spiritual classroom as a student once a year. This is one of the best decisions I've ever made. Not only has my life been deeply enhanced by these ongoing classes, but being a student has allowed me to feel supported, guided, and helped in this plane in so many profound ways. I will always be an active spiritual student, because the more I learn, the more I realize there is more to know, and the happier and more peaceful and creative I become. I want to enjoy this for as long as possible.

I'm often amused at how people ignore the advice from their spirit teachers, especially when it would clearly help them. Alex, a promising theater major, made no effort to pursue this as a career once he graduated. Instead, he settled on being a financial advisor, selling services he didn't care much about. It was no wonder he was unfulfilled and bored. I tried countless times to relay a message from his spirit teachers to take some creative risks and join an improvisational theater class, but he tuned me out each time. "It's not practical," he'd say, even though my sixth sense said it was. He ignored me, maybe because he was afraid of failure or disappointment. We had the same conversation over and over for three years with no change.

One day Alex showed up with several catalogs from the Chicago Center for the Performing Arts. Smiling, he shook the literature at me and asked, "Are you responsible for sending me these?"

Looking them over, I said, "No, but I wish I were because it's exactly where you need to go."

"I started receiving copy after copy of the same catalog every day for the past two weeks," he said. "I felt like the school was stalking me. Do you think someone's trying to tell me something?"

"Gee, I don't know, Alex. But given the past five intuitive readings you've had with me, what do you think?"

Alex took the hint and signed up for an introductory improvisational class that day. The last I heard was that he loved acting and was still pursuing it. I don't know if he ever got any professional work, but that wasn't the point—what he got from the class was the opportunity to express his true self.

Spirit teachers are here to guide you to be your extraordinary self, but to benefit from their messages you have to be open to learning. A willingness to be a student throughout your entire life is fundamental to true intuitive living. It opens up the avenues for your spirit teachers to help you discover fantastic opportunities and new facets of yourself every day.

In every reading I do, a spirit teacher shows up, offering recommendations for growth that would greatly benefit my client's soul. In my view, this is the point of getting a reading. Yet despite these suggestions, many people tune this guidance out and refuse to listen. They use excuses such as, "I'll just read a book," "I don't like groups," or "I don't have the time," even though being a student would bring new tools, forward movement, and open them up to more ways to enjoy life.

The most common response I hear is, "I know I have to learn this. I don't know why I don't." I do. Soul growth is not easy. It asks us to self-reflect, change our behavior, make better choices, be honest, acknowledge our resistance, move through our discomfort, stop our co-dependencies, and clean up our act. That's *not* easy. However, I do like to remind my clients that it's easier than not learning these things and having our problems just get worse, which they will. In the end, no one escapes their soul lessons, although, for some of us, it takes lifetimes to learn them.

One of my favorite sayings, which I often cite to students and clients who resist being open to learning, comes from the *I Ching*, and it says: "There is something very limited about an exclusively self-taught man."

With a beginner's mind and heart, a student mindset makes us available to assistance from all directions, both from above and on earth. Ask your ego to step aside and let your spirit enjoy being a student of life. See this as your endless opportunity to make life better. Embody the saying "I don't know, but I'm willing to learn." Then let your spirit teachers lead you to where you can do just that.

Woo-Woo Workout

Become aware of your spirit teachers. Notice how they are communicating as well as what you are being invited to learn. They're not very far away—in fact, they're some of the first guides who will come through and get your attention. And to grease the wheels of learning, why not attend at least one new class?

To get started, try my free online course Card Deck for Beginners, at soniachoquette.net/courses, with the access code **Vibes**. This course will teach you how to work with my oracle decks to learn your soul lessons in any situation that arises in life. From there, call to mind other things you've always wanted to learn. From French to tango, Reiki to rock-climbing, learning keeps you young, creative, and present to the best things in life. It doesn't really matter what you are learning as long as you see life as your classroom and sit in the front row, ready to go.

Also, notice if your spirit teachers have been trying to contact you. Have any books fallen on your head lately? Has anyone invited you to a lecture or a class or made you aware of a group that focuses on a specific area of learning that interests you? Have you happened upon any podcast that opened you to new horizons? I have a weekly podcast with my two daughters, Sonia and Sabrina, called *It's All Related: Welcome to the Family*, all about trusting your vibes and being intuitive. It's a lot of fun to listen to.

Be honest. Can you comfortably become a student without feeling small or inferior? If so, you're on your way to intuitive expansion. Don't make this difficult—start by studying something fun. Attaining knowledge is a way to make your life richer. Learning isn't intended to "fix" you, because you're not broken. It only serves to empower you . . . and that's the whole point of becoming more intuitive in the first place.

Woo-Woo Wisdom

Be willing to learn.

PART VI

THE INTUITIVE
ADVANTAGE

EXPECT THE BEST

Perhaps one of the more significant distinctions between five-sensory and six-sensory people is that five-sensories worry a lot about how they're going to make it in the world. In contrast, six-sensories, the woo-woos of the world, just know in their hearts that the Universe will be there to help them in every way. In other words, five-sensory people experience life more as a battle to fight, while six-sensories often see it as a game to play, enjoy, and win.

The greatest advantage of letting intuition lead is feeling free of the need to figure life out. Trying to mentally control the world is an all-consuming and exhaustive effort, and quite frankly, it's a useless pursuit. Those who need to figure things out before taking a risk never live in the way they want to. Fear of making a mistake or losing control—or any number of other imagined ego failures—keeps people playing it safe without venturing into what speaks to their hearts.

Take my client Yvonne, for instance. Yvonne was miserable being an airline agent and longed to work with animals instead, yet she couldn't figure out how to secure a job with animals that matched her present pay. Fear of going broke, of not finding a good job, and of losing her insurance, among other things, kept her from pursuing her dream. She ignored her strong intuition and didn't do anything to even explore the possibilities, even as a side hobby. My encouragement didn't make a dent in her strong belief that she wouldn't make it in a field she loved—her ego simply wouldn't let her consider quitting her job or doing something part-time.

Now contrast this with my client Cleo, who was also unhappy in her job and drawn to work with animals. Unlike Yvonne, Cleo was willing to trust her vibes and follow her feelings even though she wasn't sure where they'd lead. She told me, "I know it's right, even if I don't have a job. Do you think that if I trust my vibes and go on faith alone, I'll be okay?"

I had no doubt—I knew that Cleo would prosper because her spirit would guide her toward open doors. I was her most enthusiastic cheerleader and suggested that the sooner she followed her vibes, the better. She soon began dog sitting and dog walking for a few friends. Then, one afternoon, her guides spoke in her ear, telling her: *doggie daycare.* The idea struck her as amusing, and at that moment, she decided to expand her services and start a daycare service for dogs. She advertised in the local pet stores and newspapers, offering dog owners a place where she'd walk, feed, and play with their pooches for the day.

Within a month, Cleo had 10 new clients (some of whom were famous) clamoring for their dogs to get into her doggie daycare. She was running a full-time business before she'd even printed up her business cards, and she's been prospering and having fun with the dogs ever since. Unlike Yvonne, Cleo expected support from the Universe and received it. Now she's riding the energy waves of life, doing exactly what she wanted and loving every minute of it.

Living an intuitive life definitely takes a leap of faith. Like soaring through the air on a trapeze, you have to let go of five-sensory fears and grab on to spirit, who catches you. There will be a brief moment when you'll be cut free from the known, but guess what? At that moment, you'll be flying and then caught by the Universe. It's only when you don't let go that you'll dangle in midair doing nothing.

Knowing that the Universe will always help you creates a vacuum of positive expectation. Whenever a vacuum is created, the Universe will rush in to fill it with its vibratory equivalent. In other words, you get what you expect. So if two people drive into

Manhattan on a Friday night, and one expects to find a parking space and the other doesn't, they'll both be right: the person who expects support will get it, while the one who doesn't won't.

Expecting support from the Universe instantly raises your vibration to a six-sensory level because in doing so you acknowledge the truth of who you are: a beautiful beloved spirit, not some lost and random barking dog paddling adrift at sea. In this way, you'll bloom in the garden of life and open up to receiving the blessings and support available to you. Even though some people are cynical and doubt this, I suggest they try before they decide. Expectation is an energy magnet that draws to you whatever you ask for. Because I've always expected the best, I attract it again and again. Some call this luck; it's actually Divine Law.

Five-sensory people obsess endlessly over the *how*s of life: How will I make it? How will I meet someone who loves me? How can I sustain the romance I have now? How can I be sure of anything and everything? Six-sensory people don't concern themselves with how—they focus on what they want and what they can do to get it. They leave the *how*s up to Divine Mystery.

In my 50 years of teaching people the way to an extraordinary life, I've never heard a single success story from a person who needed to know how before following a dream. My mother used to say, "If God gives you the idea, He'll show the way as well." I know from experience that this is absolutely true—the Universe has always been more creative about making my dreams come true than I could have ever been.

One common illusion five-sensory folks have about six-sensory people is that we know everything in advance. The truth is that we rarely do, but we don't need to. We know what isn't working now, and we feel and trust that if we follow our inner wisdom, the Universe will take care of us like it does all its beautiful creations. The only thing we can guarantee is that ignoring our spirit and clinging to our fears will steal our joy and waste our life. If we're willing to follow our heart, the Universe will show us the way to success.

Woo-Woo Workout

Expect the best from the Universe. Allow your mind and heart to open and ask yourself how many beautiful gifts you can receive. Raise the mental and emotional ceiling of good things you allow yourself, and invite more support each hour of the day.

When you go to work, expect the commute to be painless; expect to get the best parking space or seat on the train; expect your boss, co-workers, and clients to appreciate you; expect people to smile at you and greet you; expect your meetings to go smoothly and your work to be brilliant.

If you're single and looking for love, expect to meet someone fabulous and interested in you. If you're in a relationship, expect your partner to dazzle you with romance. When the phone rings, expect good news. When the mail comes, expect wonderful surprises, even presents. When confronted with a problem, expect uncomplicated and fast solutions. Above all, expect love and assistance to rain upon you for all of your days.

Woo-Woo Wisdom

Be open to positive surprises.

EMBRACE THE ADVENTURE

Five-sensory people often go through life with their foot on the brake. In contrast, six-sensories have their foot on the gas. They're open, enthusiastic, and adventurous. They expect the best from life, plan positively, and are open to life's gifts and opportunities. They simply cannot get enough of it!

Being passionate and optimistic about life changes your vibration from resistance and defense to attraction and receptivity. When you love life, life loves you back. So when you dive into it with exuberance and joy, life returns the same back to you, in the extraordinary way of people and opportunities and serendipitous connections. The more you love life by fully engaging in what feeds your soul, and the more you spread that love around, the more love comes back with things that feed your soul. Your inner compass follows your attitude and values. If you have a positive expectation, your inner compass leads you to it.

Negative people have trouble with what I'm saying because it doesn't match their experience at all. "How can you deny all the horrible things happening in the world with your rose-colored glasses?" someone wrote to me last week. I do not deny the horrible things; I am simply not part of the energy creating or contributing to these awful things. They are not the only things happening in the world. There are just as many fabulous, awe-inspiring events, discoveries, love affairs, and beautiful creations happening, as well. I am busy contributing to those energies and asking my vibes to lead me to more and more ways to do that. If you are committed to a negative world outlook, that is what you will experience. If you are a hammer, everything becomes a nail. My teacher Dr. Tully once said, "If you want to help the miserable of the world, don't be one of them."

Life lovers have incredible charisma and charm, drawing people to them because their vibration is compelling and positive. They elevate your vibration to where it's rising above the clouds in an airplane and into clear space. In the same way, seeing and seeking the good in life carries you above the dark cloud cover and into endless sunshine. Below the clouds in the lower frequencies, the endless dogfights of ego continue. Above the clouds is your spirit, which carries you over the drama and into a wide-open creative bandwidth.

But shifting from ego to spirit isn't easy. It comes from making a conscious choice to be in a high, loving vibration, and this takes discipline and commitment. It's much easier to be cynical and dark, which explains why so many people live miserable lives. The ego loves to suffer—and the louder, the better. Right now, the egos on the earth plane are in a barking melee. Lovers of life reject this grim death sentence, making intentional choices to appreciate and enjoy the gifts that life offers. They light up a room like the Christmas tree in Rockefeller Center. The Dalai Lama is such a lover, but so are many other folks in the world. For example, there's Remi, who worked at my boxing gym in Paris. His vibration is delightful—every other sound out of his mouth is a laugh. He's always inspiring others, telling jokes, offering suggestions, and letting people know how much he loves his life and wants them to love theirs. So some days, when I'm feeling drained and uninspired and don't feel like working out, I go anyway just to get a dose of Remi.

I have another friend named Wendy, who always looks for and sees the best in any situation. She appreciates the small stuff in life and has an open heart and door for everyone. Being with her is like taking a mini vacation—in her presence, I laugh nonstop as we find so much to enjoy. We talk about what we love, from croissants in a Parisian café to markets in Marrakesh to Italian comedies, Indian food, and bargains at resale shops. Just talking to her is food for my soul. Every time we are together, we share good vibes.

Wendy visited me in Paris just before the pandemic, and we went to our favorite café to enjoy a sandwich and a glass of white wine. Our French waiter couldn't have been nicer. That alone is a big deal in Paris, but more than being pleasant, he brought us dessert on the house. In Paris, that is a *miracle*. This made a big difference in our day. We nearly skipped home because we were in such a high, happy vibration.

I told Wendy her high vibration was contagious, and that waiter had felt her positive energy and it had opened his heart. This is why he was so nice and generous. This is how vibes work. They don't just lead us to good things, they also attract good things to us. Our frequency is a powerful force, broadcasting and beaming on a life-affirming level or a life-destroying one. People who broadcast doom and gloom are just as guilty of creating it as those they condemn.

To enter this vibration, dip your cup into the river of life and drink up joyfully, rather than turning your back on it. Most five-sensory people refuse to enjoy life's sweetness until, as one highly depressed client said, "I can get all my ducks in a row." Unfortunately, chasing and training "her ducks" to fall in line had wasted 50 years of her life—not one minute of which she had enjoyed.

Remember what makes you happy and then do that without delay—don't wait until all your problems are solved. Nurture yourself by doing what lifts your heart, tickles your funny bone, engages your curiosity, and stimulates your sense of wonder. Dance with life instead of fighting with it—don't postpone your fun because you have serious matters to suffer first. As a true life-lover once told me, "The minute a crisis hits, I go dancing. I'll deal with it better after I've danced." She's a girl after my own heart.

What do you love in life? Do you even know what brings you happiness and joy, what makes you feel content and at peace? What affirms to you that life is good and worth living? You'll never discover what it is if you wait until the rushing river of life calms down long enough for you to reflect.

I recently spoke to a client named Florence, a senior who was recovering from COVID and feeling very low and lethargic. She called to tell me she was afraid of dying and wanted to know if she was close. I was quiet for a moment, then said, "Florence, I'm not sure you are ready for the answer."

She gasped and said, "Oh no! Am I a goner?"

"No, worse," I said. "I'm sorry to say you will recover, and you have a long road ahead. But I see that you were hoping to die rather than make the changes you need to make so that you can enjoy life."

She was quiet for 10 seconds, then said, "I was half hoping I'd die because the life I have is miserable."

"The only reason you are miserable is that you choose to be," I answered. "I see you are loved, wealthy, and up until recently, healthy and strong. You will be again. But you also have no boundaries, and are being bullied by someone who is stealing your joy. What's up with that?"

Florence started crying. "I have a grandson who is addicted to meth and in jail. He has a girlfriend who is a recovering addict with three children. I let her move into a beautiful house I own worth a million dollars and she trashed it. I pay her bills, pick up their messes, and let them walk all over me. My grandson calls me from jail every chance he gets and tells me I'm selfish for not giving him more money. But he spends it all on God knows what, and the kids don't see a penny. I was half hoping if I died, I wouldn't have to deal with this nonsense anymore."

"Are you sure dying is the best solution you can come up with? It sounds extreme to me and not very creative."

Florence laughed. "What I really want to do is to sell this property, move away with my new husband, and start over in a town about fifty miles from here where we both have friends, and they can't find me. Our friends are wonderful. I just received a call that a new home came up for sale in their neighborhood. We could go tomorrow if I said yes."

"So you have the choice of saying yes to a good life or dying a martyr. Sounds like a clear choice to me."

"What about the kids?" she lamented. "I cannot leave them."

"I see they have already been moved to a foster home. They aren't with their mom."

"That's true," she admitted. "Their grandmother, the mother's mother, took the kids last week. That was a miracle I didn't expect."

"It's up to you now, Florence. Can you stand to have a good life even if the ones you love choose not to? It takes that kind of decision to step into a higher vibration. You can't force those who don't want to go to join you."

Florence was quiet and then said, "I have a confession to make. I've been feeling better for about a week. I just didn't want anyone to know so they'd leave me alone. I almost died, but I promised God if I didn't, I would let myself be happier. So I guess it's time to do that."

"If you listen to your vibes and stay out of your head, you can do that, Florence."

As we all know, the pandemic brought the world to its knees, not just Florence. We were all sent running for cover and had to find ways to move ahead in this new unknown. Some people freaked out. Their egos could not handle all this disruption. One of my longtime clients, Kay, wrote me an e-mail when the pandemic started to gain momentum in the spring of 2020, saying, "The apocalypse is here. I knew it was coming. I love you. I'm saying good-bye now before we all go up in deadly smoke." Kay is still here, by the way.

On the one hand, I think Kay was disappointed that her catastrophe didn't come. On the other, the pandemic was the most exciting thing that happened to her in ages. She had something real to worry about instead of all the imagined awful things she had previously been preoccupied with. While she buried her head under the covers and only came up to send the occasional doomsday e-mail, another friend, an Italian restaurant owner who faced potential catastrophic losses with the shutdown, had a very different response. He asked his spirit for a solution instead of freaking out. He has a big heart and wanted to help people get through this frightening time as best he could. He went to sleep one night, praying for an answer. The next morning it came to him. He got the idea to create pizza party to go, a delivered box with all the ingredients to make two large family pizzas with prepared crust, all the toppings, party hats and favors, a bottle of red wine, sodas for the kids, and a list of funny movies to watch on Netflix. It was an instant success. It was such a success, in fact, that they couldn't keep up with the demand.

This man went on to donate 1,000 pizzas to people who lost their jobs and had kids to support, which landed him in the local newspaper. Nearly everyone who read about his efforts supported the cause.

Between this new concept and the stimulus package he got from the government, he managed to keep all of his employees working and his restaurants going until the worst had passed. In the end, he made his pizza party to go a staple of his restaurants, and he is opening several new locations.

He said the pandemic was in many ways the best thing that happened to his business. Although it felt like taking a big risk, he didn't stop to think about his new plan. He just acted on his gut. "I wasn't afraid deep down," he said. "I knew it would work, and it did." Rather than wait for life to reassure him, he turned to his spirit and came up with new ways to be creative.

One of the most striking observations I've made is that countless people suffer from what I call "psychic anorexia"—that is, they starve their souls of the sweet, tasty elements of life and don't even think about what nurtures their spirits. Six-sensory spirit-guided people know that feeding their soul is as important and necessary to their well-being as feeding their body is. Soul-starvation makes people bitter, angry, and resentful, creating a toxic vibration that causes others to recoil, leaving them isolated and lonely.

Most of us starve our souls without even realizing it. We do it when we race through our days focused on the future, missing the scent of the flowers and the warmth of the sunshine; when we forget to go for a walk, look at the stars, enjoy a great conversation with a friend, or sit by the fire with a good book; when we watch too many newscasts or listen to too many tales of darkness, foregoing our bike rides, bubble baths, and playing with the dog.

Julia Cameron understands how essential it is to the intuitive and creative spirit to feed the soul and advocates what she calls an Artist Date, a once-a-week appointment to indulge in something your soul can feast on. It can be anything from scouring second-hand stores to roller skating in the park, to renting a foreign film and making a big bowl of popcorn, to gallery or museum hopping. Like a well that runs dry, the soul gets used up quickly and needs to be replenished. Doing so sprinkles "fairy dust" in your life. It makes the ordinary sparkle and attracts miracles and magic to your front door.

Are you willing to frolic in life's garden? Are you ready to feed and nurture your spirit? Are you able to address your psychic starvation and nourish your soul every day? Are you willing to sip the sweetness of life and then pass the cup of goodness to others? If you are, you'll experience all you desire and more.

If you feel stuck, change the channel to one that feeds your soul. Recognize the feast of life placed before you—enjoy a delicious meal, a fresh cup of coffee, birds singing, a warm breeze, a walk through the neighborhood, or a great novel. Only you know what nurtures your spirit, and when you find it, you'll bring light to yourself and those around you. The lovers of life are the healers of life because they're the believers of life.

Woo-Woo Workout

This week, lighten the load. Let go of the misery and have fun. Make it a spiritual value to enjoy yourself. Focus on what makes you smile and fills you with a sense of satisfaction. Once you identify what brings you joy, indulge in it every day. The more you enjoy life, the more joy life will offer you. Stop being too responsible, and make room for sweeter, more soul-soothing moments to take care of yourself. See how different life feels when you let yourself enjoy it, and notice how differently people act toward you.

Just like the song from *The Sound of Music*, name your favorite things. It will change your vibration and leave you feeling lighter. The entire world loves a lover, so this week, I encourage you to be a lover of life. Sit down at the banquet, feast, and enjoy!

Woo-Woo Wisdom

Enjoy life.

KNOW THAT THERE'S ALWAYS A SOLUTION

You can instantly tell five-sensory people from six-sensory people by their perspective on the world. Five-sensory people, peering through the viewfinder of the ego, look only at the surface of life and see obstacles and doom. Six sensories, connected to spirit, only see invitations and opportunities to be creative and grow.

Take Monica, who worked for a major airline as a flight attendant. One year she heard that her company was going to disappear off the face of the earth and she'd be losing her job any day. For the next 11 years, she fretted, fussed, and mentally rehearsed being unemployed until she convinced herself that she was a bag lady waiting to happen. Monica made herself sick with worry—never mind that the airline continued to fly and that she never missed a day of work or a paycheck. She spent all those years suffering, only to end up having another airline merge with her employer, which stabilized her job and gave her a substantial raise. Not only was all that anxiety a waste, but it also actually ruined her health.

Neil, Monica's six-sensory co-worker, viewed the instability much differently. Not wanting to be at the mercy of things outside his control, he turned the situation into an opportunity by using his days off to learn the upholstery trade. Over the next 11 years, between flights, Neil worked as a freelance upholsterer in his home studio, perfecting his skills and gaining clients and a good reputation. When the airline merger came through, Neil took an early buyout from the airline and quit, which allowed him travel benefits and left him free to continue to develop his own business. Today, he's creatively and financially comfortable, and he's his own boss to boot.

The reason I'm so familiar with this six-sensory flight attendant is that he's my brother. Even though he and Monica both started out in the same boat (so to speak), Neil focused on solutions while all Monica could see were problems. When we were growing up in a six-sensory home, our mother emphasized that there was a solution to every problem, and it was up to our sixth sense to discover it, as if it were a game. She often said that uncovering solutions was her favorite sport in life. Neil simply put that lesson to work.

Part of being intuitive means that you take the raw material life gives you and you use your creative ability to transform it into gold. My teachers taught me that when an obstacle appears in our life, it's the Universe's way of redirecting us closer to our heart's desire.

My client Matt was a particularly entrenched five-sensory being who viewed life as being against him. When the stock market took a massive downturn, he lost $200,000 in his retirement portfolio, which had taken him more than 25 years to build. The loss almost gave him a heart attack. "Why did my broker do this to me?" Matt lamented over and over again. Never mind that the entire country, and possibly the world, had suffered the same financial setback—he took it personally.

Matt failed to see what his six-sensory wife knew: they were living beyond their means. It was time to downsize, something Matt had resisted. The couple sold their home in Los Angeles and relocated to a simpler dwelling in a small town. Life was cheaper and more manageable, and the stress was significantly lower. Both

Matt and his wife were far happier, and his financial concerns eased considerably. In the meantime, the market crept back up, and in less than two years, their fiscal picture was better than ever, and the quality of their life had vastly improved. Matt still doesn't realize the gift he received; to this day, he dwells on the money he lost back in the crash.

Six-sensory people see any change of plans or unexpected setbacks as a time to grow, even when the upsets are painful. Kathy, a discontented financial consultant in New York, was on her way to an appointment at the World Trade Center on September 11, 2001. Realizing that she was a bit early, she stopped across the street for a cup of coffee, thus missing the terrorist attacks by minutes. The devastation and deep depression she felt in the aftermath eventually gave way to inspiration and creativity she'd never felt before.

Kathy's life was lonely and lacked meaning before the 9/11 tragedy, as most of her time was spent solely helping rich people make more money. She perceived being spared from death on that tragic day as a gift from God. She's since redirected her talents into a more soulful pursuit of fundraising for nonprofit organizations that work toward healing rage, racism, and abuse. While many of Kathy's five-sensory friends are still struggling to regain their footing, she's never felt more focused and full of determination to make a difference in the world. The disaster knocked her out of her five-sensory point of view and opened her heart and mind to a meaningful six-sensory, soul-based life.

On a more personal scale, Cleo and Gary changed the channel from five-sensory to six-sensory living after the tragic loss of their three-year-old daughter, Haley, to cancer. Before their little girl's death, both Cleo and Gary were strictly five-sensory, living a superficial, consumption-oriented life, adoring Haley but loathing each other. The family was thrown into chaos when Haley got sick, but Cleo's dormant psychic sense jumped into high gear. She knew in her heart that Haley wasn't going to make it, although they tried everything medically possible to keep her alive. Cleo spent the limited time they had together loving and appreciating Haley in every way. Her immature priorities gave way to learning to love others without condition. Despite the searing pain she felt, she recognized the gift her daughter's death offered. For the first time in her life, Cleo was living from her heart.

Gary had more trouble, for he felt hurt, betrayed, angry, out of control, and secretly responsible for his daughter's death. In his hopelessness, he pushed Cleo away—until she asked for a divorce. Stunned, Gary realized how controlling, angry, and selfish he'd been. He was intuitive enough to see even more devastating loss on the horizon with Cleo's leaving, so he reluctantly began to open his heart. This led the couple to completely disassemble their old life, including ending their careers, selling their home, relocating to a new town, and getting significant counseling. They not only salvaged their marriage, but Gary began the work of creating a life with new meaning. "The gift in Haley's death," he said, "is that I am slowly finding my way back to living."

Your heart-based knowledge helps you navigate life's obstacles with grace. Of course, you'll never be able to completely eliminate challenges because they're the fuel for our spiritual growth—but what the sixth sense does is wake you up to what's important. It gives you the insight and creative and psychic stamina to stay faithful to your soul's growth and recognize that all challenges are only secret highways to learning to love others without condition.

Five-sensory people often don't recognize that Divine Wisdom is always operating on their behalf. For instance, a five-sensory client called me, feeling distraught because a snowstorm had closed the roads to the airport, causing her and her family to be snowed in at a ski resort. Frustrated that everyone's plans were upset, and their lives elsewhere were marching on without them, my client forgot that usually, she, her husband, and their college-aged kids were all over the map and rarely in one place. Consequently, she missed out on enjoying the gift of two extra days with her family.

Being six-sensory is more than just being an optimist or having a good attitude. It means trusting that life is unfolding as it should and that it's leading you toward growth and opportunity. A six-sensory isn't merely willing to look on the bright side of challenging situations. Instead, they recognize that the obstacles we face or the changes we encounter are the Universe's way of prodding us to grow—even if it does seem unbearable at times. Without them, we could possibly miss life altogether. Five-sensory people take life's challenges personally, and see them as red lights and burdens, while six-sensory people see challenges as green lights and invitations for personal development.

My mother taught me that life never stops us—it just gives us a reason to come up with better ideas. We six-sensories love to come up with better ideas because we know that we have the full support and assistance of the Universe.

When I think of the things I might have pursued save for the Universe's interference, I'm incredibly grateful to have been rerouted—and for knowing in my heart that I was constantly being directed, despite my life's obstacles and disappointments, toward my highest and most creative good.

Woo-Woo Workout

This week, view every inconvenience, disappointment, challenge, and upset as an invitation to live in an extraordinary way. Embrace the opportunity and ask your spirit to guide you to the gift it holds.

Review past problems with the same scrutiny and list the positive things that have arisen from difficulties. Where were you inspired to try new ideas? When were you spared from making mistakes? How did you discover the gifts that arose from challenges? Whether it's a traffic jam, a missed appointment, a canceled date, a client who rejects you, or even an illness or death, there are new directions, new opportunities, new lessons, and new solutions that followed. Are you able to see them? Do you want to? Are you willing to stop being a victim of life and start being an inventor? Stop pushing upstream—surrender instead and learn to go with the flow. And know that for every problem, there is a solution. You just need to undertake the sport of finding it.

Woo-Woo Wisdom

Call in the solution; don't be stopped by the problem.

PART VII

TAKE THE
HIGH ROAD

ASK YOUR
HIGHER SELF
TO LEAD

By now, it should be crystal clear that letting your five-sensory, fearful barking-dog ego lead your life is a dead-end street. Even though the ego thinks it's protecting you by running all this interference, it isn't. The key to freedom is to get *around* the ego.

To bring it to heel once and for all, make the decision to allow your spirit to finally and fully take over. Otherwise, your barking-dog ego can keep you going in circles forever, stuck in what I call the "Yeah, but" syndrome: "Yeah, but what if I make a mistake? Yeah, but what if my feelings are wrong? Yeah, but what if people think I'm an idiot for being intuitive?" If you keep going along this way, you'll never trust what you've worked so hard to connect with—your spirit and your vibes.

One of my favorite strategies for overcoming blocks to the sixth sense is to engage my subconscious mind, which follows the lead of the spirit, not the ego. This is amazingly simple: I tell my subconscious mind to override any belief coming from my ego. In other words, rather than deconstructing each false belief, distorted emotion, or self-limiting behavior the ego puts in my way, I direct my subconscious, spirit mind to simply ignore my ego and step over all the blocks I have.

In my own life, for example, my ego didn't want to get a divorce from my husband because I'm not a quitter, I told myself. We said we would be married for life, and by God, we were going to be! However, my spirit was unhappy for a long time and our fights were harmful to both our souls. My six-sensory spontaneity stressed Patrick's five-sensory desire for control. There was no compromise. We lived in two separate Universes. And it became increasingly clear to me that I would never get this to change. We decided to get a divorce and go to a mediator. It was awful, to say the least. My ego did not want to do this at all. I was loyal; I was willing to go down with the ship. After we left this horrible session, Patrick called and left a message. He said, "Call me." Everything in my ego wanted to pick up the phone and agree. I asked my spirit to move me in the direction of my highest good. It moved me to walk away from the marriage and walk the Camino de Santiago a second time instead. My ego was crushed and confused for a while, but my spirit was not going back. I had to let go and move on, so my body just kept moving. I left the marriage and moved to Paris, which totally surprised me. I felt, for the first time in ages, free to be myself without a struggle. I never imagined asking my spirit to take over would move me in such a dramatic way, but I'm so happy it did. My life is rich, colorful, beautiful, exciting, calm, and extraordinary in so many ways. I am learning and growing more than I ever would have had I stayed stuck.

Directing your subconscious mind to bypass your ego makes life a lot more adventurous, to be sure, but more rewarding as well—especially if your ego has you presently jumping to conclusions, making errors in judgment, ignoring your intuition, or performing any number of self-defeating tricks. Your spirit will keep you on course and authentic. By overriding ego-based beliefs and behaviors that cut off your sixth sense, you'll overcome your self-sabotaging behavior, which leads to amazing and sometimes amusing results. When you invite your spirit to take over the reins of your life, it will, even if your ego isn't on board. Programming your subconscious mind to listen to and respond only to your spirit will keep you faithful to your vibes—and to what you really want. Finally, you will surrender entirely to Divine Will, get out of your own way, and let God's wisdom take over.

I had this in mind when I suggested to my client Roseanne that she direct her subconscious mind to listen only to her spirit. Roseanne's ego was making a terrible mess of things, and her latest dilemma concerned whether or not she should continue dating a certain man. "I don't know what to do about this guy," she said. "He's a freelance writer who scares me because that means his income isn't stable. He's been engaged twice and broken it off both times, which means he's noncommittal. He dresses like a slob, which embarrasses me. I don't know what to do. I like him, but so many things are wrong."

Instead of alleviating her relentless fears, which were clearly the product of her controlling ego, I suggested that Roseanne sidestep this ego interference by plugging directly into her spirit for guidance. It would have been fruitless to give her any other advice because her ego would have just dished up an even larger plate of confusion. To address her worries one by one would have gotten us nowhere—it was far more helpful for her to learn how to stop the flow of drivel at the source. That would open the way for her to trust her vibes and not depend on mine to guide her toward the correct answer—in this or any other situation.

After I told her all this, Roseanne asked me, wide-eyed, "Do you mean I can do that—I don't need you?"

"Yes."

"And I can trust what I get? You know I don't trust anything."

"Yes."

"Okay. What do I do?"

"Say 'I instruct my subconscious mind to only follow my spirit despite what my conscious mind says.'"

"That's it?"

"That's it."

I told Roseanne to repeat the sentence I gave her over and over again for the next few weeks, especially when she was worried or caught up in trying to figure things out. I told her to repeat it instead of calling friends and agonizing over what to do. She was skeptical, but I assured her that it would work a miracle and give her the answers she was looking for. So she did what I suggested. At first, she didn't feel any difference in her life. Then, one night, as Roseanne and her boyfriend were trying to decide their future, going around and around, and wasting time like always, her boyfriend finally pleaded, "Just tell me what you really want to do more than anything else. I'll do whatever you want."

She started to say, "I'd really like to go to a movie," but what came out was, "I'd just like to get married so that I don't have to think about whether or not you're the right one anymore."

In disbelief, he asked, "What did you say?"

Roseanne's spirit had taken over, so she continued to speak. "I know in my heart that you're right for me," she admitted, "and I don't want to screw it up with my fears like I do everything else."

He hesitated for a second, dumbfounded by her unexpected disclosure, then said, "Then that's what we should do."

And off they went and eloped, just like that. Before that moment, Roseanne had never done a spontaneous thing in her life, let alone trusted her heart and intuition, because she was such a slave to her ego's control. Yet in that instant, she was liberated. Her spirit freed her. Although she still wrestles with her ego to this day, it no longer stops her from trusting her vibes. While she's still learning how to be comfortable trusting her vibes her allegiance has permanently shifted away from her ego. (I'm happy to report that, six years later, Roseanne and her husband are still happily married and getting ready to have their first baby.)

Directing your subconscious mind to bypass your ego is not as difficult as it sounds. You do this anytime you focus on something or repeat anything over and over for a few days. We call that developing a habit. That habit imprints your subconscious mind, and the behavior starts occurring on its own.

When a newborn baby arrives, it knows nothing about taking care of itself. Yet in five to seven days, it learns how to find and suck its fingers or thumb for comfort—that's how quickly it has programmed its subconscious to create the habit of comforting itself. It takes about the same amount of time to develop any grown-up habit. So if you spend seven days programming your subconscious mind, it will override blocks to your intuition and keep you faithful to your vibes.

Years ago, when I was married, Patrick and I were flying home late one Sunday evening from Albuquerque via St. Louis on standby. When we arrived at the connecting flight's gate, we were dismayed to be told that there were 35 passengers ahead of us and the flight was already full, so our chances of getting on were zero.

Patrick thought that we should get a hotel room and try the next day. This made sense to me since it was late and there was no use standing around. Except my body wouldn't budge. He started to walk away, but I sat firmly in my chair. The flight filled up, a few standby passengers were called, and the attendant said, "That's it, folks. Try again tomorrow."

All the remaining passengers had gone—only he and I remained. "Let's go," Patrick said impatiently. I said okay, but my body still wouldn't budge, even though the plane was taxiing away. Finally, looking very annoyed, Patrick asked, "Well, are you coming?"

I said yes, but I still sat there. I wondered what on earth was the matter with me. Just then, the plane started returning to the terminal and the agent disappeared behind the door. Thirty seconds later, she got off with three passengers following her, two adults and a young child. She looked at us and said, "We made a mistake—there were only two seats left, and this family didn't want to split up."

Seeing that all the other passengers had left, she said, "I guess it's your lucky night." We hurriedly boarded and we were back in Chicago an hour later. I was extremely grateful to my spirit that night because my ego wanted to leave, and it wouldn't let me. It kept me right in that chair despite myself. *Thank you, God*, I thought as I snuggled into my comfortable bed just a few hours later.

The great thing about programming your subconscious mind to listen only to your spirit and not your ego is that it simplifies following your vibes and being six-sensory in a five-sensory world. When you invite your spirit to take charge of your life, you don't have to worry about goofing up and staying stuck in your ego, even if you want to. Your spirit can override your negative ego patterns if you ask it to, and then living a six-sensory life will become second nature.

Interestingly, many people do this already (although they may not realize it) when they spend time on those pursuits that move them into their hearts. For example, I have a friend who's a singer-songwriter. He's never taken a formal lesson in his life, yet he composes, sings, and plays beautiful, soulful ballads like a master. When asked where he gets his inspiration from, he responds, "I honestly don't know. I don't ever think about the songs—they simply show up."

My friends Loc and Carla both have that same connection to their Higher Selves regarding photography. They are artistic geniuses, but most of the time, neither can tell you how they prepared something or what inspired them—it's automatic. "I just do this and that and don't even know what I did or why, but it works," they both say. While they learned the basic mechanics of photography, their inspiration comes from a higher place.

The spirit is in charge anytime you express yourself through your talents. When you invite your spirit to run your life, the obstacles that your ego sets up disappear, or you simply hurdle over them. You stop thinking; you just know. This is how I do intuitive readings for clients. I, Sonia, the ego, don't do them—my spirit comes in and does the reading. I don't even think about what I say until I say it, but I trust that my spirit knows what it's doing. I get out of the way and let this happen. I don't even remember what I say most days, but it makes perfect sense to my clients.

Perhaps you, too, already have your spirit running some part of your life. If so, continue whatever it is and don't think about it. The best part about giving your spirit executive status to override any resistance to your intuition is that it makes the transition to living in an extraordinary way much easier. It's a lot less taxing to your emotional system, takes less energy, brings about positive outcomes, produces brilliant results, and gives your brain a break. I believe it even makes you younger.

The way to influence your subconscious mind to cooperate and shift its alliances from ego to spirit is through repetition and consistency, so repeat your intention over and over until it clicks. The simpler the mantra, the better. Mine is "Spirit, lead." And it does. Yours can too.

Woo-Woo Workout

Repeat this phrase often: "Subconscious mind, let my spirit lead." Write it on slips of paper and tape them in prominent places throughout your home and workspace as a constant visual reminder. The minute you find yourself worrying, struggling, or questioning over what to do, again repeat: "Spirit, lead."

Make a note of all those areas where your spirit is already on the job. How do things flow in these areas? Do you like it? Finally, add a little music to your mantra, singing it to yourself rather than just saying it. The subconscious mind responds best to music, so if you sing it, it will stick.

Woo-Woo Wisdom

Let your spirit lead.

ALWAYS SEEK
THE TRUTH

One of the great discoveries you'll make when you open your intuitive channel is clairvoyance, or "clear vision." But before you can activate this extrasensory perception, start by noticing what's right in front of your nose. Unfortunately, a great many five-sensory people tend to be careless in their observations of the world. They quickly glance at what is around them, invent stories, project their opinions, and make false assumptions about others, all of which are inaccurate. These mistakes can lead to all sorts of misunderstandings and lost opportunities.

The basis of clairvoyance is to study who and what's actually in front of you without projection, distortion, bias, sentimentality, or fear. In other words, seeing what's *really* there and not what you want to see. This kind of lucid and objective perception allows you to see beyond the surface and into the essence of things. This takes attention and practice. The more accurately you perceive the world and the people around you, the deeper and more profound your intuitive insights will be.

To develop your clairvoyant abilities, start by suspending your opinion of others and of things, and observe life more closely. Be curious. Watch, and learn. Study every detail, every muscle twitch, every habit a person has, like a detective. This all reveals so much about who a person is. The same goes for places and things. Clairvoyance is the art of not only being insightful in your perceptions but also seeing past a person's protective facade and defensive posturing to their true spirit. This only happens when your spirit, not your ego, is the observer. You can see what's real in others from a place that's real in *you*.

The key is to observe without overlaying your perceptions with projections, stories, and assumptions. For example, have you ever tried to tell someone about something, and 30 seconds into your account, their response is "I know." Not "I know" from a deeply intuitive place of understanding, but rather "I know" from an attitude of "I am already aware of everything there is to know about what you are talking about, so I don't have to listen or learn a thing more from you."

I had that experience very recently. I am presently revising this book from Mallorca, Spain, where I am considering a move to. Because I'm on an exploratory trip, I am using every chance to talk to the locals about various aspects of living here and investigating multiple places. One day, I took a taxi from a small town named Soller to a larger city, Palma. Since it was a 20-minute drive, I chatted with my taxi driver, Pierre, and asked him about living here. The first thing he said was, "You're lucky to ask me. I know *everything* about this area." Pierre proceeded to tell me that Soller was full of busybodies who gossiped all day long and was not a good place to live. But he said, where he lived, about 15 minutes away, closer to the sea, everyone was far more sophisticated and minded their own business. He also told me he had a boat and loved the sea, and anyone who did not was an idiot. I smiled when he said that because I don't love the sea. I'm a mountain person. When I tried to share with him some of the things I had learned from the owner of the house where I am staying, he cut me off, saying, "I know, I know," then went right back to his critique of non-sailing people outside his village.

Coming back from Palma, I chatted with another taxi driver. I posed the same questions about the area to him. This driver spent the next 25 minutes telling me that the city where he lived,

Palma, was great, but where I was going was full of arrogant snobs and ignorant people who own boats.

When I arrived at my next destination, I then spoke with a friend who has lived there for 10 years and asked about her experience. She proceeded to say Soller was the best place she had ever lived in her life and that the people were open, warm, friendly, and helpful.

All three people shared "the truth" about Soller. None was the absolute truth, however. It was their subjective truth. Each of their opinions only reflected their own perceptions and priorities, and not a complete perspective of the place. I decided to ignore everyone and use my clairvoyance to assess the area instead.

Poor observation, or ego perception, is almost always to blame for our problems with others. This is especially true when we've been hurt or feel betrayed by someone and feel it was done on purpose. For example, I spoke with a client recently who was outraged and devastated that her husband left her for his assistant. She couldn't believe he could do this to her. Yet, if she'd been objective and had viewed the situation from her spirit's vantage point, she would have remembered that he'd left two previous marriages for other women—my client being the new woman herself at one time. She also would have acknowledged that her husband had long withdrawn from being intimate with her, he'd spoken often of feeling depressed, and he suffered from several addictions that prevented him from being present to anyone. Incredibly, she didn't see any of these signs as spelling doom for her marriage. I believe that she didn't see them because she didn't want to.

I had another client who, whenever she looked at an overweight person, told herself that they must be lazy. Her judgment became a problem at work, where she had to team up with several larger-sized co-workers. Her projections prevented her from being open to their contributions. She assumed she needed to do all the work herself, rejecting their creative ideas and contributions. They, in turn, felt judged and tuned out. Ultimately, resenting her control, her team members quit, one after the other, and she did end up doing all the work. She never saw the problem until one of the "lazy" ones started an advertising agency, and in the first year won two industry awards of excellence. My client was forced to take a deeper look at how her own prejudices had blinded her to her co-workers' enormous talents.

Just as our inability to accurately see harms us when we project through negative filters, it can also backfire just as easily when we project through positive ones. For example, a student of mine ran a busy design firm. She was so desperate for a personal assistant that she called a temp agency, who sent over a woman who seemed very nice. Grateful for the help, my student latched on to this woman without asking too many questions, placing complete confidence in her before she'd properly scrutinized her. My student gave her house keys, bank deposits, and even the authority to sign contracts, all the while singing her praises.

This went on for three months until one day, the bank called to tell her that she was overdrawn by $20,000. She called her assistant, who outright admitted that she took the money.

Stunned and hurt, my student asked, "But why? I was so good to you."

"Because you're rich and don't need it, and I do," the woman said, and hung up.

Reeling from disbelief, my student called the temp agency to find out more about this woman so that she could press charges, only to discover it was no longer in business. Her carelessness was an expensive and painful lesson.

Not only do we bury our heads in the sand when it comes to life, but we also tend to do this when we fall in love. I remember once when a friend of mine called to tell me that she was madly in love and wanted me to meet her great new boyfriend. When I asked what he was like, she gushed that he was charming and charismatic, and best of all, looked exactly like Richard Gere.

When I met this man, he was insulting, barking into his cell phone throughout dinner, chewing with his mouth open, eating with his fingers, and talking over everyone at the table. As for looking like Richard Gere . . . no comment. They dated for two months, then suddenly broke up. She later said, "I don't know what I ever saw in him. He was the worst!"

Emotional blinders and assumptions are two poor habits that prevent you from gaining a clear view of what is. Without an accurate picture, you risk having a poor understanding of another person or situation and making the wrong choices. Presumptuous, ego-based observation may very well be at the root of most of your life's problems. If you'd only take the time to see into the situation correctly, from a spiritual perspective, before you draw conclusions or make plans, you could prevent many mistakes and open up to brilliant possibilities.

I once did a reading for a doctor in my apartment in Chicago years ago. After the reading, we talked about his desire to become more intuitive and I suggested he attend my six-week class, which was coming up.

"I wish I could," he said. "My wife would laugh me out of the house if I told her I was going to an intuitive development class. She doesn't believe in any of this. It makes for a lonely marriage because learning about intuition is my passion."

Then, just as he was putting on his coat, the doorbell rang. I went to the intercom to buzz my next client in and told her to come to the third floor. When I turned back, his face was totally white. "What's the matter?" I asked, surprised to see him looking so shaken.

"Oh my God. That was my wife coming in!" he gasped. Then, panicked, he gushed, "Do you have a back door so I can leave without running into her?" I showed him out the back way, laughing the entire time. He was so sure his perception of her was accurate that he was shocked to discover it wasn't. He preferred to run away rather than face reality. It showed me just how much we live in our own worlds and call it "the truth." Clairvoyance pulls us out of our warped inner theater and helps us connect to what is real at this moment in time.

My teacher Dr. Tully told me, "Never assume you know anyone completely." Doing so projects your ideas, your assumptions, and your limitations onto them. The more you practice seeing someone for who they really are, the closer you come to knowing and understanding that person. The way you look at the world is a habit, so you may be looking through some powerfully ingrained filters. Your beliefs, judgments, biases, and patterns will keep you from seeing the truth if you let them. As I've repeatedly stated, the spirit derails the ego, which doesn't want to give up the upper hand, so it runs interference to keep you from reality. Don't let it. There are ugly and painful conditions both out there and in us, and we often fear that seeing them is more than we can bear. But until we do, we can't heal them. Denial as a form of protection doesn't work. I've never known a case where ignoring the truth has served anyone. Have you? And yet I've been humbled to see how healing and powerful honest insight can be.

To activate your higher sense of clairvoyance, look past appearances and into people's hearts. Recognize that underneath the facade, each of us is simply a vulnerable human being who feels insecure and only wants to be loved and accepted. With that in mind, observe with neutral curiosity how others go about getting that love and acceptance. Watch and listen long and hard with an interested, open heart rather than a closed one, and you'll see just how similar we all are.

Ninety-nine percent of your problems could be avoided if you'd just activate your clear vision and look at your life and others more clearly and objectively. Doing so creates understanding, the foundation for clairvoyance. As Charlie, my teacher, once told me, "Sonia, your sixth sense is really a keen sense of the obvious." The more you want to see the truth, the clearer it will become. Clairvoyance develops gradually from accurate observation of the outer world to a deep and precise insight into the nonphysical world. The more you objectively observe what's real at the moment, the more you'll intuitively see what will unfold in the future. Likewise, the more you're receptive to the truth about a person, the more their truth will emerge.

To observe others accurately is to be more interested in them than in how you appear to them. If you're willing to shift your focus from yourself and place it squarely on discovering all you can about others, you'll see all you're looking for. The key to looking into others and understanding them on the deepest level is to look with loving neutrality, not with judgment or suspicion. The more you practice looking at life on this level, the more you'll activate your higher vision: clairvoyance.

I have a seven-month-old granddaughter, Sufi, who teaches me daily how to become even more clairvoyant. This morning, as she sat on my lap, she studied my face without blinking for about a full minute. She then leaned in close and examined my necklace. Next, she turned and grabbed my wrist and slowly observed my thin gold bracelet. Sufi took her time, first leaning in closely, then sitting back, affording herself two perspectives of the same things. She thoroughly and quietly studied everything. Then she looked up at me and burst into a big smile, delighted by her discoveries.

It's a shame we lose this curious open-mindedness. We miss so much when we merely glance life over as if we've seen it all before. We haven't. This intense curiosity to discover the truth of things is the basis for clairvoyance. It is an intuitive skill that reminds us there is always more than meets the eye.

I had a client, Rob, in Kansas, who bought an old Victorian house in the country quite a few years ago. "It was seriously dilapidated and required a lot of work," he said, "but the minute I walked, I could see how this house could be a gold mine. I can't quite explain, something in me made me have to buy it. It was downright weird." His friends and family tried to talk him out of it, saying the house was a money trap, but he didn't listen. A year into what turned out to be a nightmare renovation, he realized he needed to lay new flooring and perhaps even reinforce the foundation because the present one was too rotten. Resigned to yet another cost he hadn't counted on, he began to pull up the old floorboards himself. When he did, he discovered two large burlap bags filled with moldy $100 bills hiding underneath under the kitchen floor, along with a tiny bag of jewelry, including two diamond rings and 10 gold coins. In all, his find was worth more than $200,000 and over triple what he'd paid for the house.

Doing some research on the house after this, Rob discovered that the house was said to have belonged to a reputed bootlegger back in the day. Apparently, the legend was true, and the money he found was likely to have been money the guy made and hid from the feds or the mob.

Rob had had a clairvoyant sense about this house when he bought it, proving to be accurate. "I just knew I wasn't making a mistake when I took possession," he said.

"Aren't you glad you trusted your vibes even though at the time it looked like you were taking on a big mess?" I asked rhetorically, knowing full well the challenges and stress of renovating an old Victorian house, having done it once myself.

"Darn straight I am. I used a part of the money to finish the renovation. Shortly after I was done, I heard about something called Airbnb and signed up right away. At first, I had one or two guests every few months, but now I'm making a fortune in monthly rentals since the pandemic."

With clairvoyance, not only do you see what's on the physical plane, but you'll "see" with your inner eye what's on the energy plane as well. This leads to understanding, which then leads to creative and positive opportunities and prevents mistakes. It can even lead to a pot of gold, as it did for Rob.

Woo-Woo Workout

Try pretending that you are a detective looking for clues, and take a closer, more open-minded look at what's going on around you. Discover people as much as you can. Study facial expressions and body language. Be interested in seeing their spirit instead of concerning yourself about how *you* appear to them. Try to overlook people's facades and search for clarity and insight into who they really are. Look for their greatest fears, strengths, talents, even secret hearts' desires. Search for new details you haven't noticed before.

Ask your spirit to show you what is most important. Practice this with people you interact with every day, like your family, friends, and business associates. Close your eyes and observe that person with your inner eye. Ask questions such as: *What is the most crucial thing to see about this person? What am I not seeing with my eyes alone? Show me all possibilities in this relationship and all blind spots.*

What do you see that you've never seen before? Remember to view others without judging, projecting, or telling yourself a story about them. Be neutral, as if you were looking at a beautiful landscape. Simply observe and learn.

Woo-Woo Wisdom

Never assume you know anyone completely.

LOOK FOR THE DIVINE IN EVERYTHING

To see the world through the eyes of your spirit is to look from the Divine part of yourself, which means that you'll see the world through the eyes of God. Can you imagine this? Looking at the world from this perspective will remove bias, projection, and distortion, for God does not see obstacles and defenses set up by your ego. Not only will this shift in perception allow you to accurately view the physical world, but it will also allow you to see the energetic body of others. When your spirit sees the spirit in others, you'll be amazed at how much more beauty you'll see in people.

This was not the case with Penny, who came to see me because she was sick and tired of Marshall, her "freeloading husband." Marshall hadn't held a consistent job during the 10 years of their marriage, even though Penny had found him several positions in the computer industry. She ranted about how irresponsible he was and how he "just wanted to play with his tools." Until he got an actual paycheck, she couldn't fulfill her deepest desire to have children. She was nearly consumed with frustration over his unproductive life and wanted me to help her "make something out of the louse."

When I intuitively viewed Marshall, however, I didn't see anything resembling Penny's description. Instead, I saw a frustrated man who was very gifted with his hands and had several potential artistic and healing talents that, if developed, would be pretty valuable. He just wasn't ambitious in the same material way that his wife was. Although I could see that they could teach each other about life, it would be tough until they appreciated each other's spirits.

When I looked at this man from the eyes of God, as my clairvoyant training had taught me, I saw his hands glowing as if they were made of gold. Then, searching more deeply, I perceived talent as a massage therapist and a sculptor, both of which would channel enormous healing and would fulfill his purpose. I shared these observations with Penny, but she scoffed. "Yeah, he says the same thing," she said. "That something with art or massage therapy is what he wants to do, and, hey, so would I! But that won't pay the rent. He needs a real job working on a computer or selling something like I do."

Penny's comments sadly revealed her shortsightedness, not her husband's. Because she was so five-sensory, materially insecure, and unconscious of the soul, she couldn't perceive that Marshall's beautiful healing and artistic talents had any financial value. And because she couldn't see his skills through her eyes, she mistakenly decided they weren't real.

I suggested that perhaps the problem was hers, not his, and that if she could just see and value who he really was—an artist and healer—and support that, he could get on with his work and make a decent living, and they could have the family she wanted. It was a matter of first things first.

"You mean actually encourage the nonsense he does? You're as unrealistic as he is," she said.

Sadly, Penny never did see Marshall through God's eyes—she continued to indict him as a dreamer and a freeloader, and they soon divorced. Five years later, Marshall came to see me for a reading. After the divorce, he'd gone to massage school, and at the same time, he started sculpting in earnest. He married a woman he'd met at school who recognized, appreciated, and truly loved his talents. With her support, he began a private practice in massage therapy and eventually found an agent to represent his art. He sold six sculptures (from $2,000 to $7,000 each) in only 12 months and had a piece accepted by a small museum in Canada. I wasn't surprised—his talent was always there, and with the support of someone who shared his vision, it blossomed and found its way into the world.

Marshall's second wife saw Marshall accurately and by appreciating his talent activated his potential, like water in a neglected garden. Rather than being frustrated by not seeing what she wanted to see in him (as Penny had), his second wife intuitively "got" Marshall. She saw his spirit and talent and what he could become, and with her Divine view, he became that over time.

Looking through the eyes of God does far more than merely soften our view and motivate us to look for the good in people. It gives us the ability to see to the energy body itself, which can prove to be lifesaving.

My client Beth made a spiritual decision several years ago to look at the world and everyone in it through God's eyes. Her perceptions immediately began to reveal incredible things. One day she was sitting in a board meeting when her intuition flashed an image of the company president—a seemingly healthy and relatively young guy—having a heart attack. She blinked several times and tried to shake the image, but it persisted. She wasn't sure what to do, but when the meeting was over, she took a chance and approached him, very cautiously asking how he was feeling.

"Fine," he responded. "Why?"

She hesitated, then shared her vision with him, although she toned it down a lot. He laughed and assured her that he really was okay but added, "I'll tell you what—just to respect your input, I'll take it as a sign to get a checkup soon."

Three weeks later, Beth received a memo summoning her to the president's office. As she entered, she noticed that he looked pretty shaken. "Just because I'm a superstitious guy, I got a physical," he said. "It seems that I have some major heart blockages that

I wasn't aware of. So I'm going in for surgery this week. Do you know that you may have spared me a heart attack or worse?"

Beth was astounded and grateful that she'd dared to share what she saw with her boss. So was he.

Looking through the eyes of God allows you, as a higher conscious being, to see the truth about others and yourself on both a physical and energy plane. "The minute I began to look through God's eyes, the world shifted dramatically," said Jim, a student who was taking my psychic-awakening course. "Before I shifted my perception, I realized that I wasn't really looking into people at all. Instead, I was casting sideways glances at others and then making up terrible stories about them based upon my insecure and inaccurate observations. When I decided to look with the eyes of God, as you suggested, life brightened up, and people suddenly became quite beautiful. I wasn't merely looking at physical appearances anymore—I began to look into their eyes and could actually see their souls. This recognition was so healing, profound, and moving that no matter who I looked at, my heart burst wide open. I'm embarrassed to admit that at times I even felt like crying," he said. "Not only do I now see the soul of a person, but when I look, I actually 'get' who they are. I can't explain this in words, but on some organic level, I instantly understand others like I never did before."

Jim's experience is typical of what life looks like to us six-sensory people. Our vision raises an octave, and we have more capacity to perceive the energetic richness and complexity of the objects and people around us. We sense, and ultimately see, both physical bodies and energy bodies, including their auras.

My client Miriam had an exciting surprise when she decided to view the world through God's eyes: "I saw an incredible violet light radiating from the tree in my backyard, pulsating very gently but full of energy. It actually scared me," she said. "Then I looked at my garden, and an array of similar light bounced around the tops of my flowers. Always being a nature lover, I've appreciated the beauty of the physical world, but with this change in my perspective, life became so much more intensely beautiful that it moved me to tears. How could I have missed this, I wondered. It's so awesome!"

Looking through the eyes of God enables you to perceive and comprehend everything on a much deeper level than mere intellectual viewing can because your spirit's eye responds to a different vibration, one your physical eyes don't register. It also invites you to see the shape of the world to come, which reveals what creations will unfold and what your soul's intentions will express.

One of the most powerful ways to awaken clairvoyance in you is to become what my writing mentor and friend Julia calls "believing mirrors." Many years ago, I wanted to write a book on awakening the sixth sense but doubted my writing ability. Julia had no doubt that I could do it, and for the next six months, she chose to see me as a gifted and prolific writer. Her steady gaze, full of conviction and faith, reflected unwaveringly back to me, eventually resonated in my view of myself until I, too, had no doubt. At the end of the six months, basking in the gaze of those believing mirrors, I'd written my first book, *The Psychic Pathway*. I'm absolutely convinced that Julia's view of me as a writer was the reason I became one. Without her ability to see me as I wanted to be seen, I wonder if my dream would still be merely that—a dream.

The clients I've told this story to have said that I'm so lucky to have had believing mirrors from Julia, but they don't have such luck, so they're stuck. I was indeed fortunate and am deeply grateful. But ever since receiving Julia's gift, I've studied believing mirrors. I've found that the best way to attract them is to first *become* them. Choose to see and believe in other people's heart's desires and future creations, keeping the faith until they develop faith in themselves.

While Julia held a vision of me as a writer, I held a vision of her as a clairvoyant. Our reciprocal views arising from our spirits gave birth to my book and the beginning of her clairvoyant and psychic life. The key is to see the difference you'd like to see in the world. You can either look at the world from an unconscious, superficial, five-sensory point of view—focusing on flaws, perceiving separation through judgment and fear, and scaring yourself to death; or, using your sixth sense, seek to see the soul in others, to recognize and to appreciate the beauty in everyone and have compassion for all.

Woo-Woo Workout

View the world through God's eyes, especially in situations where you don't like what you see. What difference does this change in perception bring about? Are you open to seeing others through the eyes of your spirit? What can you now see that you previously missed?

Become believing eyes for someone and ask them to do the same for you. Next, start reflecting to one another the future version of who each of you wants to become. Then, look for one beautiful thing in every person you deal with and say so—don't give false compliments or empty flattery. Then do this with yourself every morning. It's easy to dismiss this part of the practice, but when you can look at yourself with genuine appreciation, you'll know that you've made the transition.

Woo-Woo Wisdom

See the spirit in all things.

PART VIII

THE ART OF INTUITIVE LIVING

BE LIGHTHEARTED

Here's a fun secret: the more lighthearted you are, the easier it is to tune in to your vibes. A light heart quiets your ego and automatically turns on your sixth sense. This opens you to healing vibes, guidance, and insight from your spirit and spirit helpers.

One of the best ways to lighten up is simply to laugh—a lot—for this raises your energy, opens your heart, and elevates your vibration instantly and effortlessly. Laughing not only lifts your awareness to a high frequency, but it also cleanses and repairs your aura, awakens your spirit, clears your outlook, and energizes your soul. When you laugh really hard, you lose yourself and merge, letting your spirit take over your entire body. Nothing has control over you if you can laugh at it.

Laughter helps you forget your troubles, even for a moment, and when that happens, your ego calms down and your spirit takes over, clearing away negativity, confusion, and anxiety. In my studies with Dr. Tully years ago, I learned that "laughter chases the devil away"—the devil being any illusion, distortion, fear, or confusion that throws you into doubt, scares you, or causes you to question your fundamental safety, worth, and goodness.

Taking yourself too seriously is an obstacle to trusting your vibes. Your "serious" or intellectual self is your ego posturing again, relentlessly trying to stay in charge. In contrast, your lighthearted, more playful self is your spirit allowing the Universe to run the show. This doesn't mean that what your spirit concerns itself with isn't important—it's that you don't want to confuse what's profound with what's serious. The profound teaches, heals, and deepens your capacity to love yourself and others more compassionately; the serious is usually just a defense mechanism to protect your ego from feeling vulnerable. Your self-important moments require you to be on guard because they're just your ego parading around and blocking you from accessing your spirit. To the spirit, nothing is serious enough to take away your light heart, not even death. Of course, you can have somber, sad moments and passages, such as when in grief or suffering a sudden loss.

Years ago I taught an intuitive development workshop at the Omega Institute in Rhinebeck, New York. The students in this particular group, for some reason, were taking themselves way too seriously for their own good; consequently, most of them had little luck tapping into their sixth sense. To help them move out of this blocked state, I encouraged them to make each other laugh. At first, they thought this was a stupid idea, but after a lot of cajoling, they gave in and tried.

They were a little rusty and not very funny initially, but eventually, the participants loosened up and became more amusing. Some started playing trombone with their armpits, while others began crossing their eyes and making funny faces. They pretended to be animals, hopping on one foot, making silly noises, and acting like a group of crazed kindergartners. The longer they tried, the funnier they became, until genuine hilarity caught on, making them laugh even more. For 15 minutes, everyone was so consumed with lighthearted silliness that I could barely get them to stop.

Once they'd calmed down a bit, I invited them to try again to exercise their intuitive muscles. Much to their amazement, in this free, lighthearted state of mind, they were able to successfully see into each other's lives and accurately tune in to things they couldn't have known before. They were able to describe homes, jobs, secret heart's desires, travel plans, and even great loves, although they were strangers to one another. No one remained blocked, and even the most doubting Thomases were surprised at how much a little humor improved their intuition.

Laughter connects you to the big picture and expands your view, as Charlie Goodman, my first intuitive teacher, taught me. Charlie introduced laughter as the front door to my sixth sense, and when I studied with him, he sometimes made me laugh so hard that tears ran down my cheeks. "No matter what you see or feel," he'd emphasize, "always keep a sense of humor about it."

My mother said it her own way: "The situation may be critical, but it's never serious." I found that the more I looked for the humor in things, the more I saw Divine spirit lending a guiding and humorous hand.

Cultivating our sense of humor increases our intuition and improves our health. If we become too self-absorbed and serious about our problems and melodramas, we disconnect from our more profound sense of who we are as beautiful spirits. We shrink from life instead of leaning into it. Laughter brings us back to ourselves and back to life.

What makes you laugh? Discover what tickles your funny bone and do it often. And if you're feeling depressed or don't even feel like smiling, try faking it. Believe it or not, this really works. One summer when I was teaching in San Francisco, a 78-year-old man told me that he'd just spent a week at a wellness center where he and other seriously depressed people were treated by being asked to lie down on the floor and laugh for 30 minutes a day, even if they didn't feel like it. The instructors told them to fake it if they had to, but they were required to do it. This man couldn't explain why, but he soon began to feel much better. By the end of the week, he'd left behind a depressed and heavy heart that had plagued him ever since his divorce 15 years before. It's no wonder—laughing chases away the dark shadows of life and instantly raises our vibration to a more evolved, wholesome state. It heals us. We reconnect with our spirits and break free of our ego stories. Faking it works because if we fake laugh enough, the humor angels eventually show up and turn the natural laughing gas (and healing) on.

In my intuitive practice, I've seen many people acting much too seriously in the name of spiritual growth, losing all humor, spontaneity, and joy because they think this work is "holy." My client Brenda, for instance, meditated for hours each day, ate only the purest organic food, gave herself wheat-grass enemas every morning, and wrapped herself in every amulet, crystal, talisman, and titanium gadget she could get her hands on for purification and protection. In pursuit of her "holiness," she read self-help books endlessly, attended countless workshops and lectures, and was a self-appointed expert on every New Age subject (which she felt she knew more about than her instructors did).

Yet for all her efforts, Brenda was one of the most humorless, bitter, and uncreative people I've ever known. She was so controlling that intuitively she had no connection to her soul, her heart, her humor, or anything really spiritual. In short, Brenda was a total drag. I suggested several times that she stop her incessant self-improvement and lighten up. Her efforts were almost ridiculous, and I tried to get her to see the humor in them. She didn't. And she was insulted when I said that while life is important, she shouldn't be quite so serious. She stormed out of my office, offended that I'd wasted her time.

It's important not to fall into the same trap that Brenda did— that is, letting your ego trick you into believing that life is a struggle and being spiritual is the greatest struggle of all. It isn't. I say to my students, don't be spiritual—be spirited. It's more fun. The spirited way of life is an adventure, meant to be more enjoyable than not. Even though it may be scary, painful, complex, challenging, and lonely at times, you are never alone and always have help from your spirit, angels, and guides.

Some people still can't distinguish between the ego and the spirit. Here's the difference: Your spirit is relaxed, forgiving, and laughs a lot, especially at you and your own antics, while your ego is critical, noisy, controlling, and rarely laughs at anything, especially itself. The spirit gently requests and trusts, while the ego demands and is suspicious. The spirit is light and easy and loves adventures; the ego can be harsh and heavy and avoids the unknown.

When I began to develop my sixth sense, Charlie, my teacher, instructed me to find something humorous to laugh at every day for three months. The kind of humor I was to look for, however, was not sarcasm, which is passed off as humor but is really thinly disguised anger or cynicism. That's the opposite of believing in life. Instead, I was sent off to find the sweet, silly, ridiculous, and absurd in life. This opened my heart and helped me feel more compassion for myself and my fellow human beings.

I'm eternally grateful for that assignment because it permanently changed my point of view. Now I automatically look for the humor first, no matter how dark a situation may be. In doing so, I see the spirit in everyone and the light in everything, and I know that whatever obstacle I face, I'll get through it and learn.

My spiritual role models are quick to smile and are generous and easy with their laughter. Thich Nhat Hanh, the Dalai Lama, Ram Dass, and my mom when she was alive all laugh as quickly as a babbling brook. When Mother Teresa was alive, she insisted that the nuns who worked in her home for the destitute and dying stop whatever they were doing and play for an hour every afternoon. This kept her helpers healthy and devoted and filled with joy and love as they tended the dying. If Mother Teresa, the Dalai Lama, and my mom could laugh with their life challenges, then indeed we can too. Laughing doesn't stop serious issues from arising in our life—instead, it channels the wisdom to handle and heal from them.

Woo-Woo Workout

This week, laugh a lot. Look for the humor in things: sing in the shower, create shampoo sculptures with your hair in the bathtub, make funny faces while brushing your teeth, read humorous books, rent comedies, go to a karaoke club with a friend and join in, call your best pal from grade school and reminisce, goof around with your kids, and play with your dog. Get over your seriousness and let your hair down! Again, fake it if you have to, but do a good job of it. Don't worry if you look foolish—the more ridiculous you are, the more enlightened you'll feel.

Notice how laughter increases your intuition. Be prepared for intuitive flashes of genius, bright ideas, unbelievable dreams, synchronicities, and the inner peace that will surely follow.

Woo-Woo Wisdom

Laugh.

FREE YOUR CREATIVITY

Intuition is an art, not a science, because it comes from your spirit and not your ego. One of the most effective ways to stimulate your intuition is to do something artistic and outside your thinking brain. Creative efforts of any kind act as psychic jumper cables to your intuitive self.

Many of my clients have reported receiving significant intuitive inspirations and downloads when involved in a creative project because they temporarily stop thinking and are just being. Maureen said that when she and her granddaughter were finger-painting one evening, at first she was merely humoring the child, but soon she got caught up in the project and lost herself in it. As she smeared away, laughing, and having fun with the mess, Maureen suddenly realized where she'd placed some important papers that she'd been searching for for weeks. She was able to retrieve them that night.

Ron was landscaping his yard, carefully laying out bulbs in a geometric pattern that he'd designed in his mind when he got a hit to create labyrinths with flowers. He drew the idea, told people about it, and they loved it. Ron soon began selling blueprints of his labyrinth patterns to his friends and acquaintances, which led to a business creating other landscape patterns for people's gardens. Eventually his blueprints were so much in demand that it eventually allowed him to quit the warehouse job he'd wanted to leave for years.

As a newly divorced mother, Miranda was feeling very lonely and isolated, so she enrolled in a watercolor-painting class. In the third session, she got a vibe to contact her best friend from high school, whom she hadn't spoken to in 30 years. Following her hunch, Miranda tracked her old friend down on Facebook and they Zoomed the next month. Upon learning that Miranda was single, her friend said, "You should meet my neighbor—he's single and a nice guy." A blind date was arranged, and the chemistry worked: after less than a year, Miranda and this man were engaged.

Sometimes people shy away from artful expression because they were told they aren't allowed to play on that playground. They're afraid to take creative risks because they were discouraged from freely expressing themselves when they were young somewhere along the line. Maybe they were told they weren't talented, or that art wouldn't earn them a living, or make them cool or popular like sports. These people were psychically injured, and that's unfortunate. Art and vibes are both natural expressions of the Divine spirit that we are all entitled to.

Each of us is intuitive and artistic—both are integral parts of our nature, although we may have been wrongly told otherwise in the past. Forget that. We each have our own unique way of being creative that reflects our soul's personality: some paint, some write, some sing, some cook, some garden, and some do magnificent ironing. The key is to be artful as opposed to being *an artist*, much like the difference between being *psychic* and being *a psychic*. Changing our understanding of these definitions and seeing them as a part of our intuitive heritage will start us on the path to being artfully intuitive.

We create art all the time through conversation or cooking or letter writing, although it may not be what five-sensory people consider artistic. Similarly, we all have intuition, because we all have a spirit, and art and intuition are the wings of our spirit. Being "artful," like being psychic, is just another way of expressing our spirit. To access your creative Self, leave your head, open your heart, and make a beautiful mess—color outside the lines of life and do things spontaneously, whimsically, honestly, and with courage, just as you did when you were young and still connected to your intuition. The more artfully you live, the more intuitive you'll be, and the more intuitive you are, the more artful you'll be.

This reminds me of what happened when I went on a 10-city book tour in support of my book *True Balance*. Because being artful is so essential to living an intuitive life, I asked a clairvoyant artist friend, Anne, to come with me to help audiences reactivate their artful self-expression. After each talk, we introduced a small art project for everyone to try. We distributed a big pile of crayons and index cards on the floor and asked each visitor to find a partner and work together to make a collaborative piece of art with the crayons on an index card. Most of the attendees on tour approached the exercise with the same skepticism that they did when it came to trusting their intuition, but at least they were willing to try. Once they got out of their heads, they forgot their fear and had fun, and made some very creative art.

One time we faced a very tough audience in Cincinnati— reserved and suspicious, their arms and legs were rigidly crossed, their lips were pursed tight, and they avoided eye contact with each other and us. I told stories and shared my ideas for balance, including some creative and even silly suggestions, but they didn't laugh at my jokes or try the exercises. I wondered what they were even doing there. But having endured several book tours, I knew better than to let this flatlining response throw me off balance.

However, when I looked at my friend, I could see that Anne was sweating bullets and feeling seriously challenged. Yet, true to her artful spirit, she leaped up, passed out the index cards, dumped the crayons, and introduced her project with great enthusiasm. No one budged. Undeterred, Anne tried again to encourage the audience to get out of their chairs and have some fun. Still no takers.

A stone-faced older woman dryly remarked, "Honey, you're in Cincinnati. In Cincinnati, we don't do crayons." Just then, a child no more than two years of age ran down the aisle heading for the kids' section of the bookstore. With her father following her, she saw the pile of crayons and dove into it, screaming, "Crayons! Look, Dad! Crayons!" Grabbing them by the handfuls, not believing her good luck, she looked at the deadpan crowd and shouted, "Crayons! Come on, everyone! Let's color!"

The little girl started coloring furiously on one index card after the other. Then, seeing that no one was moving, she urged them again to join in. This time it worked. One by one, the adults left their chairs, mesmerized by her delight. Finally, they grabbed crayons and began to color, and at that moment, the group itself transformed from black-and-white to color. To further fan their initial flame of enthusiasm, we put on some lively African drumming music, and the miracle became full-blown: Cincinnati was coloring! Laughing, moving to the music, exchanging cards, and drawing like mad, their spirits came alive. Once everyone joined in the act, the little girl popped back on her feet, said, "Bye," and ran off as suddenly as she'd appeared.

We spent a few more moments being "artful," as Anne called it, celebrating our creative genius, showing off our brightly colored works of art, and feeling beautifully balanced. Then we shut off the music, put away the crayons, and said good-bye. Our mission was accomplished: the crowd was liberated from the sterile prison of their intellect and rewired to their spirits. From the looks on their faces, we knew that they'd had a six-sensory breakthrough. As we were about to leave, no one moved. They'd had so much fun that they didn't want us to go.

One woman shouted from the back row, "Put the music back on—we want to party some more!"

I gently insisted that it was time to go when the little girl suddenly reappeared and started yanking on the hem of my dress. "Lady," she said, looking devastated, "the crayons are gone. Where are they?" And in the most desperate, heart-wrenching voice I've ever heard, she said, "I need them!"

Hers was a good question. Where did the crayons go? Where did the color and fun go from life? Human beings need art and spontaneity because they feed our souls and inspire our intuitive genius. We are all artists, poets, painters—all creators and inventors in our own way. For six-sensory intuitive spirit beings, however, being artistic, like being soulful, is not something we do once in a while. It's a way of life. Being artful means living life with heart, style, and zest. Like my two-year-old angel, those of us who live to trust our vibes are willing to take risks, make our mark, and turn ordinary moments into extraordinary adventures.

Now take a look at your life. Do you allow yourself to have artful moments? Can you let your creative spirit express itself freely? It can happen in lots of ways: Visit your local art supply or crafts store and let your spirit run free. Play with crayons and any other artful medium you desire. What does your intuitive genius want to do? Be generous in exploring your creative outlets.

The last time I was in an art supply store, I saw a little boy of about nine nearly having a fit over all the creative possibilities: Did he want paint? Markers? Chalk? Clay? Tempera? He couldn't decide because he wanted it all. But unfortunately, his mother didn't appreciate his excitement and tried to contain it. "You can't have all of this," she snapped as he fretted over what he would love most. "Choose one thing," she said, "and if you're good at it, I'll consider letting you try more. Otherwise, it's just a waste."

"That's not fair!" he said. "How can I be good at something if I can't try it first?" This made sense to me.

They continued to argue, and I prayed for the angels to come to the rescue. My vibes told me that the reason this mother was so cranky was that she was jealous. Being controlled by her ego, she was willing to let her son have a little artful fun, while she was unwilling to let herself have any.

I had compassion for her and wanted to give her spirit a little boost. When our eyes met, she nodded at me like one condescending mother to another. "These kids," she said, shaking her head. "If I let him, he'd take it all."

"I know what you mean," I said. "But if you did let him, then there wouldn't be any for you. That's what's not fair. He should get some art tools, and so should you. So what do you want to play with?"

Surprised, she wasn't sure how to answer. "I'm not here for me," she said. "I'm no artist."

"Sure you are. Who isn't, really? You just have to be willing to be a lousy artist."

She laughed, and her entire spirit opened up, "Well, that I can do."

"I believe you. And doesn't it sound like fun?"

With that thought in mind, she stopped policing her son and went off in search of her own artistic pot of gold. You see, putting your artfulness into action is the same as getting your intuitive engines up and running. Each requires that you reach inside yourself, pull out whatever's in your heart, and let it live, breathe, and dance simply because it's part of you—not because it meets someone else's standards or ideas.

When I ask my clients to do art as a way to unlock their intuition, I inevitably hear their ego recoiling at the idea. "I can't draw," "I don't paint," or "I'm terrible at art," they say. I tell them not to worry about it. After all, have you ever known a child under the age of four who didn't like to create, speak their truth, or trust their spirit? Probably not, because it's part of who we are and the way we're born. We just get it trained out of us. So "I'm not an artist" really means "I'm not someone else's idea of an artist."

If you think about it, that "someone else" probably wasn't much of an intuitive or much fun either, so let that notion go. Besides, being a "bad artist" really means being a good risk taker and being a beginner when necessary. Also, it means expressing your feelings, inspirations, and heartfelt callings, regardless of what others think or what you've been told.

When I say that you need to be artful to activate your sixth sense and live in your spirit, I'm not saying that you should go into the gallery business. Instead, I'm suggesting that you start taking more creative time for fun, nonintellectual, artistic pursuits. Everything you do can become art if you want it to and believe it is.

Woo-Woo Workout

Visit an art store, a music shop, a dance studio, a flower farm, a baking supply store, or some other place where a form of artistic expression calls you. Give yourself permission to be a lousy artist and take the risk of enjoying a few creative tools for fun. You don't have to spend a lot of money—a box of crayons and a pad of paper is all it takes. Even a small drum can be exciting with a bit of effort.

Spend a few minutes every day making bad art: doodle, color, scribble, dance, make music, sing, and enjoy. If you really want to express your spirit, display your creations in public by posting your work on the refrigerator, dancing in the living room, singing at the table, and appreciating yourself for doing so.

Approach everything you do with an artful flair. As my friend Anne says, "Art is the beautiful voice of your spirit." Intuition expresses itself through the heart, and most directly through art. With enough opportunity to play, I guarantee that your spirit will start shining through your art, too.

Woo-Woo Wisdom

We are all artists.

GET INSTANT
FEEDBACK

As a six-sensory, you will find it valuable and practical to have as many tools and techniques for exercising your vibes as possible. So when you're in doubt, need to make a choice, or want to find out the truth about something fast, you can do it directly without wasting time thinking about it. One means is to use kinesiology or muscle testing.

Kinesiology is an established intuitive art based on testing muscle response to positive or negative stimuli. A positive stimulation provokes a strong muscle response, whereas a negative stimulus results in a radical weakening of the muscle. Muscle testing can also establish the difference between life-supporting and life-draining situations, and most interesting of all, can discern true from false in any circumstance.

Muscle testing is relatively simple, and if done correctly, foolproof: a strong muscle response means something is supportive, desirable, or accurate, while a weak muscle response indicates that something is undesirable or false. The results help you find quick, clear answers and directions without involving your intellect, which can mislead you. The premise behind muscle testing is that your body is part of nature and is energetically connected to the whole, so it can reveal accurate information about the heart of everything in the Universe, especially when thinking is kept to a minimum. In addition, the body doesn't lie; thus, it can relay accurate feedback about things that affect you.

Kinesiology has been studied by scientists and doctors worldwide and is even used as a diagnostic tool in alternative medicine. A quantum physicist could probably explain why it works so well, but we six-sensory beings don't need to know why or how to use it. Instead, we use it because it makes intuitive sense to do so, knowing that our body can act as an accurate receiver of information and guides us as a natural part of its job.

Muscle testing gives you instant, intuitive feedback on anything at any time—whether you need a particular vitamin or supplement, whether the used car you want to purchase is a lemon, or whether the vacation destination you have in mind will have good weather during your visit. The options for using muscle testing as a psychic barometer are endless.

The best way to use this technique is the two-person method, in which another person helps you. Thankfully, the assistant needn't be six-sensory, as finding one can sometimes be challenging. (Having said that, for obvious reasons, a six-sensory helper is always preferred when doing muscle testing because you'll find that two intuitive people are better than one when verifying vibes.)

After finding a helper, place your right hand over your belly, and then extend your left arm out to the side and hold it there. Next, ask your helper to push down quickly on your left wrist while you gently resist. Don't struggle to keep your arm in place— the idea is to find a point of natural resistance and strength against the pressure, which will serve as the baseline for instant feedback. Once established, bring your question or concern to mind in the most neutral way possible without emotion or bias. Don't smile, talk, nod your head, or offer any comments while testing. It also helps to remove metal from your body and have the atmosphere be as quiet as possible.

Let's say that I want to do a muscle test to discover whether a specific soy-protein product would be beneficial to my health. I'd bring the product to mind as though I were looking at it, but I wouldn't interject my feelings about it—I'd avoid thoughts such as *I love the packaging, I like the flavor,* or *I think it's too expensive,* all of which come from emotion, not intuition. It's better to simply think soy product.

Once I have the product in mind, I'd extend my arm to the side and ask my body, "Can I ask this question?" Then I'd ask my helper to press gently down on my arm. If my arm muscles remained strong and resisted the pressure quickly, the answer would be yes, my body agrees to be consulted on this topic. On the other hand, if my arm weakened under pressure and dropped to my side, then my body would reveal my secret resistance to the question and accurately suggest that no, I'm not ready to ask.

If I received a yes, the next step would be to bring the topic to mind and simply say, "Sonia, soy product." Then my helper would press down on my arm again. If the product energized and supported me, my arm muscles would remain strong and resist pressure easily and remain firmly in place. If the product wasn't energizing, my arm muscles wouldn't withstand the pressure and would weaken. My arm would fall to my side even though I might want to resist. Of course, I can override this natural weakening and force my arm to remain strong, but not without doing so willfully and with great effort. If that's the case, I'm defeating the purpose of the exercise. If we do this with an open, neutral, and natural mindset, the body can very accurately counsel us on all matters. For example, I've used muscle testing to select carpets for my home, buy food at the market, and find the best flight to take when traveling.

When I go to the health-food store and see what's available, I tend to get overwhelmed and confused. I've been known to buy all sorts of vitamins and minerals that sound interesting at the time, but most of them end up sitting on the shelf unused. Since discovering muscle testing, however, that's no longer the case. If a product appeals to me, I simply muscle test it to determine whether I need it and if it's right for me. Doing this has simplified the matter of choosing vitamins and remedies significantly for me—I'm now down to a few supplements, and I feel great. I also muscle tested each of my daughters for the right vitamins as well.

They each had different results (my older daughter needed more of one thing than my younger one did), so muscle testing them helped me customize their supplements as well.

A six-sensory friend of mine used muscle testing to lose weight. With it, she discovered that wheat, cheese, and meat weren't good for her system, so she gave them up. On her new diet, she began to slim down instantly and has regained her energy, too. "With muscle testing, my diet nightmare was finally over once and for all," she said, "something that's been a problem for me ever since I was a teenager."

Another six-sensory client uses muscle testing to determine where to place investments. "I figured that my broker was only making educated guesses anyway," she said, "and his suggestions weren't infallible. So I don't ignore or disagree with what he suggests—I just muscle test it now. Between the two of us, I feel that I have all my bases covered."

When my daughter Sonia was entering high school, she was faced with the task of choosing which school would be best for her. She agonized over her decision for several weeks and finally approached me to muscle test her choices. Once we did, and she identified a specific school, she was relieved. "That's the school I've been most interested in all along," she told me. "This just confirms my vibes and makes it easier to decide."

I've used muscle testing to help locate people and things, and even used it once to determine whether a missing friend was still alive. My brother Anthony contacted me one evening, extremely upset, to say that a mutual friend of ours, Randy, an antique collector and dealer, had gone from his home in Colorado to Detroit to attend an antique show several weeks earlier and hadn't returned when he was scheduled to. He was driving alone, and my brother hadn't heard one word from him in several days.

Because Randy may have been transporting valuable antiques, Anthony was worried that maybe Randy had been robbed or had an accident and was unconscious and unknown in a hospital. To make matters worse, Randy's father had just died, and Anthony had no one to contact for information. So he came to me for help.

With the assistance of my daughter, we muscle tested for the answers. The results said that Randy was alive, safe, and strangely enough, back home in Colorado. I told Anthony the results and asked to be kept informed. The following day, my brother called to say that Randy had indeed arrived home safe and sound late the previous evening, just as I'd said. It turns out that our pal had decided to be spontaneous on his way home—he took the scenic route, stopping in small towns along the way looking for treasures, and he didn't think to notify anyone of his delay. Furious at Randy but greatly relieved, Anthony thanked me for at least one good night's sleep during our buddy's disappearance.

I muscle test for travel decisions, such as asking for hotel guidance, timing, weather information, and even how to pack. Why not? It's practical and highly accurate, as I found out when I ignored my answers when planning a trip to Albuquerque one spring. My muscle test said to pack for cold weather, although the news said that the city had enjoyed record warm temperatures for the previous 10 days. I believed the newspaper and figured that the good weather would continue, so I packed shorts and T-shirts.

When I arrived at the Albuquerque airport, it was 75 degrees, but by the time I picked up the rental car, the temperature had dropped 30. By the following day, it had snowed, so I had to go to a Walmart to get outfitted with long pants, boots, a sweatshirt, a hat, and a fleece jacket. Never again would I question what my muscle tests advised, I declared, as I stood there looking like Frosty the snowman.

My client Georgine had a similar experience with muscle testing versus logic, and thankfully she chose to heed the test results. Georgine had discovered a tiny lump in her left breast, so she went to her doctor for an exam. He ordered a mammogram, but it determined that nothing was wrong. Georgine's muscle test disagreed, suggesting that it was cancerous. She returned to her doctor and pushed for more tests, which he wouldn't approve. He said that she was imagining things and should relax. Georgine couldn't relax, so she got a second opinion. This time she had an ultrasound and a biopsy, which showed that she did have early-stage cancer. She was treated and is now on the mend.

I'm not saying that you should muscle test instead of getting a medical diagnosis, but it doesn't hurt to use it as a backup if you're in doubt. Doing so can, as in Georgine's case, shed light on areas that otherwise aren't very clear.

I have a friend who muscle tests for which bulbs to plant in his garden, which mechanic to work on his car, and even which client to contact on what day. It doesn't override or take the place of his rational mind—it just takes the place of doubt and insecurity. So if a choice is not clear and you're left to guess anyway, why not muscle test? Doing so is another way of tapping into the Universal mind for direction, which intuitive people love to do most.

The key to accurate muscle testing is to keep your subjective mind out of it. Don't ask your body for its opinion; ask your body for the truth. Try it yourself and you'll see what I mean. Someone once told me that real genius lies in making the complex simple. If that's the case, muscle testing is a genius tool for tuning in to your vibes.

Woo-Woo Workout

This week, muscle test every choice you have to make. Find your helpers and work together, and don't forget to start by asking your body, "May I ask this question?" This will eliminate all subconscious resistance and give you a clear channel. Once you get feedback, check it against your vibes: Do they resonate? Does it ring true? Does it feel right, even if it isn't what you want to hear? Take your information and use it. And see how much more peaceful you are when you remove doubt.

Woo-Woo Wisdom

Muscle test.

PART IX

THE HEART OF INTUITIVE LIVING

WATER THE AFRICAN VIOLETS

As you fully trust your vibes, you'll learn that what propels you beyond illusion and fear and enables you to live in a higher way is simply love. Love heals old wounds and clarifies your vision to help you tune in to what's genuine and authentic in others and yourself. Love activates your sixth sense best—when you operate from love, you live from your heart, awaken your spirit, and express yourself authentically to the world. Love allows you to feel, hear, understand, and flow with the hidden world of spirit with grace, style, and ease.

There are four basic ways in which energy from the heart flows, but only one opens you to fully function at your best as a creative, intuitive human being:

The first is when you love others freely; however, when it comes to receiving love in return, you block it and don't take it in. This way of loving flows one-way alone, outward, in what I call the "chronic exhale mode." People can get stuck in this mode if they've been taught that giving love is superior to receiving it, even though this isn't accurate and is, in fact, very damaging to one's spirit. Giving others love without allowing your store to be replenished will leave you physically burned out and psychically tuned out. Without enough love, your higher centers of awareness can't open and function properly.

Do you easily give love to others while neglecting your own heart and what it needs? Are you the first to offer help but the last to ask for it? If so, then, believe it or not, you're being controlled by your ego. Receiving love without guilt or resistance is fundamental to balanced intuitive living. Your spirit wants you to accept your vulnerability—your need to be loved—with grace and appreciation. In other words, don't perceive your need for love as a burden, but as an expression of your humanity.

Receiving love gracefully isn't easy, as I was reminded many years ago. It was my birthday, so Patrick and my daughters gave me an incredible celebration that began at five in the afternoon. To my surprise, my daughters and I were whisked away in a limousine on a birthday scavenger hunt. And to my utter embarrassment, at every stop along the way, one of my friends was waiting with confetti, cookies, and other treats for me. Next, the limo arrived at a beautiful hotel where Patrick was waiting for us. He escorted us to the penthouse, which had a magnificent view of the city, and we were served a private candlelit dinner.

You'd think that this would have been one of the happiest days of my life, but it wasn't. It was almost painful to be showered with so much love and attention, fanfare, and luxury. It was uncomfortable to be so indulged. I know it was only my defensive ego and not my spirit feeling this, but it was challenging, nonetheless. Instead of enjoying myself, I could hardly wait for it to be over.

The anxiety I felt from receiving so much more than was comfortable at the time finally leaked out when my kids presented me with their gifts. "Stop it," I pleaded. "This is too much." My daughter Sabrina got really frustrated. "You stop it, Mom," she said. "You always do nice things for us. Let us have a turn, and don't spoil our fun."

When I saw her expression and felt her heart, I understood. It was highly satisfying and empowering for my family to give me this big surprise. I knew how they felt, as I've enjoyed the same feelings many times in my life. For me to block my family's efforts would have robbed them of joy. So, rather than continue to let my ego control and block their love, I acknowledged how selfish it would be for me not to accept it. So I let go and jumped right into my heart . . . and loved every minute of the experience that remained.

The second way to experience love is when you accept love freely from others, but you hold your love back and refuse to give it in return. My spiritual teachers said that withholding love is actually a severe form of soul abuse. I agree. Our souls require love just as our bodies need oxygen, and withholding love is the psychic equivalent of suffocating someone. When we keep our love from others, we stifle their spirit. This is an insidious ego strategy for remaining in control, and it really does terrible psychic damage.

I'm sure that you've experienced the pain of being with a person with this type of heart. You probably became anxious and struggled harder to get their heart to open. If the withholding person kept it up, you might have panicked, gotten frantic, and wondered if you're even worthy of love, which is a grave soul injury. The person who kept their feelings locked up may feel temporarily powerful, but the human heart isn't designed to withhold love, which puts a terrible strain and pressure on it. Locking love away results in stress and heartache that can eventually cause physical damage if done chronically.

Very few conscious soul seekers imagine themselves withholding love, and most are more likely to be over-givers, if anything. But sometimes we hold back our love in such unconscious ways that even we are unaware of it. For example, my friend Klaus, one of the most aware people I know, told me the following story. He had some beautiful African violets in his office that he loved very much. One day, as he was rushing about, Klaus noticed that the blooms looked a little droopy and it occurred to him that they needed to be watered. He made a mental note to do so, but decided it wasn't worth stopping for at that moment. Days flew into each other, and Klaus kept seeing that his violets were drooping badly and seriously needed water. Each time, he noted that he needed to water them and then went on about his business.

A few more days whizzed by with no water for the flowers. By the end of the week, the poor plants had died. Seized with guilt, Klaus realized how he'd chosen to deny them what they needed and wondered why he'd done such a thing. He'd known in his heart that the violets required water, and although he believed he'd get around to it eventually, he never did.

Withholding love, like keeping water from a plant, is death to our spirit. When we disconnect from our hearts, get stuck in our heads, and fall back into following the ego's rules again, our ability to feel and respond to the truth dramatically diminishes. Klaus's spirit could see that his flowers were dying, but his heart couldn't feel it. Sadly, it took the loss of his prized plants to open his heart.

To live intuitively is to realize that love is the most important thing in the world and should never be put on hold. A six-sensory being loves first and lets other things follow. But, like Klaus, we're all guilty of withholding love without realizing it. We do it when we don't play with our kids, don't walk the dog, or forget to feed the fish or water the plants on time. We do it when we don't take a moment to chat with our neighbor, call our mom, or send condolences to a sick friend. Worst of all, we do it to ourselves when we don't stop to go to the bathroom when we have to, eat when we're hungry, or exercise. We do it when we work tirelessly and never play. We, like African violets, are hearty and can live a long time without what we need. But when we start to die, it's tough to revive us.

The third way to experience love is to neither give nor receive love. In this case, there's no energy exchange on a heart level at all. This is energetically known as being cold- or stone-hearted, and people like this are profoundly ill. They've completely succumbed to their very harsh and hurt ego and are in the dark night of the soul. Unfortunately, cold-hearted people are too isolated to receive help directly, but you can send them love to warm their hearts at a distance—and you should. We're all connected on a soul level, so when one of us is hurting, we all are. To send love, imagine the other person's heart warming and responding to your energy.

A cold heart occurs when people have been so violated or injured that they shut down completely. When you're around a cold-hearted person, don't take it personally—and for heaven's sake, don't take it upon yourself to heal this person on your own because you probably won't be able to. Instead, just expect the love you send to do its job and leave it up to the Universe to do the healing.

A cold heart is difficult to experience, and if you're exposed to such a person, be extra loving and compassionate to yourself as well as the bearer. Your intuitive battery can get drained very fast, so watch out. On the other hand, cold-hearted people need patience, and given time and love, their hearts will open.

The last way to love is the most joyous. When you give and receive love equally, this clearly reflects living in a higher way. When I was eight, after the frenzy of opening presents on Christmas morning, my younger sister, Soraya (who was two at the time), disappeared into the kitchen. She was gone for about 15 minutes, returning with presents of her own that she handed out as gleefully as the ones she had received. She gave everyone a piece of toast with butter, wrapped in toilet paper and thread. Hers was as sweet a gift as any I'd ever received, and I envied her giving them. Even then, I wondered which was more fun, giving or receiving. As I ate the toast and played with my new Charmin' Chatty doll, I decided that I loved both.

Six-sensory people know that love is the grease that lubricates the wheels of life. It's the magic elixir that empowers us to operate freely, joyously, and consciously in our surroundings. It transforms the world from a scary, dangerous place into a connected, beautiful Universe that's synchronistic and blessed.

If you feel frustrated about not having enough love in your life, you'll be happy to know that it's a self-generating vibration: the more you choose to love, the more love you'll create and the more love you'll attract. Love yourself first and fully, then love others without hesitation or stinginess, and see what happens. Like a magnet, it will draw you to more and more love and healing.

Love is the true foundation of intuitive living—so give it, accept it, inhale it, exhale it, and bask in it. And remember to water the African violets.

Woo-Woo Workout

Practice alternating between giving and receiving love. In the morning, make it your aim to show love immediately and without hesitation wherever you can. Through appreciation, compliments, assistance, patience, and acts of kindness and generosity, love whatever you're invited to love.

In the afternoon, open your heart to receiving love—expect and recognize it wherever and however it shows up. If you're given a compliment, accept it and say thank you. If someone asks you if you need anything, say yes, and identify it. Practice loving yourself: take a break, have a nap, or enjoy a few minutes of meditation. Appreciate yourself and say "I love myself," out loud.

Note how you feel. Is there any difference in your comfort between giving and receiving love? If so, strive to narrow the difference, and note, as you do this, how you begin to feel the power of spirit move you in life.

Woo-Woo Wisdom

Act on intuition before it's too late.

BE GENEROUS

The more we trust our vibes, the more we'll allow our Divine spirit to run our lives. It's not something to do occasionally if you want your life to shift upward and into a magical flow. Trusting your vibes is a way of life, one you get used to with practice. The more you trust your vibes, the more aligned with your spirit you become, the more aligned with your authentic self you become, and the better life goes. Guaranteed.

The quickest way to step into the spirit and get into this flow is to be generous and give freely rather than being stingy and withholding. This is not about the amount you share. It's about having a generous, giving attitude and love to share. When I began my metaphysical studies with Dr. Tully, one of the first lessons I learned was the law of reciprocity—that is, we get from life what we give to it. If we offer support, we'll get support. If we take an interest in others, others will be interested in us. The more we open our hearts to share ideas, time, kindness, enthusiasm, love, and appreciation, the more the same will return to us. It's that simple.

The secret to the law of reciprocity is to share freely, with no strings attached, no secret agenda, and no unspoken expectation of "now you owe me"—it's the art of giving in a way that's honest and willing, with no thought of return. Giving from the heart and sharing who you are and what you have with others creates opportunity, synchronicity, friendship, and harmony with others in life. You build balanced relationships this way and enter a gentler, more abundant way of living.

I don't think I've met many people who don't want to give. Most people want to be generous but may have a hard time doing so because they fear they don't have enough for themselves, let alone have anything to give anyone else. Much of this stems from how they were influenced as children. If people were taught to be generous by their parents, they're usually quite generous, but sharing becomes much more of a challenge if they were told to take care of number one and ignore the rest.

I had a friend who grew up in a large, poor family, where the child who cleaned the house the most, ran the most errands, and babysat the most was openly most loved. There was even a contest for "kid of the week" set up by their mother. While it may have gotten the kids to do everything needed to keep the bustling house in order (which was probably needed), to make the children compete for the love of their siblings was a terrible idea. This created the sense that love was as scarce as everything else, leading to competition for what little there was. As a result, the kids were both competitive and resentful of one another. Not surprisingly, attached to my friend's over-the-top generosity was an expectation of being loved that could never be satisfied. When I realized that whenever she gave anyone something, she resented it, I told her to stop giving me anything because I couldn't stand the bad vibes that came with the gift.

Meanwhile, another of my friends seemed hyper-focused on not spending a penny more than she had to. At lunch, she'd whip out the calculator to pay only for what she'd eaten and not a cent more. When we traveled together, she never paid the cab fares or tips. I eventually tired of being the expected giver, so I called her on it. She admitted that she rarely gave her fair share, but she explained that when she was young, debt collectors would show up on her doorstep to repossess things that her parents couldn't pay for. Consequently, she developed such a fear that her security would be taken away that she couldn't give anything without feeling great anxiety.

Both of my friends were stuck in a past where their anxious inner child ego said there was never enough, which made them afraid to give. And that's precisely what they got—not enough. Our spirit knows that there's always enough, and the more you give, the more you'll get. Jesus demonstrated this with the loaves and fishes: he fed thousands of people with five fish and two loaves because he just kept giving.

Being unwilling to give or stingy is a psychic wound that arises from either having your basic needs neglected as a child or simply refusing to stop being a child. In either case, the core of this wound is being disconnected from the true source, living from the ego and not your spirit, and relying on people and not your creative spirit and the Universe to provide for you. You can begin to heal this psychic injury by focusing on those areas in your life where you can and do give comfortably.

My client Magdalena came from a large Mexican household that struggled to make ends meet, so she has a problem spending money. Yet she's the first to make a huge batch of tamales and take it to the church potluck, or invite her children's friends over for homemade pizza, or arrange a bouquet of flowers from her own backyard and bring them to the shut-in down the block. In those ways, she gives with tremendous ease, and it makes her feel happy and secure. I also have a client who's tight with a dollar, but he'll show up when someone is moving and carry every last box up and down several flights of stairs. His generosity comes in the form of service with a smile. And I know a woman who hates volunteering—she'll do anything to avoid helping at her kid's school, but she never hesitates to write them a big check. All three of these people are being genuinely generous where they can be, and that's what matters. Generosity is our love language, and we each need to learn what ours is. If you haven't read Gary Chapman's terrific book *The Five Love Languages*, know that it can help you discover your love language, what kind of giving comes most effortlessly to you, and appreciate other people's love languages too. We are all different, and one size does not fit all when it comes to giving. There are many ways to give and express love, and the more ways we know to do this, the happier and more secure we feel. This is because the Universe gets in on the exchange and starts to be more and more generous with us in return. That's when extraordinary things start happening.

During the first lockdown of the pandemic, my client's son, Joshua, a junior in high school and math whiz, saw that parents needed help managing their kids' online schooling and juggling that with their new work-from-home routine. Rising to the occasion, Joshua offered free math tutoring classes for 7- to 10-year-olds in his neighborhood via Zoom. He made it more fun for the kids than the teachers at school by playing math games and telling jokes. It kept him sane and the kids learning. When the pandemic eased, one of the neighbor's families invited Joshua to join them on a five-star vacation to Mexico as a thank-you for his help. This was something he could never have dreamed up, and he had the time of his life.

Identify ways in which being generous comes easily to you and go from there. The thing to know is that the more authentically generous you are, the more you link into the eternally abundant web of life. The more you empty your cup to share with others, the more your cup will refill, not just materially, but in every way. The more giving you are, the more you'll activate your intuition, because generosity opens the heart, where your sixth sense originates, leading to more and more beautiful experiences and open doors than you can imagine.

Those who are generous in spirit and give fully without holding back are positively charismatic, and they draw things and people to them like magnets. These are the ones who easily share a laugh, give a compliment, take a moment to listen, appreciate those around them fully, and really notice what others do—and tell them so. This kind of benevolence costs nothing but gives everything. It comes from the spirit and leaves the ego behind. Anyone can afford to be generous in this way.

When you open your heart, you'll learn that there's no more spiritual merit in giving than in receiving—they're both equal facets of love. Practice being generous, beginning in small ways and gradually expanding. Then, every time you decide to give to another, open your heart to receive from others, as well. Whenever you are generous with another, be generous with yourself, too. As an example, I happily take my daughters to lunch or shopping whenever we are together, but I also give myself time to go on a long walk alone or get a pedicure.

Another measure of balance is giving spirit generously but not doing more for people than they're willing to do for themselves. For instance, if your friend constantly calls you for support in a crisis but never addresses or fixes the root problem, then going forward, listen with compassion, but don't try to solve her problem for her. Trust she will do it for herself—when she is ready. That's why it's *her* crisis, not *yours*. Now, of course, I'm not talking about a real crisis such as being in an accident or getting ill. I'm talking about creating perpetual drama that never goes away. If you take on someone else's problem, even in the spirit of generosity, another problem will simply follow behind it.

Giving is an art form that elevates your vibration an entire octave. Contributing from an authentic and generous place opens the heart and tunes you in to your spirit. To live generously is to live "full out" rather than be inhibited or restrained in any way. This means no holding back "just in case." Dive into the pool of life and make a splash instead of only putting your toes in the water. Allow and trust your spirit to run your life completely. Once you do, you'll never look back because that's when the extraordinary life begins.

Being generous means taking your attention off your ego and focusing it on those around you. If you don't feel charitable, the best cure is to be grateful. Stop thinking about what's in it for you and notice how much is already given to you. It can even be helpful to make a list of all that you've received in life. Instead of worrying about what you don't have, think of the Sufi master who, when his house burned down, said, "Good. Now I can appreciate the night stars."

Woo-Woo Workout

Pay attention to ways in which you naturally give, then do more of that. Next, observe how your generosity affects you physically, emotionally, and psychically. Note the areas in which you're not charitable and how that particular energy feels. Then, practice giving in those areas a little at a time: if you're cheap with money, invite someone to lunch and pay; if you're always rushed, give a loved one a few minutes more of your time; and if you're critical, give other people compliments, appreciation, and affection.

Play full out in life instead of holding back from life, fearing that you'll lose control. When you're with people, really be with them—help those who help you, listen to those who share their problems with you, and offer others more than you usually do. Begin each day by naming at least three things you're grateful for, striving for new ways to express gratitude each day.

Finally, be generous with yourself. Say yes instead of no to things you love, and let in more love, appreciation, and fun each day. Notice how these choices influence your intuition, your creativity, and your sixth sense. Write down all the intuitive gifts that show up this week.

Woo-Woo Wisdom

You get what you give.

SLOW DOWN

One of the great paradoxes of six-sensory living is that to amplify our intuition and get more accomplished, we must slow down. Conducting our life at a breakneck pace as we push into the future or obsess over the past only shuts down our vibes and scrambles our intuitive sensibilities. These behaviors are symptoms of living in our head—we're disconnected from our heart and not trusting the wisdom of the Universe. But by slowing down and focusing on the present, we shift our energy back to our heart, which opens up to provide inspiration and guidance again.

Sometimes simply stepping away from a situation and allowing a little space is all that's needed. As my teacher, Dr. Tully, often said, "Sometimes the most powerful thing you can do is nothing." What I've humbly come to understand after experiencing 50-plus years of intuitive living is that just because we're not doing something doesn't mean that something isn't being done. Something is being done behind the scenes in the unseen realm, and we need to make room for it.

Sometimes the mystery ingredient we need to bring the backstage action onstage is simply time. The sacred element of time can save us volumes of wasted adrenaline, not to mention emotional wear and tear. Time reflects God's wisdom, which works in God's way. When you connect with God's Divine pace, you connect with what I call the "Divine Inhale." It's that sacred pause or quiet space that allows all synchronistic pieces to assemble.

I once attended a Chicago Symphony Orchestra concert, and it was a wonderful and enriching experience. As the orchestra played the last brilliant phrases of the final work on the program, I held my breath because I was so moved. The final note climaxed in an intense crescendo, like a bolt of lightning crackling through the auditorium, and it left the audience completely silent. The audible music ended, but its energy lingered. It took 15 seconds before its full impact was absorbed. Then, like a rush of oxygen, applause broke out, and the audience leaped to its feet, wildly cheering the musicians for their extraordinary performance.

Coming home after the concert, I couldn't help but notice that the most powerful moment of the evening for me was the silence after the last note was played. More happened during those 15 seconds than in the entire program. What happened was that I got it: I was able to cellularly absorb not only the performance but the feeling that went with it. Had the crowd rushed to applaud, I would have missed the heart and soul of the performance. So instead, I got to take the Divine Inhale.

Time is the Divine's way of again reminding us that we co-create with the Universe—we aren't doing it alone. We plant and water the seeds of creativity, but we don't have the power to make them grow, let alone grow according to our schedule. How it all unfolds is up to God. God's wisdom will fulfill our deepest intentions once we set them in motion. Our part is to create the perfect conditions for the Universe to flow through us—much as our job is to create the ideal conditions for the garden to grow—but that's all we can do. God flows through us and develops our gardens according to his own timetable. And thank goodness for that because God knows and grows better than we do.

Because I'm a very intense and willful person, slowing down has been one of the hardest lessons for me to learn. I want what I want now, and I'll do whatever it takes to create it. Yet, I've learned that to embrace my dreams, I often must just sit and wait. Our soul path unfolds on its own terms, in its own time, and with its own magic.

My client Caitlyn also learned this lesson when she applied and interviewed for what she perceived to be the ideal job at a start-up company in San Francisco. She felt so sure that she was the perfect choice that she announced she was even willing to quit her present position and move in three weeks if she were hired. When she didn't hear from the company immediately, she started calling and campaigning for the job, yet despite her confidence and over-the-edge crusade of persuasion, she didn't get hired.

Caitlyn was stunned. She'd told everyone that she was getting a new job and moving, so now she faced the embarrassment of admitting her failure. Feeling demoralized and angry, Caitlyn stopped looking to change jobs and reluctantly began to focus her energies on making herself happier in Chicago. She settled back into her apartment and put her career on the back burner. She spent her newfound free time painting, reading, walking, making friends, and fixing up her condo.

Four months later, the company that had interviewed her disappeared overnight. All she could do was thank God she hadn't been hired and left stranded. Even better, her readjusted ambitions caused her not only to slow down but to stop climbing the career ladder and get a life outside her job. She quit working for companies altogether and realized she'd rather have a more balanced life.

She began her own business coaching people who wanted to transition from corporate employment to self-employment. She was just busy enough to survive for the first several years, then the pandemic sent everyone home and the Great Resignation of 2021 followed. Like Caitlyn, thousands and thousands of people also didn't want to return to corporate work, and to jobs where their voice and needs weren't honored, so they quit their jobs. A lot of them looked to her to for guidance on starting their own businesses instead. Suddenly Caitlyn was off-the-charts busy. When we last spoke, she marveled, "It took a decade for the Universe to validate my intuition that one day everyone would want to quit and work for themselves like I did." Caitlyn is now writing her first book and creating online courses for people like her who are ready to go their own way and live extraordinary lives.

Waiting peacefully and patiently for the Universe to work for you is a sign that you're genuinely starting to move into the spiritual consciousness. You're intuitively sensing and comprehending the truth that everything is exactly as it should be, moving in exactly the right direction to deliver the best openings and opportunities for your soul's growth. The wisdom of the Universe is bigger, better, brighter, more generous, and infinitely more efficient than your ego is. You just have to be patient as it works its magic. By slowing down and backing off, you trust that God is on the job, so you can relax and let go. Slowing down is an act of faith, wisdom, and surrender. And waiting is a show of respect and humility for supportive Divine forces of the Universe as they weave your beautiful life together for you and bring it back in their own time as a gift.

When you slow down and get comfortable with the pauses of the unknown, you will have genuinely gotten the hang of trusting your vibes, knowing that in doing so, all is and will always be better than fabulous. But by then, you won't need me to tell you that—you'll know it in every cell of your body.

Woo-Woo Workout

Occasionally it is time to step back, pause, relax, let go, give everything a rest, and let the Universe take over. You'll know when because you will feel it in your body, especially in your heart. Turn all your plans, dreams, hopes, fears, and ambitions over to God and your guides, and trust that if you've been following your guidance and doing your part fully, things will work out. If there are delays, know they are for a reason. It may just be the Universe needs more time. It may be that you are being rerouted to a better plan. Stay off the phone and computer or keep it to a minimum. And have some fun: sleep late; see a foreign film; window-shop; go for a long, leisurely walk; or take a bike ride. Rather than fight the river, get in a kayak, and ride it! Better yet, let someone else paddle for you. Trust that the Universe will deliver all you need when the timing is right. Don't fret or stress—simply open your heart and wait.

Woo-Woo Wisdom

Let the Universe help.

DANCE IN THE FIRE

The year after my then-husband Patrick and I were newly married, we were living in Chicago and decided to buy our first house. Using the power of visualization and trusting my vibes, it wasn't long before I found the perfect place for us. It had all the features that we envisioned—three bedrooms, a fireplace, a large basement, a big backyard—and was in a lovely neighborhood right next to the Chicago River. I immediately insisted we buy it. Patrick was hesitant because the price was beyond our means. Still, I used all my powers of persuasion to convince him we could make it work, then used the same influence to convince the Realtor to offer the sellers a price we could afford. Neither was easy, but I succeeded, and soon we had a deal.

Needless to say, we were thrilled. I was really looking forward to owning this house until one morning, a few weeks after our offer was accepted, I woke up with a terrible feeling of dread and knew that we had to call off the purchase. My vibes told me it was no longer perfect for us but gave me no more information than that. I didn't need more information. I trusted my vibes and knew them to be the most essential guidance in my life, so I immediately told my husband that we had to cancel the deal, and I didn't know why. Confused because I was so adamant just a few weeks earlier that this was the perfect house for us, he argued with me, suggesting that I just had buyer's remorse. I knew it was more than that and told him he was wrong. I insisted that under no conditions would I agree to buy the house because my vibes told me not to.

Angry and frustrated, but knowing I wouldn't change my mind, Patrick left it up to me to inform our Realtor and the sellers that we were calling off the deal and get us out of the contract without losing our deposit money. Not letting his confusion and resentment deter me from what I felt was in our best interest, I called the Realtor and told her the deal was off. I was met with the same incredulous response from her as I had been with Patrick.

"What do you expect me to tell them when closing is only three weeks away?" she cried. I said, "Tell them the truth. I'm psychic, and I have bad vibes about buying the house, so we need to call off the contract." She agreed but gave me no assurance that we would get our deposit money back. She further told me what a nut case she thought I was. Not wanting to get into litigation or waste any more time having the house off what was at the time a hot market, the sellers agreed to cancel the deal and gave us our $1,000 deposit back.

Relieved, I still had to live with what I had just done. None of the intense resentment and irritation that came with my decision to rescind the deal was easy to withstand, nor did it subside. Still, my vibes were so clear that I was willing to withstand the anger and judgment coming my way rather than ignore my vibes and go ahead with the deal.

The would-be closing date came and went without fanfare, but a week after we were to have closed, the weather changed.

Suddenly we were soaked by an unprecedented three weeks of relentless heavy rain. As a result, the house we were to have purchased and would have owned for only a week was completely flooded. The Realtor called to share the news. "I don't know how, but you surely dodged a bullet by not closing on that house a week ago," she said. "I know I gave you a hard time, but I couldn't help but be impressed when I heard the news from the sellers this morning. They, too, thought it was uncanny that you called off the deal and were spared the misery of owning the house for only a week only to have it destroyed by a flood."

Even my husband said, "Thank God we didn't own that house, or we would have been financially destroyed." All I could do was thank the Universe for protecting us and giving me the strength to withstand other people's disapproval, as doing so saved us from a financial catastrophe.

Hopefully, the tools you've discovered in this book have helped you sharpen your sixth sense and strengthen your intuition. However, the final commitment you must make if you truly want to live an extraordinary life is to trust your vibes no matter what harassment, disapproval, or resistance comes your way. Growing up, my mom called this "dancing in the fire" because facing others' disapproval or attempts to get us to ignore our vibes feels like energetic fire coming our way, trying to stop us away from acting on our authentic feelings. Rather than be intimidated by the fire of others' negative reactions, my mom told us if we simply "danced in their fire," or in other words, stuck to our authentic truth and kept going no matter what potential consequences we'd face, we'd be protected in the end. She was right. This is the most important decision you can ever make when it comes to trusting your vibes, because unless you follow your vibes, they cannot work their magic.

Pressure to ignore your vibes will arise again and again because your vibes reveal what is not yet apparent to the eye nor evident from the conditions at hand, so others will naturally doubt you. For example, when buying my house, my vibes warned me of the weather pattern heading our way long before the meteorologists picked it up. This is how vibes work. They tune in to energy as it is gathering and moving in your direction and prepare you to respond to this energy ahead of time. As a result, you step away from harm and into opportunity instead of being blindsided by the outwardly unforeseen.

Think about moments in your own life when you had an intuitive feeling, yet you let yourself or others talk you out of listening to it, only to regret it later. Life improves dramatically when you muster the courage to overcome your own doubt or others' disapproval and not abandon your inner guidance and truth for convenience, to please or appease others, or to assuage your own uncertainty.

A willingness to trust your vibes is the most empowering decision you can make if you want to lead a truly extraordinary life. There will be countless moments when you receive guidance with no evidence to back it up. In these cases, your rational mind may kick in and try to interfere. It will ask you for a sensible reason for trusting your vibes, which you cannot provide . . . yet. In such moments, you may be tempted to abandon your vibes and take the path of least resistance even though it doesn't feel correct inside. Please don't. You'll regret that you did.

I have a client named Colleen, the mother of 10-year-old twins, a boy and a girl. One day, her son complained of an intense backache and said he didn't feel like going to school. Since he wasn't normally a complainer, this was unusual. For a brief moment, Colleen intuitively felt she should listen to him and let him stay home. Yet she had grown up in a family where the ethic was to basically "Suit up, shut up, and show up," meaning essentially that if you're in pain, suck it up and do what you have to do anyway. Because of this, she automatically told her son it was out of the question to stay home and assured him he would be okay once he got to school.

At 10:00 A.M. that morning, Colleen received a call from the school nurse informing her that her son was in terrible pain, and they had called an ambulance to come and get him. She should go to the hospital immediately. Her son's appendix had burst sometime that morning, and he was now in grave danger. Colleen was horrified to receive the news and felt terrible because she had ignored her son's complaints and her own vibes. Grateful that her son didn't die from sepsis, Colleen resolved never again to ignore her vibes.

Can you recall any moment when you, too, had a strong intuition but were overwhelmed by conditioning that dismissed your vibes so fast you barely registered them? This is a trap to beware of. It's all too easy to automatically dismiss your vibes by force of habit or family conditioning, even when you feel you shouldn't.

DANCE IN THE FIRE EVEN IF IT MAKES YOU UNPOPULAR

My client Julie attained her dream job when she was hired by a prized social media company. She loved the people, the camaraderie, and the fun that she experienced working in this new place. After work, her colleagues met for drinks at a local pub across the street from the office. They invited Julie to join them soon after she started. Happy to be part of the crowd, Julie agreed, even though she came from a very alcoholic family and knew that drinking was not good for her. Not wanting to appear to be a drag, however, she ignored her vibes and soon found herself drinking heavily five days a week after work before going home. Several times Julie feebly tried to say no to another drink, but her work colleagues wouldn't listen and insisted she have another, then another, all in the name of a good time. Ignoring her inner voice, she caved in to the pressure. Every night on the train home, her vibes rose up and told her to stop drinking like this now! She didn't listen. She wanted to be accepted and considered "cool" by her colleagues and was afraid that not drinking would make her unpopular. Never mind that drinking this much made her feel sick.

Three months into the job and indulging daily in way too much alcohol, Julie's work deteriorated. She made one mistake after another, followed by sad excuses for her failed performance. Finally, in her fourth month, Julie was fired from her job and left in shame.

When she came to me for a reading, she said her vibes repeatedly screamed at her to stop drinking and enjoy the fun without the alcohol. Unfortunately, she was too insecure to listen. By blatantly ignoring her vibes, not only did she lose her dream job, but she now also had a bad job review on her resumé. "I feel like such a fool," Julie cried. "I knew I shouldn't drink. Before this job, I rarely drank. I don't even like drinking. Why didn't I listen to my vibes and drink water when they were nearly screaming in my ear to stop drinking alcohol and go home?"

I knew why. Intuitive people tend to be highly empathic and keenly sense the emotions of people around them. Not wanting to feel her colleagues' disappointment, Julie took care of them and put their wants over her own needs. Ask yourself if you can think of a moment when you might have abandoned yourself and ignored your vibes, seeking group approval instead of standing in the truth of what feels suitable for you. If the answer is yes, what were the consequences, and was the approval of others worth the cost to you of ignoring your vibes? Once you recognize that the price of neglecting your intuition is not worth anyone's approval, it becomes easier to respect what you feel even if others don't agree or understand.

The good news is that once you decide to dance in the fire of others' disapproval or coercion to ignore your vibes, you discover that it feels really great to do so. It means you are empowering, honoring, and trusting in yourself no matter what. You become the leader of your life instead of a sheep, blindly following others. People who trust their vibes even when it's challenging lead the most extraordinary lives. They may have to temporarily withstand the heat of disapproval and pressure because they have no immediate evidence to back them up. But in the end, the evidence usually does appear, and there is no sweeter sense of victory when it does.

The bottom line is that you do not need evidence to listen to your intuition. The important thing is that if you feel something is right or wrong for you, respect that feeling no matter what. Trust your vibes because, in the end, it is only you who has to live with your decisions, not the people who tried to convince you to abandon your inner truth and guidance for their sake.

Start withstanding the little pressures that come from both outside and within by affirming out loud, "I trust my vibes because doing so works for me." That's a good enough reason. Rarely will someone challenge this. But they may judge it. My advice is to not put that much importance on other people's judgments because the cost of self-abandonment to gain another's approval is much too high. It's just not worth it.

My teacher Charlie taught me to respect the first commandment and not to have false gods. He said other people's approval is a false god. We learn as children that we need the approval of others to survive in our families of origin because we are powerless and depend on our parents or other adults to meet our needs. But once you become an adult yourself, that is no longer the case.

This was good advice for me as I learned to dance in the fire. While not easy in the beginning, it does get easier with practice. It's worth the short-term discomfort to experience the long-term gain as well as the deep feeling of self-love and integrity that comes with respecting the voice of your spirit guiding your life.

The best way to trust your vibes is to slow down and check in with yourself before jumping in and agreeing to anything. Take a deep breath and feel for your vibes before saying yes or no to the circumstances before you. Don't listen to your head, your barking dog. Listen to your body, listen to your heart, and ask yourself, "What do my vibes say?" Express them aloud if possible. If you are guided to make a decision that could be unpopular or challenged, and you are asked to defend your choice or explain your reasoning, just say, "I trust my vibes because they work for me, and that's the only reason I have, but I'm willing to stand by it."

TAKE CARE OF YOU FIRST

Last week I traveled with my daughter Sonia to Sedona, Arizona, to teach our first post-pandemic in-person workshop. We were excited to go for several reasons, among which, for me, was being in such a gorgeous natural wonder. In addition, my daughter was excited that it was such a short flight from Phoenix to San Diego, as after the event, she planned to visit her college roommate, who had just had a baby.

As we drove into the car rental return on Sunday afternoon, after the demanding workshop and a two-hour-fifteen-minute drive from Sedona to the Phoenix airport, Sonia received a notice from American Airlines that her flight would be delayed for four hours. This was not good news, as Sonia was utterly exhausted and didn't feel she had it in her to wait that much longer for her flight. I instantly had a vibe that she should abandon her plans to go to San Diego and go home instead. "Sonia," I said, "your flight is going to be canceled. You need to quickly book a ticket home to New Orleans."

"I really want to," she said, "because I'm so tired, but I don't want to disappoint Mary. I've been looking forward to this for a month."

"It's not about disappointing Mary," I answered. "I feel this delayed flight isn't going at all. If you don't hurry and buy a ticket home now, you will be stuck here." Sonia was torn, but at the same time, said, "I think you are right. I have the same vibe. It may be too late to buy anything, but I'll try." She quickly got on the Internet and looked for a flight. Only one option would get her home, a Southwest flight leaving in 55 minutes and connecting through Las Vegas, arriving in New Orleans after midnight. It was tight, but if she hurried, she might make it. There were only minutes left to buy the ticket before the chance was gone.

"I feel so bad canceling like this," she cried, while at the same time booking the flight. "I'm going through with this even though my emotions are fighting me. If I can purchase the ticket, it's my sign it's the right choice." The minute she said that, she got confirmation that she had secured a ticket. "I guess I'm going home. I hope Mary understands and doesn't think I just blew her off." Then she grabbed her bag and ran.

She disappeared into the Southwest terminal, and I went in the other direction to my flight to Chicago, then Paris. Four hours later, I received a text from Sonia saying, "I just received a text from American saying the flight was canceled after all. Good thing I didn't wait and decided to go home. I'm glad I trusted my vibes."

The point of this story is that your vibes are not your emotions, and you may have to even ignore your emotions when listening to your vibes. In Sonia's case, she needed to face her fear of disappointing her friend. Willing to face her friend's potential hurt feelings, Sonia trusted her vibes to take care of her, and they did. For someone else, dancing in the fire may mean saying no to a relationship that isn't good for you, even though every emotion in you wants to hold on for fear of being alone. For another, it may mean saying yes to a challenging new job even though your emotional self would rather remain in its comfort zone, however underpaid and unstimulating it may be.

I have a client named Emma who was proposed to by a wonderful guy—a doctor by profession and devoted father to a teenage daughter. Emma felt loved, and her vibes told her he was a good match for her. However, her fearful emotions had other things to say. She worried that he worked too hard and wasn't spiritual enough. She stressed that he would pay more attention to his teenage daughter than to her or their future children and leave her feeling abandoned and alone. She got so worried she could not sleep at night. That's when she called me. "Is this the right partner for me? I am so worried about so many things I can't relax. And yet he is the most loving, kind, generous man I've ever known. What is wrong with me?"

I asked Emma, "What do your vibes say?"

She answered without missing a beat. "Marry him and relax."

"What does your barking-dog ego say?"

"It says I should hold out because I can find someone better."

"How do you feel when you listen to your vibes?"

"I feel relieved."

"And your barking dog?"

"I feel anxious like I do most of the time. Terrible."

"Emma, you know what is right for you. You just have to allow yourself to relax and be loved."

I don't know what Emma will do. I hope she trusts her vibes and moves on with her relationship because she is adored and loves her partner. I have no idea what her barking-dog ego is afraid of, but it certainly could ruin her chances of happiness if she isn't willing to trust her vibes over listening to her fearful emotions.

BE LOW-KEY

You don't have to announce your vibes as if Elvis just made an appearance. Instead, quietly make the choices that respect and honor your inner guidance and don't feel the need to explain or defend. Just say, "This works for me." Of course there will be moments when you will be met with resistance, teasing, joking, and pushback, with rolled eyes and criticism, or even with a fight. But, if you remain calm and resolved, this resistance will eventually give way. If you are genuinely unwavering in your decision to trust your vibes, people will stop trying to get you to change your mind and will respect your conviction.

The quickest way to learn to dance in the fire is to say out loud, "I choose to trust my vibes. They work for me," and offer no other explanation. Then breathe and smile. While you may be braced for a considerable pushback, more often than not, you'll get no more than a shrug. Others will say, "Okay, whatever," and that's about as bad as it'll get.

I also want to point out that vibes are a moment-to-moment experience—they can and do change. When I tried to buy our first house, it felt absolutely right at one moment, then absolutely wrong a couple of weeks later. We need to allow for that when it comes to trusting our vibes. Intuition is like surfing the waves of life, and those waves are in constant motion. Very often, what's correct one day could shift, and we need to allow for that. Your intuition reflects what feels true now and not forever; it depends entirely on the situation. Rather than get tangled up in your head about this and stressed out, just surrender and know that your vibes will work properly if you pay attention to and respect them. We don't have to orchestrate how and what our vibes are conveying. They work perfectly well on their own. Our job is simply to listen and respect them as they arise, however uncomfortable that may be at times, no matter what.

Don't overthink this. Instead, stay in your heart, feel the energy in your body, and simply trust your vibes. They will alert you if things change and invite new decisions. Indeed, one of the most important and rewarding aspects of your vibes is that they do alert you to moment-by-moment changes so that you can make the best possible decisions rather than get blindsided by life.

After working with all the tools in this book, you will discover that dancing in the fire of others' disapproval or the disapproval of your own ego without abandoning your true Self will feel more and more natural. Making the decision to trust your vibes is worth all the difficulty it occasionally brings. In my experience, the more you trust your vibes even when met with others' skepticism and judgment, the less it happens. If anything, those very same skeptical, disapproving people will watch you thrive and will soon begin to ask you how to do the same. This is when trusting your vibes becomes really magical, fulfilling your purpose in life, which is to share your gifts and be an uplifting force of good in the world for others.

Once you decide to trust your vibes, even when it's difficult, your life improves dramatically. Making that decision empowers you to take charge of your life, and with this, extraordinary things begin to happen. The most extraordinary of all is that you truly love who you are and the life you have created.

GOING FORWARD

I hope that by reading this book, you've learned that trusting your vibes is an art and not a science, and that, with practice, it will turn your life into a more fulfilling, peaceful, meaningful, and truly extraordinary adventure. Furthermore, trusting your vibes is not something to do on occasion if you expect them to work. Instead, trusting your vibes is a way of life, centered on fundamental intuitive practices and based upon the wisdom I've shared in this book.

Trusting your vibes creates a partnership with the Universe that moves you through each day as though it were a dance with the Divine. What you will discover when practicing these six-sensory secrets is that by surrendering control over to your Divine spirit, the Universe will partner with you—and together, you'll create a life of grace, harmony, simplicity, and abundance. While this may seem far-fetched, risky, and unlikely to the five-sensory person, for the six-sensory intuitive and soulful person, this is your natural design, guaranteed to make life better and better.

I invite—even urge—you to join me in living a divinely guided, confident, creative life. It is the way of the future and necessary if we ever hope to achieve peace and harmony for all on this planet.

Woo-Woo Commitment

Slow down, take a breath, and make the decision to trust your vibes even when it feels uncomfortable. Commit to following your inner guidance one vibe at a time. Be prepared to stand in the fire of your own and others' objections *before* you find yourself in a situation where you need to dance as fast as you can. Each time you trust your vibes, even when difficult, you gain evidence and confidence that this is the best decision you will ever make in your life. You will also gain personal power.

A Final Piece of Woo-Woo Wisdom

Always trust your vibes.

ACKNOWLEDGMENTS

I'd like to thank my beautiful mother in spirit, Sonia Choquette, for parting the veil to the world of spirit and introducing me to the ever available and extraordinary love and support of the heavens. And to my father's spirit for being a steady, grounded guide in my highly spirited and unpredictable world. To my daughters, Sonia and Sabrina, for your enduring friendship, love, willingness, and joyful companionship and for joining me in this life's work. To my beloved teachers in spirit Dr. Tully and Charlie Goodman, for sharing their wisdom and tools with me for establishing the highest level of spirit-guided communication. To my beloved soul sister, Lu Glatzmaier, for being my continuous support for over 50 years in always trusting my vibes.

To Reid Tracy, my constant publishing earth angel, and the entire staff at Hay House for your dedication and tireless support. To my fabulous editors and shining beings, Linda Kahn and Sally Mason-Swaab, for working your magic on this present manuscript. And to all my clients for lending me your stories. Above all, I'd like to thank God and all blessed bright beings of the Universe for your love, guidance, and hard work on my behalf as you perpetually guide me on my path. I am a grateful and humble servant.

ABOUT THE AUTHOR

Sonia Choquette is a celebrated worldwide author, spiritual teacher, and intuitive guide who has devoted herself to teaching people to honor their spirit, trust their vibes, and live in the grace and glory of an extraordinary spirit-guided life. A fourth-generation intuitive guide, beginning her public work with spirit at age 15, Sonia has spent over 45 years traveling the world on her mission to help others lead confident, authentic lives with intuition as their guiding light. She is the author of 27 internationally best-selling books and numerous audio programs on intuitive awakening, personal and creative growth, and spiritual transformation, most notably with the *New York Times* bestseller *The Answer Is Simple.*

Sonia's work has been published in over 40 countries, translated into 37 languages, making her one of the most widely read authors and experts in her field of work. Sonia's legacy is continued by her two daughters, Sonia and Sabrina, both who have their own careers in spiritual coaching and guidance and are published authors of the Hay House book *You Are Amazing: A Help-Yourself Guide for Trusting Your Vibes and Reclaiming Your Magic.* Sonia and her daughters also currently host a weekly lively podcast called *It's All Related: Welcome to the Family* found on iTunes, Spotify, and YouTube.

Sonia is an avid traveler, passionate dancer, prolific storyteller, and a natural comedian. She prides herself on her endless pursuit of learning, growing, and living full-out every day. Sonia loves everything about Paris and currently calls it her home.

Website: soniachoquette.com

Hay House Titles of Related Interest

YOU CAN HEAL YOUR LIFE, the movie,
starring Louise Hay & Friends
(available as an online streaming video)
www.hayhouse.com/louise-movie

THE SHIFT, the movie,
starring Dr. Wayne W. Dyer
(available as an online streaming video)
www.hayhouse.com/the-shift-movie

***

*A BEGINNER'S GUIDE TO THE UNIVERSE: Uncommon Ideas
for Living an Unusually Happy Life,* by Mike Dooley

*THE ART OF EXTREME SELF-CARE: 12 Practical
and Inspiring Ways to Love Yourself More,*
by Cheryl Richardson

*LETTERS TO A STARSEED: Messages and Activations
for Remembering Who You Are and Why You Came Here,*
by Rebecca Campbell

*HAPPY DAYS: The Guided Path from Trauma
to Profound Freedom and Inner Peace,*
by Gabrielle Bernstein

All of the above are available at your local bookstore,
or may be ordered by contacting Hay House (see next page).

***

We hope you enjoyed this Hay House book. If you'd like to receive our online catalog featuring additional information on Hay House books and products, or if you'd like to find out more about the Hay Foundation, please contact:

Hay House, Inc., P.O. Box 5100, Carlsbad, CA 92018-5100
(760) 431-7695 or (800) 654-5126
(760) 431-6948 (fax) or (800) 650-5115 (fax)
www.hayhouse.com® • www.hayfoundation.org

———

Published in Australia by: Hay House Australia Pty. Ltd.,
18/36 Ralph St., Alexandria NSW 2015
Phone: 612-9669-4299 • *Fax:* 612-9669-4144
www.hayhouse.com.au

Published in the United Kingdom by: Hay House UK, Ltd.,
The Sixth Floor, Watson House, 54 Baker Street, London W1U 7BU
Phone: +44 (0)20 3927 7290 • *Fax:* +44 (0)20 3927 7291
www.hayhouse.co.uk

Published in India by: Hay House Publishers India,
Muskaan Complex, Plot No. 3, B-2, Vasant Kunj, New Delhi 110 070
Phone: 91-11-4176-1620 • *Fax:* 91-11-4176-1630
www.hayhouse.co.in

———

Access New Knowledge.
Anytime. Anywhere.

Learn and evolve at your own pace
with the world's leading experts.

www.hayhouseU.com